Learning Java Functional Programming

Create robust and maintainable Java applications
using the functional style of programming

Richard M Reese

[PACKT] open source *

PUBLISHING   community experience distilled

BIRMINGHAM - MUMBAI

Learning Java Functional Programming

First published: October 2015

Production reference: 1091015

Published by Packt Publishing Ltd.
Livery Place
35 Livery Street
Birmingham B3 2PB, UK.

ISBN 978-1-78355-848-3

www.packtpub.com

Credits

Author
Richard M Reese

Reviewers
Jose Luis Ordiales Coscia
David Greco
Hossein Kazemi
Amar Potghan

Commissioning Editor
Veena Pagare

Acquisition Editor
Vivek Anantharaman

Content Development Editor
Susmita Sabat

Technical Editor
Prajakta Mhatre

Copy Editor
Charlotte Carneiro

Project Coordinator
Judie Jose

Proofreader
Safis Editing

Indexer
Rekha Nair

Graphics
Jason Monteiro
Abhinash Sahu

Production Coordinator
Aparna Bhagat

Cover Work
Aparna Bhagat

About the Author

Richard M Reese has worked in both industry and academics. For 17 years, he worked in the telephone and aerospace industries, serving in several capacities, including research and development, software development, supervision, and training. He currently teaches at Tarleton State University, where he has the opportunity to draw on his years of industry experience to enhance his teaching.

Richard has written several Java books and a C pointer book. He uses a concise and easy-to-follow approach to the topics at hand. His Java books have addressed EJB 3.1, updates to Java 7 and 8, certification, jMonkeyEngine, and Natural Language Processing.

Richard would like to thank his daughter, Jennifer, for her numerous reviews and contributions; his wife, Karla, for her continued support; and the staff at Packt for their work in making this a better book.

About the Reviewers

Jose Luis Ordiales Coscia is a software engineer with much experience in both academia and the private industry. He has a master's degree in computer science, focusing his research on helping developers improve their service-oriented applications.

He has more than 7 years of experience working in backend development with Java and other JVM languages.

David Greco is a software architect with more than 27 years of working experience. He started his career as a researcher in the field of high-performance computing; thereafter, he moved to the business world, where he worked for different enterprise software vendors and helped to create two start-ups. He played different roles, those of a consultant and software architect and even a CTO. He's an enthusiastic explorer of new technologies, and likes to introduce new technologies into enterprises to improve their businesses. Over the past 5 years, he has fallen in love with big data technologies and typed functional programming—Scala and Haskell. When not working or hacking, he likes to practice karate and listen to jazz and classical music.

Hossein Kazemi is an entrepreneur and software engineer based in Amsterdam, the Netherlands. He holds a master's in artificial intelligence with a major in machine learning and minor in Natural Language Processing (NLP) from the University of Amsterdam. He has more than 5 years of hands-on experience in software development and has worked on projects for large-scale machine learning and NLP using Java and Scala.

Amar Potghan is a polyglot functional programming enthusiast. He has vast experience in building scalable distributed systems. Amar is currently working on Haskell and ClojureScript to build a next generation P2P lending platform for a fintech company in Singapore. Before that, he was working as a consultant at ThoughtWorks and as a senior software engineer for a couple of other global software consultancies where he worked on continuous delivery, microservices, big data, and analytics product development projects. Amar's current interests are functional programming, distributed systems, and machine learning.

www.PacktPub.com

Support files, eBooks, discount offers, and more

For support files and downloads related to your book, please visit www.PacktPub.com.

Did you know that Packt offers eBook versions of every book published, with PDF and ePub files available? You can upgrade to the eBook version at www.PacktPub.com and as a print book customer, you are entitled to a discount on the eBook copy. Get in touch with us at service@packtpub.com for more details.

At www.PacktPub.com, you can also read a collection of free technical articles, sign up for a range of free newsletters and receive exclusive discounts and offers on Packt books and eBooks.

https://www2.packtpub.com/books/subscription/packtlib

Do you need instant solutions to your IT questions? PacktLib is Packt's online digital book library. Here, you can search, access, and read Packt's entire library of books.

Why subscribe?

- Fully searchable across every book published by Packt
- Copy and paste, print, and bookmark content
- On demand and accessible via a web browser

Free access for Packt account holders

If you have an account with Packt at www.PacktPub.com, you can use this to access PacktLib today and view 9 entirely free books. Simply use your login credentials for immediate access.

Table of Contents

Preface	**vii**
Chapter 1: Getting Started with Functional Programming	**1**
Aspects of functional programming	**2**
Functions	3
Function composition	6
Fluent interfaces	7
Strict versus non-strict evaluation	8
Persistent data structures	9
Recursion	10
Parallelism	11
Optional and monads	13
Java 8's support for functional style programming	**14**
Lambda expressions	15
Default methods	16
Functional interfaces	17
Method and constructor references	18
Collections	20
Summary	**20**
Chapter 2: Putting the Function in Functional Programming	**23**
Lambda expressions usage	**24**
Functional programming concepts in Java	**26**
High-order functions	26
Returning a function	29
First-class functions	31
The pure function	33
Support repeated execution	33
Eliminating dependencies between functions	36
Supporting lazy evaluation	37

Referential transparency	37
Closure in Java	38
Currying	40
Lambda expressions revisited	**43**
Java 8 type inference	44
Exception handling in lambda expressions	46
Functional interfaces revisited	**47**
Creating a functional interface	47
Common functional interfaces	47
Function-type functional interfaces	48
Predicate-type functional interfaces	49
Consumer-type functional interfaces	50
Supplier-type functional interfaces	51
Operator-type functional interfaces	51
Summary	**53**
Chapter 3: Function Composition and Fluent Interfaces	**55**
Introduction to function composition	**56**
Creating composite functions prior to Java 8	**56**
Creating composite functions in Java 8	**58**
Using the Function interface for function composition	59
Using the Functional interface to supplement methods	60
Passing instances of the Functional interface	61
Fluent interfaces	**64**
Fluent interfaces in Java 8	64
Method chaining and cascading	65
Contrasting method cascading and fluent interfaces	67
Creating and using fluent interfaces	68
Using fluent interfaces to hide older interfaces/classes	72
Using fluent interfaces with the Properties class	74
Extending fluent interfaces	76
Default methods and functions	**80**
Static default methods	81
Default methods in Java 8	81
Multiple inheritance in Java 8	83
Summary	**84**
Chapter 4: Streams and the Evaluation of Expressions	**85**
The Stream class and its use	**86**
Intermediate and terminal methods	88
Creating streams	**89**
Fixed length streams	90

Infinite streams   90
    Using the iterate method to create an infinite stream   91
    Using the generate method to create an infinite stream   94
Using the Stream class methods   **95**
Filter methods   96
    Using the filter method   97
    Using the skip method   98
Sorting streams   99
Mapping methods   100
    Understanding the mapping operation   100
    Implementing the map-reduce paradigm   101
    Using the flatmap method   103
Lazy and eager evaluation   **106**
Stream and concurrent processing   **109**
Understanding non-inference   110
Understanding stateless operations   111
Understanding side effects   112
Understanding the ordering   113
Summary   **114**

Chapter 5 Recursion Techniques in Java 8   **117**
Recursive data structures   **118**
Types of recursion   **120**
Using direct recursion   120
Head and tail recursion   121
Understanding recursion   **123**
The Node class   124
Using head recursion   126
Using tail recursion   127
Using the head and tail recursion   128
Creating a recursive solution based on a formula   129
Converting an iterative loop to a recursive solution   131
Merging two lists   132
Understanding the program stack   133
Recursive lambda expressions   137
Common problems found in recursive solutions   137
    Absence of a base case   138
    Using static or instance variables   138
    Using the pre- and post-increment operators   139
Recursion implementation techniques   **139**
Using a wrapper method   140
Using short circuiting   140

Tail call optimization	141
Converting to a tail call	142
When to use recursion	**143**
Recursion and humor	**144**
Summary	**146**
Chapter 6: Optional and Monads	**147**
Using the Optional class	**147**
Creating Optional instances	148
Using the Optional class to support return values	149
Handling missing values	153
Using the orElse method to get a substitute value	153
Using the orElseGet method to use a function to get a substitute value	154
Using the orElseThrow method to throw an exception	154
Filter and transforming values	155
Using the Optional class's filter method	155
Using the Optional class's map method	156
Optional solution to the Customer problem	157
Disadvantages of the Optional class	159
Monads	**160**
Monads in Java 8	163
Using the of method as the unit function	164
Using the flatMap method	164
Using the map method	165
Using the Optional class with strings	166
Using monads with the Part class	167
A formal discussion of monads	168
Associativity	171
Left identity	171
Right identity	172
Summary	**173**
Chapter 7: Supporting Design Patterns Using Functional Programming	**175**
Implementing the execute-around-method pattern	**177**
Object-oriented solution to the execute-around-method pattern	177
Functional solution to the execute-around-method pattern	178
Using the execute-around-method pattern with a stream	181
Implementing the factory pattern	**182**
Object-oriented solution to the factory pattern	183
Functional solution to the factory pattern	185
Implementing the command pattern	**185**
Object-oriented solution to the command pattern	186
Functional solution to the command pattern	188

Implementing the strategy pattern   **189**
Object-oriented solution to strategy pattern   190
Functional solution to the strategy pattern   194
Using the Function interface   195
Implementing the visitor pattern   **196**
Object-orient solution to the visitor pattern   197
Functional solution to the visitor pattern   200
Implementing the template pattern   **202**
Object-oriented solution to the template pattern   203
Functional solution to the template pattern   205
Summary   **208**

Chapter 8: Refactoring, Debugging, and Testing   **209**
Refactoring functional code   **210**
NetBeans support for refactoring   211
Converting anonymous inner classes to lambda expressions   211
Refactoring multiple code instances   212
Support of other refactoring operations   214
Eclipse support for refactoring   215
Converting anonymous inner classes to lambda expressions   215
Refactoring multiple code instances   217
Support of other refactoring operations   219
Debugging lambda expressions   **220**
Using the println method to assist debugging   **221**
Using the peek method to assist debugging   222
Debugging lambda expressions using NetBeans   222
Debugging lambda expressions using Eclipse   225
Debugging recursive lambda expressions   227
Debugging parallel streams   229
Testing functional programs   **230**
Testing lambda expressions   230
Copying the lambda expression   232
Using a method reference   233
Reorganizing the test class   234
Testing exceptions using a fluent style   236
Summary   **237**

Chapter 9: Bringing It All Together   **239**
Functional Zork   **239**
Playing the game   240
The game's architecture   **243**
Understanding the GameElements class   243
Introducing the Item, Direction, and NPC classes   244

Implementing the FunctionalZork class	246
Initializing the game	247
Initializing the commands	250
Getting a command from the console	252
Parsing the command	255
Executing the command	255
Implementing the Character class	258
Implementing the pickup method	258
Implementing the drop method	259
Implementing the walk method	260
Implementing the inventory method	261
Implementing the Location class	262
Handling items	263
Handling NPCs	263
Handling directions	264
Summary	**265**
Epilogue	**266**
Index	**267**

Preface

With the introduction of Java 8, many functional programming techniques have been added to the language. However, functional programming may seem unfamiliar to developers who are used to using imperative and object-oriented techniques. The new additions to Java 8 offer the opportunity to develop more maintainable and robust applications than that offered by earlier versions of Java.

The goal of this book is to introduce functional programming techniques to developers who are not familiar with this technology. You will be guided through the use of functional programming techniques with the help of numerous examples. Older imperative and object-oriented approaches will be illustrated and contrasted with equivalent functional programming solutions.

What this book covers

Chapter 1, *Getting Started with Functional Programming*, introduces the essential elements of functional programming as supported by Java 8. This includes the introduction of functional terms complemented by Java 8 examples.

Chapter 2, *Putting the Function in Functional Programming*, covers the types of functions found in functional programming languages such as high-order functions, first-class functions, and pure functions. The use of lambda expressions in support of functions is explained.

Chapter 3, *Function Composition and Fluent Interfaces*, addresses how to use functional composition. Also covered are fluent interfaces and the use of default methods.

Chapter 4, *Streams and the Evaluation of Expressions*, covers the basics of their creation and use. Streams are an important addition to Java.

Chapter 5, Recursion Techniques in Java 8, demonstrates recursion, a very useful functional programming technique. While not new to Java, we explore the topic in depth and examine the use of recursive lambda expressions.

Chapter 6, Optional and Monads, covers the use and the nature of monads in creating fluent interfaces and producing resilient code. The Optional class provides a better way of working with missing data.

Chapter 7, Supporting Design Patterns Using Functional Programming, illustrates design patterns. They play an important role in Java programming. The impact of the functional style of programming and lambda expressions is illustrated.

Chapter 8, Refactoring, Debugging, and Testing, demonstrates how these tools have been affected by the new functional programming techniques and how IDEs support them. These are valuable tools in the development process.

Chapter 9, Bringing It All Together, summarizes many of the functional programming techniques presented earlier that are used in the creation of a demonstration application. Such an application provides a concise illustration of how these techniques support the development of robust and maintainable software.

What you need for this book

Java SDK 1.8 is needed for the functional programming examples encountered in the book. Some of the examples use NetBeans 8.02 and Eclipse IDE for Java developers, Mars Release Version 4.5.0.

Who this book is for

This book is for developers who are already proficient in Java and want to learn how to use the functional programming features of Java 8. Familiarity with basic Java object-oriented programming concepts is all that is needed. You will learn how to apply lambda expressions and other functional programming techniques to create a more elegant and maintainable code.

Conventions

In this book, you will find a number of text styles that distinguish between different kinds of information. Here are some examples of these styles and an explanation of their meaning.

Code words in text are shown are follows: "As you may remember, the `forEach` method accepts a lambda expression which matches the `Consumer` interface's `accept` method."

A block of code is shown as follows:

```
list.forEach(new Consumer<String>() {
    @Override
    public void accept(String t) {
        System.out.println(t);
    }
});
```

The output of code sequences is formatted as shown here:

```
Starting FPS Game

Generating FPS Image

Rendering FPS Image

Updating FPS Game
```

New terms and **important words** are shown in bold. Words that you see on the screen, for example, in menus or dialog boxes, appear in the text like this: "There is the text form as entered by the user such as: **drop Axe**."

> Warnings or important notes appear in a box like this.

> Tips and tricks appear like this.

Reader feedback

Feedback from our readers is always welcome. Let us know what you think about this book — what you liked or disliked. Reader feedback is important for us as it helps us develop titles that you will really get the most out of.

To send us general feedback, simply e-mail feedback@packtpub.com, and mention the book's title in the subject of your message.

If there is a topic that you have expertise in and you are interested in either writing or contributing to a book, see our author guide at www.packtpub.com/authors.

Customer support

Now that you are the proud owner of a Packt book, we have a number of things to help you to get the most from your purchase.

Downloading the example code

You can download the example code files from your account at `http://www.packtpub.com` for all the Packt Publishing books you have purchased. If you purchased this book elsewhere, you can visit `http://www.packtpub.com/support` and register to have the files e-mailed directly to you.

Errata

Although we have taken every care to ensure the accuracy of our content, mistakes do happen. If you find a mistake in one of our books—maybe a mistake in the text or the code—we would be grateful if you could report this to us. By doing so, you can save other readers from frustration and help us improve subsequent versions of this book. If you find any errata, please report them by visiting `http://www.packtpub.com/submit-errata`, selecting your book, clicking on the **Errata Submission Form** link, and entering the details of your errata. Once your errata are verified, your submission will be accepted and the errata will be uploaded to our website or added to any list of existing errata under the Errata section of that title.

To view the previously submitted errata, go to `https://www.packtpub.com/books/content/support` and enter the name of the book in the search field. The required information will appear under the **Errata** section.

Piracy

Piracy of copyrighted material on the Internet is an ongoing problem across all media. At Packt, we take the protection of our copyright and licenses very seriously. If you come across any illegal copies of our works in any form on the Internet, please provide us with the location address or website name immediately so that we can pursue a remedy.

Please contact us at `copyright@packtpub.com` with a link to the suspected pirated material.

We appreciate your help in protecting our authors and our ability to bring you valuable content.

Questions

If you have a problem with any aspect of this book, you can contact us at
questions@packtpub.com, and we will do our best to address the problem.

1
Getting Started with Functional Programming

Functional programming languages have been used successfully for decades and present a different and often more elegant way of expressing the program logic. Functional languages, such as Lisp, Clojure, or Haskell, incorporate techniques that may seem odd and hard to follow by programmers who are used to imperative programming techniques.

A language such as Java, while not initially developed with a functional orientation, can incorporate functional techniques. This is the major change to the language made with the release of Java 8. Java now incorporates imperative, procedural, object-oriented, and functional techniques.

It is possible to write a non-object-oriented program in Java. Likewise, it is possible to write a nonfunctional program in Java 8. The goal of this book is to enlighten the reader to the nature of functional programming techniques and how to incorporate these techniques in Java 8 applications.

We will start with a discussion of the attributes commonly associated with functional programming. From there, we will examine the support, Java provides for developing applications using a functional-style programming approach.

A predominant feature of functional programming languages is the use of functions. The term, function, is generally understood to be:

- A way of expressing an algorithm
- A mathematical function
- Where the goal is to avoid state changes and mutable data

In functional programming, applications are constructed using only pure functions. A pure function is a function which does not have side effects. A side effect occurs when a function does something else besides simply returning a value, such as mutating a global variable or performing IO. In this chapter, we will examine the major aspects of functional programming including:

- Functions and function composition
- Fluent interfaces
- Strict and non-strict evaluation
- Persistent data structures, monads, and the `Optional` class
- Recursion and parallelism

This is followed by the support Java 8 provides for functional programming, including:

- Lambda expressions
- Default methods
- Functional interface
- Method and constructor references
- Collections

In addition, to our discussion of functional programming support as provided by Java 8, refactoring, debugging, and testing Java 8 code are also important topics, which need to be addressed. These topics are covered in *Chapter 8, Refactoring, Debugging, and Testing*.

So, let's begin with an overview of what constitutes the functional programming approach.

Aspects of functional programming

Functions can be simple or complex, but simpler functions are preferred. The function should ideally not change the state of memory or perform I/O, and consequently work with immutable data. These later two concepts are explored in *Chapter 6, Optional and Monads*.

There are several aspects of functional programming languages that we will explore here. They include:

- Functions
- Function composition
- Fluent interfaces

- Strict versus non-strict evaluation
- Parallelism
- Persistent data structures
- Recursion
- Optional and monads

Each of these concepts will be introduced in the following sections. We will explore the nature of each concept, explain why it is important, and when practical provide simple examples using Java.

Functions

Functions are the foundation of functional programming languages. They play a central role in supporting other functional programming concepts. In this section, we will introduce many of the terms used to describe functions including high-order, first-class, and pure functions. The concepts of closure and currying will also be explained.

First-class and high-order functions are associated with functional programming. A first-class function is a computer science term. It refers to functions that can be used anywhere a first-class entity can be used. A first-class entity includes elements such as numbers and strings. They can be used as an argument to a function, returned from a function, or assigned to a variable.

High-order functions depend upon the existence of first-class functions. They are functions that either:

- Take a function as an argument
- Return a function

Java 8 has introduced the concept of lambda expressions to the language. These are essentially anonymous functions that can be passed to and returned from functions. They can also be assigned to a variable. The basic form of a lambda expression follows where a parameter, such as x, is passed to the body of the function. The lambda operator, ->, separates the parameter from the body. This function is passed a value, which is multiplied by two and then returned, as follows:

```
x -> 2 * x
```

In this lambda expression, it is assumed that an integer is passed and that integer is returned. However, the data type is not restricted to an integer as we will see later. In the following lambda expression, an argument is passed and nothing is returned:

```
x->System.out.println(x)
```

Lambda expressions must be used in the proper context. It would not be appropriate to pass a lambda expression, which returns a value to a method, to a function that cannot use the returned value.

We can use the previous expression in many places that expect a single value being passed and nothing to be returned as shown next. In the following example, an array of integers is converted to a list. The lambda expression is then used as an argument to the `List` class's `forEach` method, which displays each element of the list. The `forEach` method applies the lambda expression to each element in the list, avoiding having to create an explicit loop to achieve the same effect:

```
Integer arr[] = {1,2,3,4,5};
List<Integer> list = Arrays.asList(arr);
list.forEach(x->System.out.println(x));
```

> **Downloading the example code**
>
> You can download the example code files from your account at http://www.packtpub.com for all the Packt Publishing books you have purchased. If you purchased this book elsewhere, you can visit http://www.packtpub.com/support and register to have the files e-mailed directly to you.

The output will list the numbers one to five on separate lines.

Changing a program's state is avoided in functional programming. Calling a function with the same input values should result in the same behavior each time. This makes it easier to understand the function. Imperative programming changes the state using statements such as the assignment statement.

A **pure function** is a function that has no side effects. This means that memory external to the function is not modified, IO is not performed, and no exceptions are thrown. With a pure function, when it is called repeatedly with the same parameters, it will return the same value. This is called **referential transparency**.

With referential transparency, it is permissible to modify local variables within the function as this does not change the state of the program. Any changes are not seen outside of the function.

Advantages of pure function include:

- The function can be called repeatedly with the same argument and get the same results. This enables caching optimization (memorization).
- With no dependencies between multiple pure functions, they can be reordered and performed in parallel. They are essentially thread safe.

- Pure function enables lazy evaluation as discussed later in the *Strict versus non-strict evaluation* section. This implies that the execution of the function can be delayed and its results can be cached potentially improving the performance of a program.

- If the result of a function is not used, then it can be removed since it does not affect other operations.

There are several other terms associated with functions, such as the term **closure**. This refers to a function passed around along with its environment. The environment consists of the variables it uses. Java 8 supports a form of closure, and will be illustrated in *Chapter 2, Putting the Function in Functional Programming*.

Currying is the process of evaluating multiple arguments of a function one-by-one, producing intermediate results. In the process, we introduce a new function with one less argument than the previous step. For example, let's start with this function:

$$f(x, y) = x + y$$

We can evaluate it for the value of 3 and 4 as follows, returning a result of 7:

$$f(3, 4) = 3 + 4$$

If we substitute 3 for *x* we get:

$$f(3, y) = 3 + y$$

Next, if we define *g(y)* as:

$$g(y) = 3 + y$$

Then, the following is also true:

$$f(3, y) = g(y) = 3 + y$$

We reduced the number of arguments from two to one. Using a value of 4 for *y* yields the original result of 7. The process of currying, and partially applying functions, permit high-order functions to be used more effectively. This will become clearer in *Chapter 2, Putting the Function in Functional Programming*.

Function composition

Imperative programming places emphasis on a step-by-step process to implement an application. This is typified by a logical set of steps where code is executed using basic control constructs and is often encapsulated in functions or procedures.

Functional programming places more emphasis on how these functions are arranged and combined. It is this composition of functions, which typifies a functional style of programming. Functions are not only used to organize the execution process, but are also passed and returned from functions. Often data and the functions acting on the data are passed together promoting more capable and expressive programs.

We will illustrate this technique using the `Function` interface as defined in the `java.util.function` package. This interface possesses a `compose` and `andThen` methods. Both of these methods return a composed function.

The `compose` method will execute the function passed to it first, and then uses its result with the function the `compose` method is executed against. The `andThen` method will execute the first function and then execute the function passed as an argument to the `andThen` method.

The next code sequence demonstrates the `compose` method, which is passed as a function to take the absolute value of a number. The `absThenNegate` variable is assigned a function that will also negate the number. This variable is declared as a `Function` type, which means that the function assigned to it expects to be passed as an integer and returns an integer.

This function will execute the argument of the `compose` method and the `Math` class's `abs` method first, against some value, and then apply the `negateExact` method to this result. In other words, it will take the absolute value of a number and then negate it. Both of these methods are expressed as method references, which are new to Java 8. A method reference consist of the class name followed by a set of double colons, and then a method name providing a simpler form of method invocation:

```
Function<Integer,Integer>absThenNegate =
    ((Function<Integer,Integer>)Math::negateExact)
        .compose(Math::abs);
```

This is illustrated with the following sequence. The `Function` interface's `apply` method is used to invoke the composed function:

```
System.out.println(absThenNegate.apply(-25));
System.out.println(absThenNegate.apply(25));
```

Both of these statements will display a -25. In the first statement, the absolute value of a -25 is obtained and then negated. The second statement works the same way except its argument is +25.

The negateThenAbs variable that follows, illustrates the andThen method. The function used as an argument to the andThen method is applied after the first function is executed. In this case, the negateExact method is executed first and then the abs function is applied:

```
Function<Integer,Integer>negateThenAbs =
    ((Function<Integer,Integer>)Math::negateExact)
        .andThen(Math::abs);
System.out.println(negateThenAbs.apply(-25));
System.out.println(negateThenAbs.apply(25));
```

The output of both display statements will be 25.

We could have obtained the same results with a series of imperative statements. However, this does not result in as much flexibility as can be obtained using function composition. The ability to pass functions will provide the enhanced flexibility. We will postpone a detailed discussion of this approach until *Chapter 3, Function Composition and Fluent Interfaces*.

Fluent interfaces

Fluent interfaces constitute a way of composing expressions that are easier to write and understand. A fluent interface is often implemented using method chaining, sometimes called method cascading, where the returned value is used again in the same context.

In Java 8, the use of fluent interfaces is found in numerous places. We will illustrate this style with an example using the new Date and Time API.

Suppose we want to calculate a new date that is 2 years in the future, minus 1 month plus 3 days. We can use the following code sequence to achieve this result. The LocalDate class's method now returns an instance of the LocalDate class representing the current date. This date is the base for creating a new day called futureDate:

```
LocalDate today = LocalDate.now();
LocalDate futureDate = today.plusYears(2);
futureDate = futureDate.minusMonths(1);
futureDate = futureDate.plusDays(3);
System.out.println(today);
System.out.println(futureDate);
```

This will generate the following output:

```
2015-03-22
2017-02-25
```

Contrast this with the next code sequence, which takes advantage of the APIs fluent interface and produces the same output:

```
LocalDatefutureDate = LocalDate.now()
    .plusYears(2)
    .minusMonths(1)
    .plusDays(3);
```

The code flow is easy to read and flows in a more natural way. You will see repeated usage of fluent interfaces in the book. Streams use this approach consistently.

Strict versus non-strict evaluation

Functional languages can be classified as either using strict or non-strict evaluation of expressions. With strict evaluation, sometimes called eager evaluation, the expressions are evaluated as they are encountered.

With non-strict evaluation, they are not evaluated until necessary. Non-strict evaluation is sometimes called lazy evaluation. However, these terms are not always strict synonyms. Non-strict evaluation is concerned with the semantics of the expression, while lazy evaluation deals more with how the expression is evaluated.

Lazy evaluation is supported using streams. A stream can be thought of as a series of elements that flow like a river or stream. They add a convenient means of processing data in an easy-to-use and natural manner. The stream concept is support in Java 8 with the `Stream` class.

In the following sequence, a stream is created by generating five random numbers, sorting these numbers, and then displaying them:

```
Random random = new Random();
random.ints()
    .limit(5)
    .sorted()
    .forEach(x->System.out.println(x));
```

The `ints` method returns an `IntStream` instance. The `limit` method will restrict the stream to the first five numbers, and the `sorted` method will sort these numbers. However, the stream is not evaluated until a terminal method such as the `forEach` method is encountered. The use of streams will be demonstrated in more detail in *Chapter 4, Streams and the Evaluation of Expressions*.

One possible output follows:

```
-1790144043
-1777206416
23979263
801416357
874941096
```

A stream is processed lazily, which enables the runtime system to optimize how the stream's component operations are executed. In addition, they are used in a fluent manner.

Persistent data structures

Persistent data structures maintain previous versions of itself. As changes to the data structure occur, a new version of the data structure is created while maintaining the older version. These structures are effectively immutable.

Avoiding the mutation of data obviously has no side effects. This means that they are thread-safe and enable various optimization techniques.

One consequence of mutable data is that, when accessed from multiple threads, many threading issues arise that can make a program less reliable and maintainable. If the data is immutable, then these threading issues such as the need to synchronize data access largely go away.

One approach used by functional programming languages to simulate state is using a data structure, which is passed to a function. The data structure is copied and any changes made are reflected in the new copy of the data structure. This is referred to a state-passing style and can use a considerable amount of memory unless appropriate optimization techniques are applied.

There are immutable collections that support the concept of persistent data structures. However, when a language is entirely immutable, then a large amount of garbage is generated requiring extensive optimization to be useful. Some of these collections are not practical when they contain a significant number of elements.

We are not able to show how Java can support this concept here. However, in *Chapter 6, Optional and Monads* we will examine techniques that can be used in Java 8 to support data structures, such as some monads, in more detail.

Recursion

A loop is used in an imperative language to perform repeated calculations. Recursion is a technique that can achieve the same effect but often in a more elegant manner. A function is recursive if it calls itself either directly or indirectly. For example, calculating the factorial of a number can be accomplished using either iteration or recursion. The factorial of a number is defined as follows:

$$f(1) = 1$$

$$f(n) = n * f(n-1)$$

where n>0

An iterative solution follows:

```
int result = 1;
for (int i = 5; i >= 1; i--) {
    result = result * i;
}
System.out.println(result);
```

The output will be 120. The equivalent recursion solution starts with a recursive factorial function:

```
public int factorial(int n) {
    if(n==1) {
        return 1;
    } else {
        return n * factorial(n-1);
    }
}
```

This solution is more succinct than the iterative version and more closely matches the problem definition. The function can be invoked as follows:

```
System.out.println(factorial(num));
```

It will generate the same output: `120`.

Indirect recursion occurs when a function calls itself but not immediately. For example, if function *A* calls function *B*, which then calls function *A*, we have indirect recursion.

A recursion function needs to be bounded. This means that it must stop calling itself at some time. Otherwise, it will exceed the system's resources and result in an exception being thrown and the program terminating abnormally. In the `factorial` function, the test for an `n` value of `1` stopped the recursion.

Frequently, recursion is implemented using a program stack. However, if tail recursion is used, then the compiler can avoid the use of a program stack and use essentially the same technique used to implement an imperative loop. Tail recursion involves a tail call, which is where the recursive call is the last statement of the function.

Parallelism

One area where the use of functional programming can be useful is handling parallel, also called concurrent, programming tasks. Consider the following sequence:

```
result = a.methodA() + b.methodB() + c.methodC();
```

In what order can these methods be executed? If they have side effects, then they will most likely need to be computed sequentially. For example, the effect of `methodA` may affect the results of the other methods. However, if they do not have side effects, then the order of execution is not important and can be executed concurrently. Conceivably, they might not be executed at all until the value of `result` is needed, if ever. This is another potential application of lazy evaluation.

Java has steadily improved its support of concurrent programming over the years. These approaches built upon the underlying `Thread` class and provided various classes to support specific concurrent task such as pools.

The problem with these earlier approaches has been the need to learn these models and decide if they are a good fit for the problem at hand. While this is necessary and works well for many problem areas, it does require more effort on the part of the developer to learn these techniques.

In Java 8, much of the effort requires to add concurrent behavior to a program has been lessened allowing the developer to focus more on the problem at hand. This support comes in the use of functions in conjunction with streams and collections.

For example, the next code sequence illustrates how a lambda expression can be applied to each member of a stream. The `Stream` class's `of` method will generate a stream of integers. The `map` function applies the lambda expression, `x->x*2`, to each element of the stream:

```
Stream<Integer> stream = Stream.of(12, 52, 32, 74, 25);
stream.map(x->x*2)
    .forEach(x ->System.out.println(x));
```

The output follows:

24

104

64

148

50

This can be parallelized easily using the `parallel` method as shown here:

```
stream = Stream.of(12, 52, 32, 74, 25);
stream.parallel().map(x->x*2)
    .forEach(x ->System.out.println(x));
```

One possible output follows. However, since the stream operations are executed in parallel, a different output ordering is possible:

64

148

50

104

24

When the lambda expression is executed concurrently on different elements of the stream, the operations can be assigned to different processors and at different times. There is no guarantee with regard to the order in which the operations will be executed.

Humans are not very adept at multitasking, let alone writing concurrent programs that are reliable. By moving some of the decision-making process to the compiler and runtime system, more capable and efficient programs can be created.

Optional and monads

Null pointer exceptions are common, and their very existence is problematic to many developers. They introduce a slew of problems, including the need to handle them gracefully. The Optional class has been introduced in Java 8 to help deal with null pointer exceptions. It helps preserve type safety. The approach will ease the use of functions, provide an opportunity for using fluent interfaces, and avoid exception handling boilerplate code.

The intent of the Optional class is to help programmers deal with situations where a failure may occur. One way of handling this type of problem has been to return a null reference indicating a missing value. Using the Optional class forces the programmer to explicitly deal with the possibility that a function might not return a value. The Optional type should be used as the return type of a method or function that might not return a value.

Consider the situation where we would like to return an instance of a Customer class based on an ID using the following method:

```
public Optional<Customer>findCustomerWithID(long id) {
    //...
    return someValue;
}
```

Later when we invoke the function, a value of the Optional<Customer> type will be returned. We need to use the isPresent method to explicitly determine if a value is returned. If it is present, then the get method returns the actual Customer instance as shown next:

```
Optional<Customer>optionalCustomer = findCustomerWithID(123);
if (optionalCustomer.isPresent()) {
    Customer customer = optionalCustomer.get();
    // Use customer
} else {
    // handle missing value
}
```

The problem with simply returning null is that the programmer may not realize that a method may return null and may not attempt to handle it. This will result in a null pointer exception. In this example, since the findCustomerWithID method explicitly used the Optional type, we know and must deal with the possibility that nothing may be returned.

The `Optional` type allows chained function calls where a method might not return a value. We will demonstrate this in *Chapter 6, Optional and Monads* where the `Optional` type is discussed in more detail.

The `Optional` type has a monadic structure. A **monad** is basically a structure containing a set of computations represented as a series of steps. These computations are chained together effectively forming a pipeline. However, there is more to monads than this. Monads are a very useful technique and promote more reliable programs than most imperative programming techniques are capable of doing. You will learn more about the nature of monads and how to use them in *Chapter 6, Optional and Monads*.

In the same way, as you need to choose the right hammer for a job, you also need to choose the right language and programming style for the programming task. We don't want to use a sledge hammer to put a small nail in the wall for a picture. Since most jobs consist of multiple tasks, we need to use the right programming style for the specific task at hand.

Hence, a major focus of the book is how to blend the various programming styles available in Java 8 to meet an application's need. To be able to decide which technique is best for a given job, one needs to understand the nature of the task and how a technique supports such a task.

The incorporation of these functional programming techniques does not make Java a functional programming language. It means that we now have a new set of tools that we can use to solve the programming problems presented to us. It behooves us to take advantage of these techniques whenever they are applicable.

Java 8's support for functional style programming

So, what is the foundation for functional style programming in Java 8? Well, it comes from a number of additions and modifications to the language. In this section, we will briefly introduce several concepts that Java 8 uses. These include:

- Lambda expressions
- Default methods
- Functional interfaces
- Method and constructor references
- Collections

Understanding these concepts will enable you to understand their purpose and why they are used.

Lambda expressions

Lambda expressions are essentially anonymous functions. They can be considered to be one of the most significant additions to Java 8. They can make the code easier to write and read.

We have already seen a lambda expression in the previous examples. In this section, we will provide additional detail about their form and use. There are three key aspects to lambda expressions:

- They are a block of code
- They may be passed parameters
- They may return a value

The following table illustrates several different forms a simple lambda expression can take:

Lambda expression	Meaning
`()->System.out.println()`	It takes no arguments and displays a single line
`x->System.out.println(x)`	It takes a single argument and displays it on a line
`x->2*x`	It takes a single argument and returns its double
`(x,y)->x+y`	It takes two arguments and returns their sum

`x -> {`
`int y = 2*x;`
`    return y;`
`}`
	It takes a single argument and returns its double using multiple statements

These examples are intended to provide some indication of what forms they may take on. A lambda expression may have zero, one, or more parameters and may return a value. They can be a concise single-line lambda expression or may consist of multiple lines. However, they need to be used in some context to be useful.

You can use a lambda expression in most places where a block of code needs to be executed. The advantage is that you do not need to formally declare and use a method to perform some task.

Lambda expressions are often converted to a functional interface automatically simplifying many tasks. Lambda expressions can access other variables outside of the expression. The ability to access these types of variables is an improvement over anonymous inner functions, which have problems in this regard. Lambda expressions will be discussed in more detail in *Chapter 2, Putting the Function in Functional Programming*.

Default methods

A default method is an interface method that possesses an implementation. Traditionally, interfaces can only contain abstract methods or static and final variables. This concept provides a way of defining a set of methods that a class can implement, and by doing so, it provides an enhanced form of polymorphic behavior.

Adding a default method to an interface is simple. The method is added using the `default` keyword along with its implementation. In the following example, an interface called `Computable` is declared. It has one abstract method and two default methods:

```
public interface Computable {
    public int compute();

    public default int doubleNumber(int num) {
        return 2*num;
    }

    public default int negateNumber(int num) {
        return -1*num;
    }
}
```

To use a default method, we create a class that implements its interface and executes the method against an instance of the new class. In the next sequence, the `ComputeImpl` class is declared that implements the `Computable` interface:

```
public class ComputeImpl implements Computable {

    @Override
    public int compute() {
        return 1;
    }
}
```

Next, an instance of ComputeImpl is declared, and the default method is executed:

```
ComputeImplcomputeImpl  = new ComputeImpl();
System.out.println(computeImpl.doubleNumber(2));
```

The result will be a 4. We did not have to provide an implementation of the doubleNumber method in the ComputeImpl class before we used it. However, we can override if desired.

In Java 8, we can add default and static methods to interfaces. This has a number of advantages, including the ability to add capability to previous interfaces without breaking the existing code. This has allowed interfaces declared prior to Java 8 to be augmented with a default method that supports functional-type operations.

For example, the forEach method has been added as a default method to the java.lang package's Iterable interface. This method takes a lambda expression that matches the Consumer interface's accept method and executes it against each member of the underlying collection.

In the next code sequence, an array list is populated with three strings. The ArrayList class implements the Iterable interface enabling the use of the forEach method:

```
ArrayList<String> list = new ArrayList<>();
list.add("Apple");
list.add("Peach");
list.add("Banana");
list.forEach(f->System.out.println(f));
```

The addition of a default method will not break code that was developed before the method was added.

Functional interfaces

A functional interface is an interface that has one and only one abstract method. The Computable interface declared in the previous section is a functional interface. It has one and only one abstract method: compute. If a second abstract method was added, the interface would no longer be a functional interface.

Functional interfaces facilitate the use of lambda expressions. This is illustrated with the Iterable interface's forEach method. It expects a lambda expression that implements the Consumer interface. This interface has a single abstract method, accept, making it a functional interface.

This means that the `forEach` method will accept any lambda expression that matches the `accept` method's signature as defined here:

```
void accept(T t)
```

That is, it will use any lambda expression that is passed a single value and returns void. As seen with the `ArrayList` class used in the previous section and duplicated next, the lambda expression matches the signature of the `accept` method.

```
list.forEach(f->System.out.println(f));
```

This is possible because Java 8 uses a technique called **type inference** to determine if the lambda expression can be used.

Java 8 has introduced a number of functional interfaces. However, conceptually they have been present in earlier version of Java, but were not identified as functional interfaces. For example, the `Runnable` interface, with its single abstract `run` method, is a functional interface. It has been a part of Java since the very beginning, but until Java 8 was not labeled as a functional interface.

The advantage of functional interfaces is that Java is able to automatically use a lambda expression that matches the signature of the abstract method found in a functional interface. Consider the creation of a thread as illustrated in the following code sequence:

```
new Thread(()-> {
    for(inti=0; i<5; i++) {
        System.out.println("Thread!");
    }
}).start();
```

The argument of the `Thread` class's constructor is a lambda expression that implements the `Runnable` interface's `run` method. This method takes zero argument and returns void. The lambda expression used matches this signature.

Method and constructor references

A method or constructor reference is a technique that allows a Java 8 programmer to use a method or constructor as if it was a lambda expression. In the following sequence, a stream is generated, its elements are doubled, and then displayed using a lambda expression:

```
Stream<Integer> stream = Stream.of(12, 52, 32, 74, 25);
Stream
```

```
        .map(x -> x * 2)
        .forEach(x ->System.out.println(x));
```

The output follows:

24

104

64

148

50

We can duplicate this sequence using a method reference in place of the lambda expression as shown next. A method reference takes the form of a class name followed by a double colon and then the method name. The parameter is implied, and the code will produce the same output as the previous example.

```
Stream<Integer> stream = Stream.of(12, 52, 32, 74, 25);
Stream
    .map(x -> x * 2)
    .forEach(System.out::println);
```

In the following example, two method references are used where the first one invokes the sin method against each element of the list:

```
stream
    .map(Math::sin)
    .forEach(System.out::println);
```

The output follows:

-0.5365729180004349

0.9866275920404853

0.5514266812416906

-0.9851462604682474

-0.13235175009777303

We can also use constructors in a similar manner. Method and constructor references provide a convenient and easy way of using methods and constructors where lambda expressions are used.

Collections

The `Collection` interface has been enhanced in Java with the addition of methods that return a `Stream` object based on the collection. The `stream` method returns a stream executed in sequential order while the `parallelStream` method returns a stream that is executed concurrently. The following example illustrates the use of the `stream` method as applied against the `list` object. The `List` interface extends the `Collection` interface:

```
String names[] = {"Sally", "George", "Paul"};
List<String> list = Arrays.asList(names);
Stream<String> stream = list.stream();
stream.forEach(name ->System.out.println(name + " - "
    + name.length()));
```

This sequence output follows:

```
Sally - 5
George - 6
Paul - 4
```

In addition, since the `Collection` interface inherits the `Iterable` interface's `forEach` method from the iterator. We can use this with the previous `List` object:

```
list.forEach(name ->System.out.println(name + " - "
    + name.length()));
```

There are other enhancements to collections in Java 8, which we will present as they are encountered.

Summary

In this chapter, we introduced many of the features that constitute a functional programming language. These included functions and the idea that they can be combined in more powerful ways than are possible in an imperative type language.

Functional languages frequently allow the expression of program logic using a fluent style where function invocations build upon each other. The expression of parallel behavior is simplified in functional programming languages allowing better optimization of code.

An important goal of functional programs has been to minimize the use of mutable data and avoid side effects. This also promotes certain optimizations and makes functional code more maintainable. Recursion is central to functional programming languages, and we hinted at how it can be used. The use of optional types and monads were also introduced.

Java 8 introduced several new language features that support the use of functions. These include lambda expressions, which underlie functions and functional interfaces with type inferences. The introduction of default methods enables the newer functional techniques to be used with older interfaces and classes. Method and constructor references provide a way of using these constructs where lambda expressions are expected.

With many of these topics, we provided simple examples of how Java can support these concepts. The remainder of the book provides a much more detailed discussion of how Java can be used.

Java is not a pure functional programming language. However, it supports many functional style techniques, which a knowledgeable developer can use. The use of these techniques require a different way of thinking about and approaching problems. We will convey these techniques in this book starting with a more detailed discussion of functions in *Chapter 2, Putting the Function in Functional Programming*.

2
Putting the Function in Functional Programming

In the first chapter, the basic concept of functions and how they are supported by lambda expressions in Java 8 were introduced. In this chapter, we will cover lambda expressions in more depth. We will explain how they satisfy the mathematical definition of a function and how we can use them in supporting Java applications.

In this chapter, you will cover several topics, including:

- Lambda expression syntax and type inference
- High-order, pure, and first-class functions
- Referential transparency
- Closure and currying
- Common functional interfaces

Our discussions cover high-order functions, first-class functions, and pure functions. Also examined are the concepts of referential transparency, closure, and currying. Examples of nonfunctional approaches are followed by their functional equivalent where practical.

While we used lambda expression extensively in our examples, in the last part of this chapter, a little time will be spent examining their syntax and variations. We will also examine functional interfaces and many of the standard functional interfaces added to Java 8.

Lambda expressions usage

A lambda expression can be used in many different situations, including:

- Assigned to a variable
- Passed as a parameter
- Returned from a function or method

We will demonstrate how each of these is accomplished and then elaborate on the use of functional interfaces. As you may remember from *Chapter 1, Getting Started with Functional Programming*, a functional interface is an interface that has one and only one abstract method.

Consider the `forEach` method supported by several classes and interfaces, including the `List` interface. In the following example, a `List` interface is created and the `forEach` method is executed against it. The `forEach` method expects an object that implements the `Consumer` interface. This will display the three cartoon character names:

```
List<String> list = Arrays.asList("Huey", "Duey", "Luey");
list.forEach(/* Implementation of Consumer Interface*/);
```

More specifically, the `forEach` method expects an object that implements the `accept` method, the interface's single abstract method. This method's signature is as follows:

```
void accept(T t)
```

The interface also has a default method, `andThen`, which is passed and returns an instance of the `Consumer` interface. We will discuss this in *Chapter 3, Function Composition and Fluent Interfaces*.

We can use any of three different approaches for implementing the functionality of the `accept` method:

- Use an instance of a class that implements the `Consumer` interface
- Use an anonymous inner class
- Use a lambda expression

We will demonstrate each method so that it will be clear how each technique works and why lambda expressions will often result in a better solution. We will start with the declaration of a class that implements the `Consumer` interface as shown next:

```
public class ConsumerImpl<T> implements Consumer<T> {
    @Override
```

```
    public void accept(T t) {
        System.out.println(t);
    }
}
```

We can then use it as the argument of the `forEach` method:

```
list.forEach(new ConsumerImpl<>());
```

Using an explicit class allows us to reuse the class or its objects whenever an instance is needed.

The second approach uses an anonymous inner function as shown here:

```
list.forEach(new Consumer<String>() {
    @Override
    public void accept(String t) {
        System.out.println(t);
    }
});
```

This was a fairly common approach used prior to Java 8. It avoids having to explicitly declare and instantiate a class, which implements the `Consumer` interface. However, it is not easily reused and has issues accessing variables outside of the inner class as we will illustrate in the *Closure in Java* section.

A simple statement that uses a lambda expression is shown next:

```
list.forEach(t->System.out.println(t));
```

The lambda expression accepts a single argument and returns void. This matches the signature of the `Consumer` interface. Java 8 is able to automatically perform this matching process. This process is covered in more detail in the *Java 8 type inference* section.

This latter technique obviously uses less code, making it more succinct than the other solutions. If we desire to reuse this lambda expression elsewhere, we could have assigned it to a variable first and then used it in the `forEach` method as shown here:

```
Consumer consumer = t->System.out.println(t);
list.forEach(consumer);
```

Anywhere a functional interface is expected, we can use a lambda expression. Thus, the availability of a large number of functional interfaces will enable the frequent use of lambda expressions and programs that exhibit a functional style of programming.

While developers can define their own functional interfaces, which we will do shortly, Java 8 has added a large number of functional interfaces designed to support common operations. Most of these are found in the `java.util.function` package. We will use several of these throughout the book and will elaborate on their purpose, definition, and use as we encounter them. In the *Functional interfaces revisited* section, we will briefly introduce many others.

Functional programming concepts in Java

In this section, we will examine the underlying concept of functions and how they are implemented in Java 8. This includes high-order, first-class, and pure functions.

A first-class function is a function that can be used where other first-class entities can be used. These types of entities include primitive data types and objects. Typically, they can be passed to and returned from functions and methods. In addition, they can be assigned to variables.

A high-order function either takes another function as an argument or returns a function as the return value. Languages that support this type of function are more flexible. They allow a more natural flow and composition of operations. The use of composition is explored in *Chapter 3, Function Composition and Fluent Interfaces*.

Pure functions have no side effects. The function does not modify nonlocal variables and does not perform I/O.

High-order functions

We will demonstrate the creation and use of the high-order function using an imperative and a functional approach to convert letters of a string to lowercase. The next code sequence reuses the `list` variable, developed in the previous section, to illustrate the imperative approach. The for-each statement iterates through each element of the list using the `String` class' `toLowerCase` method to perform the conversion:

```
for(String element : list) {
    System.out.println(element.toLowerCase());
}
```

The output of this sequence will display each name in the list, in lowercase and on a separate line.

To demonstrate the use of a high-order function, we will create a function called `processString`, which is passed a function as the first parameter and then apply this function to the second parameter as shown next:

```
public String processString(Function<String,String>
operation,String target) {
    return operation.apply(target);
}
```

The function passed will be an instance of the `java.util.function` package's `Function` interface. This interface possesses an `accept` method that passes one data type and returns a potentially different data type. With our definition, it is passed `String` and returns `String`.

In the next code sequence, a lambda expression using the `toLowerCase` method is passed to the `processString` method. As you may remember, the `forEach` method accepts a lambda expression, which matches the `Consumer` interface's `accept` method. The lambda expression passed to the `processString` method matches the `Function` interface's `accept` method. The output is the same as produced by the equivalent imperative implementation.

```
list.forEach(s ->System.out.println(
    processString(t->t.toLowerCase(), s)));
```

We could have also used a method reference as show next:

```
list.forEach(s ->System.out.println(
    processString(String::toLowerCase, s)));
```

The use of the high-order function may initially seem to be a bit convoluted. We needed to create the `processString` function and then pass either a lambda expression or a method reference to perform the conversion. While this is true, the benefit of this approach is flexibility. If we needed to perform a different string operation other than converting the target string to lowercase, we will need to essentially duplicate the imperative code and replace `toLowerCase` with a new method such as `toUpperCase`. However, with the functional approach, all we need to do is replace the method used as shown next:

```
list.forEach(s ->System.out.println(processString(
    t->t.toUpperCase(), s)));
```

This is simpler and more flexible. A lambda expression can also be passed to another lambda expression.

Let's consider another example where high-order functions can be useful. Suppose we need to convert a list of one type into a list of a different type. We might have a list of strings that we wish to convert to their integer equivalents. We might want to perform a simple conversion or perhaps we might want to double the integer value. We will use the following lists:

```
List<String> numberString = Arrays.asList("12", "34", "82");
List<Integer> numbers = new ArrayList<>();
List<Integer> doubleNumbers = new ArrayList<>();
```

The following code sequence uses an iterative approach to convert the string list into an integer list:

```
for (String num : numberString) {
    numbers.add(Integer.parseInt(num));
}
```

The next sequence uses a stream to perform the same conversion:

```
numbers.clear();
numberString
        .stream()
        .forEach(s -> numbers.add(Integer.parseInt(s)));
```

There is not a lot of difference between these two approaches, at least from a number of lines perspective. However, the iterative solution will only work for the two lists: numberString and numbers. To avoid this, we could have written the conversion routine as a method.

We could also use lambda expression to perform the same conversion. The following two lambda expression will convert a string list to an integer list and from a string list to an integer list where the integer has been doubled:

```
Function<List<String>, List<Integer>> singleFunction = s -> {
    s.stream()
            .forEach(t -> numbers.add(Integer.parseInt(t)));
    return numbers;
};

Function<List<String>, List<Integer>> doubleFunction = s -> {
    s.stream()
            .forEach(t -> doubleNumbers.add(
                Integer.parseInt(t) * 2));
    return doubleNumbers;
};
```

We can apply these two functions as shown here:

```
numbers.clear();
System.out.println(singleFunction.apply(numberString));
System.out.println(doubleFunction.apply(numberString));
```

The output follows:

```
[12, 34, 82]
[24, 68, 164]
```

However, the real power comes from passing these functions to other functions. In the next code sequence, a stream is created consisting of a single element, a list. This list contains a single element, the numberString list. The map method expects a Function interface instance. Here, we use the doubleFunction function. The list of strings is converted to integers and then doubled. The resulting list is displayed:

```
Arrays.asList(numberString).stream()
        .map(doubleFunction)
        .forEach(s -> System.out.println(s));
```

The output follows:

```
[24, 68, 164]
```

We passed a function to a method. We could easily pass other functions to achieve different outputs.

Returning a function

When a value is returned from a function or method, it is intended to be used elsewhere in the application. Sometimes, the return value is used to determine how subsequent computations should proceed. To illustrate how returning a function can be useful, let's consider a problem where we need to calculate the pay of an employee based on the numbers of hours worked, the pay rate, and the employee type.

To facilitate the example, start with an enumeration representing the employee type:

```
enum EmployeeType {Hourly, Salary, Sales};
```

The next method illustrates one way of calculating the pay using an imperative approach. A more complex set of computation could be used, but these will suffice for our needs:

```
public float calculatePay(int hourssWorked,
        float payRate, EmployeeType type) {
    switch (type) {
```

```
        case Hourly:
            return hourssWorked * payRate;
        case Salary:
            return 40 * payRate;
        case Sales:
            return 500.0f + 0.15f * payRate;
        default:
            return 0.0f;
    }
}
```

If we assume a 7 day workweek, then the next code sequence shows an imperative way of calculating the total number of hours worked:

```
int hoursWorked[] = {8, 12, 8, 6, 6, 5, 6, 0};
int totalHoursWorked = 0;
    for (int hour : hoursWorked) {
        totalHoursWorked += hour;
    }
```

Alternatively, we could have used a stream to perform the same operation as shown next. The `Arrays` class's `stream` method accepts an array of integers and converts it into a `Stream` object. The `sum` method is applied fluently, returning the number of hours worked:

```
totalHoursWorked = Arrays.stream(hoursWorked).sum();
```

The latter approach is simpler and easier to read. To calculate and display the pay, we can use the following statement which, when executed, will return `803.25`.

```
System.out.println(
    calculatePay(totalHoursWorked, 15.75f,
    EmployeeType.Hourly));
```

The functional approach is shown next. A `calculatePayFunction` method is created that is passed the employee type and returns a lambda expression. This will compute the pay based on the number of hours worked and the pay rate. This lambda expression is based on the `BiFunction` interface. It has an `accept` method that takes two arguments and returns a value. Each of the parameters and the return type can be of different data types. It is similar to the `Function` interface's `accept` method, except that it is passed two arguments instead of one.

The `calculatePayFunction` method is shown next. It is similar to the imperative's `calculatePay` method, but returns a lambda expression:

```
public BiFunction<Integer, Float, Float> calculatePayFunction(
        EmployeeType type) {
```

```
        switch (type) {
            case Hourly:
                return (hours, payRate) -> hours * payRate;
            case Salary:
                return (hours, payRate) -> 40 * payRate;
            case Sales:
                return (hours, payRate) -> 500f + 0.15f * payRate;
            default:
                return null;
        }
    }
```

It can be invoked as shown next:

```
System.out.println(
    calculatePayFunction(EmployeeType.Hourly)
        .apply(totalHoursWorked, 15.75f));
```

When executed, it will produce the same output as the imperative solution. The advantage of this approach is that the lambda expression can be passed around and executed in different contexts. In addition, it can be combined with other functions in more powerful ways as we will see in *Chapter 3, Function Composition and Fluent Interfaces* .

First-class functions

To demonstrate first-class functions, we use lambda expressions. Assigning a lambda expression, or method reference, to a variable can be done in Java 8. Simply declare a variable of the appropriate function type and use the assignment operator to do the assignment.

In the following statement, a reference variable to the previously defined BiFunction-based lambda expression is declared along with the number of hours worked:

```
BiFunction<Integer, Float, Float> calculateFunction;
int hoursWorked = 51;
```

We can easily assign a lambda expression to this variable. Here, we use the lambda expression returned from the calculatePayFunction method:

```
calculateFunction = calculatePayFunction(EmployeeType.Hourly);
```

The reference variable can then be used as shown in this statement:

```
System.out.println(
    calculateFunction.apply(hoursWorked, 15.75f));
```

It produces the same output as before.

One shortcoming of the way an hourly employee's pay is computed is that overtime pay is not handled. We can add this functionality to the `calculatePayFunction` method. However, to further illustrate the use of reference variables, we will assign one of two lambda expressions to the `calculateFunction` variable based on the number of hours worked as shown here:

```
if(hoursWorked<=40) {
    calculateFunction = (hours, payRate) -> 40 * payRate;
} else {
    calculateFunction = (hours, payRate) ->
        hours*payRate + (hours-40)*1.5f*payRate;
}
```

When the expression is evaluated as shown next, it returns a value of `1063.125`:

```
System.out.println(
    calculateFunction.apply(hoursWorked, 15.75f));
```

Let's rework the example developed in the *High-order functions* section, where we used lambda expressions to display the lowercase values of an array of string. Part of the code has been duplicated here for your convenience:

```
list.forEach(s ->System.out.println(
    processString(t->t.toLowerCase(), s)));
```

Instead, we will use variables to hold the lambda expressions for the `Consumer` and `Function` interfaces as shown here:

```
Consumer<String> consumer;
consumer = s -> System.out.println(toLowerFunction.apply(s));
Function<String,String> toLowerFunction;
toLowerFunction= t -> t.toLowerCase();
```

The declaration and initialization could have been done with one statement for each variable. To display all of the names, we simply use the `consumer` variable as the argument of the `forEach` method:

```
list.forEach(consumer);
```

This will display the names as before. However, this is much easier to read and follow. The ability to use lambda expressions as first-class entities makes this possible.

We can also assign method references to variables. Here, we replaced the initialization of the `function` variable with a method reference:

```
function = String::toLowerCase;
```

The output of the code will not change.

The pure function

The pure function is a function that has no side effects. By side effects, we mean that the function does not modify nonlocal variables and does not perform I/O. A method that squares a number is an example of a pure method with no side effects as shown here:

```
public class SimpleMath {
    public static int square(int x) {
        return x * x;
    }
}
```

Its use is shown here and will display the result, 25:

```
System.out.println(SimpleMath.square(5));
```

An equivalent lambda expression is shown here:

```
Function<Integer,Integer> squareFunction = x -> x*x;
System.out.println(squareFunction.apply(5));
```

The advantages of pure functions include the following:

- They can be invoked repeatedly producing the same results
- There are no dependencies between functions that impact the order they can be executed
- They support lazy evaluation
- They support referential transparency

We will examine each of these advantages in more depth.

Support repeated execution

Using the same arguments will produce the same results. The previous square operation is an example of this. Since the operation does not depend on other external values, re-executing the code with the same arguments will return the same results.

This supports the optimization technique call **memoization**. This is the process of caching the results of an expensive execution sequence and retrieving them when they are used again.

An imperative technique for implementing this approach involves using a hash map to store values that have already been computed and retrieving them when they are used again. Let's demonstrate this using the `square` function. The technique should be used for those functions that are compute intensive. However, using the `square` function will allow us to focus on the technique.

Declare a cache to hold the previously computed values as shown here:

```
private final Map<Integer, Integer> memoizationCache =
    new HashMap<>();
```

We need to declare two methods. The first method, called `doComputeExpensiveSquare`, does the actual computation as shown here. A display statement is included only to verify the correct operation of the technique. Otherwise, it is not needed. The method should only be called once for each unique value passed to it.

```
private Integer doComputeExpensiveSquare(Integer input) {
    System.out.println("Computing square");
    return 2 * input;
}
```

A second method is used to detect when a value is used a subsequent time and return the previously computed value instead of calling the `square` method. This is shown next. The `containsKey` method checks to see if the input value has already been used. If it hasn't, then the `doComputeExpensiveSquare` method is called. Otherwise, the cached value is returned.

```
public Integer computeExpensiveSquare(Integer input) {
    if (!memoizationCache.containsKey(input)) {
        memoizationCache.put(input,
            doComputeExpensiveSquare(input));
    }
    return memoizationCache.get(input);
}
```

The use of the technique is demonstrated with the next code sequence:

```
System.out.println(computeExpensiveSquare(4));
System.out.println(computeExpensiveSquare(4));
```

The output follows, which demonstrates that the `square` method was only called once:

```
Computing square
16
16
```

The problem with this approach is the declaration of a hash map. This object may be inadvertently used by other elements of the program and will require the explicit declaration of new hash maps for each memoization usage. In addition, it does not offer flexibility in handling multiple memoization. A better approach is available in Java 8. This new approach wraps the hash map in a class and allows easier creation and use of memoization.

Let's examine a memoization class as adapted from `http://java.dzone.com/articles/java-8-automatic-memoization`. It is called **Memoizer**. It uses `ConcurrentHashMap` to cache value and supports concurrent access from multiple threads.

Two methods are defined. The `doMemoize` method returns a lambda expression that does all of the work. The `memorize` method creates an instance of the `Memoizer` class and passes the lambda expression implementing the expensive operation to the `doMemoize` method.

The `doMemoize` method uses the `ConcurrentHashMap` class's `computeIfAbsent` method to determine if the computation has already been performed. If the value has not been computed, it executes the `Function` interface's `apply` method against the function argument:

```
public class Memoizer<T, U> {
    private final Map<T, U> memoizationCache = new
        ConcurrentHashMap<>();

    private Function<T, U> doMemoize(final Function<T, U>
            function) {
        return input -> memoizationCache.computeIfAbsent(input,
            function::apply);
    }

    public static <T, U> Function<T, U> memoize(final Function<T,
            U> function) {
        return new Memoizer<T, U>().doMemoize(function);
    }
}
```

A lambda expression is created for the square operation:

```
Function<Integer, Integer> squareFunction = x -> {
    System.out.println("In function");
    return x * x;
};
```

The `memoizationFunction` variable will hold the lambda expression that is subsequently used to invoke the square operations:

```
Function<Integer, Integer> memoizationFunction =
    Memoizer.memoize(squareFunction);
System.out.println(memoizationFunction.apply(2));
System.out.println(memoizationFunction.apply(2));
System.out.println(memoizationFunction.apply(2));
```

The output of this sequence follows where the square operation is performed only once:

In function

4

4

4

We can easily use the `Memoizer` class for a different function as shown here:

```
Function<Double, Double> memoizationFunction2 =
    Memoizer.memoize(x -> x * x);
System.out.println(memoizationFunction2.apply(4.0));
```

This will square the number as expected. Functions that are recursive present additional problems. Recursion will be addressed in *Chapter 5, Recursion Techniques in Java 8*.

Eliminating dependencies between functions

When dependencies between functions are eliminated, then more flexibility in the order of execution is possible. Consider these `Function` and `BiFunction` declarations, which define simple expressions for computing hourly, salaried, and sales type pay, respectively:

```
BiFunction<Integer, Double, Double> computeHourly =
    (hours, rate) -> hours * rate;
Function<Double, Double> computeSalary = rate -> rate * 40.0;
BiFunction<Double, Double, Double> computeSales =
    (rate, commission) -> rate * 40.0 + commission;
```

These functions can be executed, and their results are assigned to variables as shown here:

```
double hourlyPay = computeHourly.apply(35, 12.75);
double salaryPay = computeSalary.apply(25.35);
double salesPay = computeSales.apply(8.75, 2500.0);
```

These are pure functions as they do not use external values to perform their computations. In the following code sequence, the sum of all three pays are totaled and displayed:

```
System.out.println(computeHourly.apply(35, 12.75)
        + computeSalary.apply(25.35)
        + computeSales.apply(8.75, 2500.0));
```

We can easily reorder their execution sequence or even execute them concurrently, and the results will be the same. There are no dependencies between the functions that restrict them to a specific execution ordering.

Supporting lazy evaluation

Continuing with this example, let's add an additional sequence, which computes the total pay based on the type of employee. The variable, `hourly`, is set to `true` if we want to know the total of the hourly employee pay type. It will be set to `false` if we are interested in salary and sales-type employees:

```
double total = 0.0;
boolean hourly = ...;
if(hourly) {
    total = hourlyPay;
} else {
    total = salaryPay + salesPay;
}
System.out.println(total);
```

When this code sequence is executed with an hourly value of `false`, there is no need to execute the `computeHourly` function since it is not used. The runtime system could conceivably choose not to execute any of the lambda expressions until it knows which one is actually used.

While all three functions are actually executed in this example, it illustrates the potential for lazy evaluation. Functions are not executed until needed. Lazy evaluation does occur with streams as we will demonstrate in *Chapter 4, Streams and the Evaluation of Expressions*.

Referential transparency

Referential transparency is the idea that a given expression is made up of subexpressions. The value of the subexpression is important. We are not concerned about how it is written or other details. We can replace the subexpression with its value and be perfectly happy.

With regards to pure functions, they are said to be referentially transparent since they have same effect. In the next declaration, we declare a pure function called `pureFunction`:

```
Function<Double,Double> pureFunction = t -> 3*t;
```

It supports referential transparency. Consider if we declare a variable as shown here:

```
int num = 5;
```

Later, in a method we can assign a different value to the variable:

```
num = 6;
```

If we define a lambda expression that uses this variable, the function is no longer pure:

```
Function<Double,Double> impureFunction = t -> 3*t+num;
```

The function no longer supports referential transparency.

Closure in Java

The use of external variables in a lambda expression raises several interesting questions. One of these involves the concept of **closures**. A closure is a function that uses the context within which it was defined. By context, we mean the variables within its scope. This sometimes is referred to as **variable capture**.

We will use a class called `ClosureExample` to illustrate closures in Java. The class possesses a `getStringOperation` method that returns a `Function` lambda expression. This expression takes a string argument and returns an augmented version of it. The argument is converted to lowercase, and then its length is appended to it twice. In the process, both an instance variable and a local variable are used.

In the implementation that follows, the instance variable and two local variables are used. One local variable is a member of the `getStringOperation` method and the second one is a member of the lambda expression. They are used to hold the length of the target string and for a separator string:

```
public class ClosureExample {
    int instanceLength;

    public Function<String,String> getStringOperation() {
        final String seperator = ":";
```

```
        return target -> {
            int localLength = target.length();
            instanceLength = target.length();
            return target.toLowerCase()
                + seperator + instanceLength + seperator
                + localLength;
        };
    }
}
```

The lambda expression is created and used as shown here:

```
ClosureExample ce = new ClosureExample();
final Function<String,String> function =
    ce.getStringOperation();
System.out.println(function.apply("Closure"));
```

Its output follows:

`closure:7:7`

Variables used by the lambda expression are restricted in their use. Local variables or parameters cannot be redefined or modified. These variables need to be *effectively final*. That is, they must be declared as final or not be modified.

If the local variable and separator, had not been declared as final, the program would still be executed properly. However, if we tried to modify the variable later, then the following syntax error would be generated, indicating such variable was not permitted within a lambda expression:

`local variables referenced from a lambda expression must be final or effectively final`

If we add the following statements to the previous example and remove the `final` keyword, we will get the same syntax error message:

```
function = String::toLowerCase;
Consumer<String> consumer =
    s -> System.out.println(function.apply(s));
```

This is because the `function` variable is used in the `Consumer` lambda expression. It also needs to be effectively final, but we tried to assign a second value to it, the method reference for the `toLowerCase` method.

Closure refers to functions that enclose variable external to the function. This permits the function to be passed around and used in different contexts.

Currying

Some functions can have multiple arguments. It is possible to evaluate these arguments one-by-one. This process is called currying and normally involves creating new functions, which have one fewer arguments than the previous one.

The advantage of this process is the ability to subdivide the execution sequence and work with intermediate results. This means that it can be used in a more flexible manner.

Consider a simple function such as:

$$f(x, y) = x + y$$

The evaluation of *f(2,3)* will produce a 5. We could use the following, where the 2 is "hardcoded":

$$f(2, y) = 2 + y$$

If we define:

$$g(y) = 2 + y$$

Then the following are equivalent:

$$f(2, y) = g(y) = 2 + y$$

Substituting 3 for *y* we get:

$$f(2,3) = g(3) = 2 + 3 = 5$$

This is the process of currying. An intermediate function, *g(y)*, was introduced which we can pass around. Let's see, how something similar to this can be done in Java 8.

Start with a `BiFunction` interface's `apply` method that can be used for concatenation of strings. This method takes two parameters and returns a single value as implied by this lambda expression declaration:

```
BiFunction<String, String, String> biFunctionConcat =
    (a, b) -> a + b;
```

The use of the function is demonstrated with the following statement:

```
System.out.println(biFunctionConcat.apply("Cat", "Dog"));
```

The output will be the `CatDog` string.

Next, let's define a reference variable called `curryConcat`. This variable is a `Function` interface variable. This interface is based on two data types. The first one is `String` and represents the value passed to the `Function` interface's `accept` method. The second data type represents the `accept` method's return type. This return type is defined as a `Function` instance that is passed a string and returns a string. In other words, the `curryConcat` function is passed a string and returns an instance of a function that is passed and returns a string.

```
Function<String, Function<String, String>> curryConcat;
```

We then assign an appropriate lambda expression to the variable:

```
curryConcat = (a) -> (b) -> biFunctionConcat.apply(a, b);
```

This may seem to be a bit confusing initially, so let's take it one piece at a time. First of all, the lambda expression needs to return a function. The lambda expression assigned to `curryConcat` follows where the ellipses represent the body of the function. The parameter, a, is passed to the body:

```
(a) ->...;
```

The actual body follows:

```
(b) -> biFunctionConcat.apply(a, b);
```

This is the lambda expression or function that is returned. This function takes two parameters, a and b. When this function is created, the a parameter will be known and specified. This function can be evaluated later when the value for b is specified. The function returned is an instance of a `Function` interface, which is passed two parameters and returns a single value.

To illustrate this, define an intermediate variable to hold this returned function:

```
Function<String,String> intermediateFunction;
```

We can assign the result of executing the `curryConcat` lambda expression using it's `apply` method as shown here where a value of `Cat` is specified for the a parameter:

```
intermediateFunction = curryConcat.apply("Cat");
```

The next two statements will display the returned function:

```
System.out.println(intermediateFunction);
System.out.println(curryConcat.apply("Cat"));
```

The output will look something similar to the following:

packt.Chapter2$$Lambda$3/798154996@5305068a

packt.Chapter2$$Lambda$3/798154996@1f32e575

Note that these are the values representing this functions as returned by the implied toString method. They are both different, indicating that two different functions were returned and can be passed around.

Now that we have confirmed a function has been returned, we can supply a value for the b parameter as shown here:

```
System.out.println(intermediateFunction.apply("Dog"));
```

The output will be CatDog. This illustrates how we can split a two parameter function into two distinct functions, which can be evaluated when desired. They can be used together as shown with these statements:

```
System.out.println(curryConcat.apply("Cat").apply("Dog"));
System.out.println(curryConcat.apply(
    "Flying ").apply("Monkeys"));
```

The output of these statements is as follows:

CatDog

Flying Monkeys

We can define a similar operation for doubles as shown here:

```
Function<Double, Function<Double, Double>> curryAdd =
    (a) -> (b) -> a * b;
System.out.println(curryAdd.apply(3.0).apply(4.0));
```

This will display 12.0 as the returned value.

Currying is a valuable approach useful when the arguments of a function need to be evaluated at different times.

Lambda expressions revisited

In this section, we will explore the syntax of lambda expression in more depth. So far, we used them without formally describing them. We will also examine other forms they can take.

As mentioned earlier, a lambda expression is essentially an anonymous function. They can be passed to another function or method, returned from a function or a method, and assigned to variables.

A lambda expression consists of an optional parameter list, followed by the lambda operator, and then a body. The lambda operator is a dash followed by the greater than symbol. The body of a lambda expression may be one or more statements and may optionally return a value.

Let's examine several variations of a simple lambda expression. A single value is passed to the function. This value is incremented and then returned. Several equivalent variations of this function are illustrated in the following table:

Variation	Comment
`x -> x + 1`	The simplest form of the function
`(x) -> x + 1`	The parameter(s) can be enclosed in parentheses
`(Integer x) ->` `    x + 1`	A data type can be declared for parameter(s)

`x -> {`
`    x + 1;`
`    return x;`
`}`
	A multiline function which is verbose

`x -> {`
`    Integer y;`
`    y = x + 1;`
`    return y;`
`};`
	A multiline function which uses a local variable

Multiple parameters are possible as illustrated in the following table:

Variation	Comment
`(x,y) -> x + y`	Multiple parameters must be placed in parentheses
`(Integer x, Integer y) -> x + y`	Data types can be declared
`(Integer x, Double y) -> x + y`	The parameter's data types can be different
`(x,y) -> System.out .println(x+y)`	A return value is not required

A lambda expression's parameter list does not necessarily need a data type or a set of parentheses. A data type is used when it is necessary to clarify the type of data being passed. Parentheses are needed when a data type is used or when multiple parameters are passed.

Java 8 type inference

When a lambda expression is used, it goes through a process of inferring the types of its arguments based on its context. Its context depends on which functional interface it matches. More specifically, it depends on the signature of the functional interface's abstract method.

Consider the following example where we define a `concatenate` method, which combines two string, integers, or doubles together:

```
public interface StringConcatenation {
    public String concatenate(String s1, String s2);
}

public interface IntegerConcatenation {
    public String concatenate(Integer n1, Integer n2);
}

public interface DoubleConcatenation {
    public String concatenate(Double n1, Double n2);
}
```

In the following code sequence, lambda expressions are declared, which implement the concatenation functionality by returning a string containing the two arguments separated by a colon:

```
StringConcatenation sc = (s, t) -> s + ":" + t;
IntegerConcatenation ic = (m, n) -> m + ":" + n;
DoubleConcatenation dc = (m, n) -> m + ":" + n;
```

With each assignment, the lambda expression is matched against the signature of the concatenate method. Should a mismatch occur, then a syntax error will be produced. You may note that the same lambda expression is assigned to both the IntegerConcatenation and DoubleConcatenation variables. Since the data type of the lambda expression's parameters are not specified, the system can infer that they be treated as either an Integer or a Double types.

Likewise, the lambda expression used with the StringConcatenation variable could be used in place of the other lambda expressions since it matches the concatenate method's signature.

The following illustrates their use:

```
System.out.println(sc.concatenate("Cat", "Dog"));
System.out.println(ic.concatenate(23, 45));
System.out.println(dc.concatenate(23.12, 45.12));
```

The following output is generated:

CatDog

23:45

23.12:45.12

We can create another functional interface that eliminates the need for the previous three interfaces using generics as shown here:

```
public interface Concatenation<T> {
    public String concatenate(T u, T v);
}
```

Lambda expressions are assigned to an instance of this interface as shown next:

```
Concatenation<String> stringConcatenate = (s,t) -> s+":"+ t;
Concatenation<Integer> integerConcatenate = (s,t) -> s+":"+t;
System.out.println(
    stringConcatenate.concatenate("Cat", "Dog"));
System.out.println(integerConcatenate.concatenate(23, 45));
```

When a lambda expression is assigned to a variable, the left-hand side of the assignment is called the lambda expression's target type. There are several rules for target types:

- It must be a functional interface
- It must be compatible with the abstract method's parameter and return types
- It must throw only those exceptions thrown by the abstract method

We will address exception handling and functional interfaces in the next two sections.

Exception handling in lambda expressions

Lambda expressions can throw exceptions. However, they must only be those specified by its functional interface's abstract method.

To illustrate how to throw an exception in a lambda expression, we modified the IntegerConcatenation interface as developed in the previous section. This will throw an instance of IllegalFormatException as shown here:

```
public interface IntegerConcatenation {
    public String concatenate(Integer n1, Integer n2)
        throws IllegalFormatException;
}
```

A lambda expression is then declared, which will throw the exception when the first argument is zero:

```
IntegerConcatenation ic = (m, n) -> {
    if(m==0) {
        throw new IllegalArgumentException();
    } else {
        return m + ":" + n;
    }
};
System.out.println(ic.concatenate(0, 45));
```

While we will not be using exceptions very frequently, it is useful to know how they are handled.

Functional interfaces revisited

We used several functional interfaces in the previous examples. In this section, we will examine in more detail how they are created and illustrate a number of predefined functional interfaces available for immediate use in Java 8.

As mentioned earlier, a functional interface is an interface that has one and only one abstract method. It may have zero or more default methods. Since the interface has only one abstract method, the system is able to know which method to match to a lambda expression. This abstract method is called the **functional method**.

Creating a functional interface

The IntegerConcatenation interface is duplicated here as an example. Note the use of the @FunctionalInterface annotation. While not required, it will generate a syntax error if the interface is not a functional interface:

```
@FunctionalInterface
public interface IntegerConcatenation {
    public String concatenate(Integer n1, Integer n2);
}
```

Functional interfaces are easy to create. After working with functional interfaces for a while, some common patterns quickly emerged suggesting the need for some standard definitions. By defining these standard functional interfaces, there is less of a need to reinvent the wheel and common names can be used, which facilitates communication. For example, we used the Function functional interfaces several times in previous examples and hopefully its meaning is clear. The next section explores many of these standard interfaces.

Common functional interfaces

The java.util.function package was added to Java 8. In this package, 42 functional interfaces have been defined. We will not exhaustively examine every functional interface here, but we will discuss how they are categorized and detail a few of the more commonly used ones.

We can group these interfaces into five categories:

- **Function**: These transform their arguments and return a value
- **Predicate**: These are used to perform a test, which returns a Boolean value

- **Consumer**: These use their arguments, but do not return a value
- **Supplier**: These are not passed data, but do return data
- **Operator**: These perform a reduction type operation

We will examine each of these types in the following sections.

Function-type functional interfaces

We have seen the Function interface used in several of the previous examples. Its abstract method is called apply. As its name implies, it performs a transformation type operation against its arguments. Its signature is as follows:

```
R apply(T)
```

There are several other interfaces related to the Function interface that accept one or two arguments and return a single value. Some of these are designed to work with specific input and output data types such as DoubleToIntFunction, which is passed a double and returns an integer.

The DoubleToIntFunction interface has been added as a convenience. We could have used the Function interface to achieve the same result: Function<Double, Integer>. However, having a specialized interface eliminates the need to declare the data types explicitly.

Conversion between wrapper classes, such as Double and the primitive data type double, occurs automatically using boxing/unboxing. Boxing converts a primitive type to its wrapper equivalent while unboxing performs the opposite conversion.

These functional interfaces are listed in the following table:

Functional-type interfaces	Return type	Functional method
Function<T,R>	R	apply(T t)
BiFunction<T,U,R>	R	apply(T t, U u)
DoubleFunction<R>	R	apply(double value)
DoubleToIntFunction	int	applyAsInt(double value)
DoubleToLongFunction	long	applyAsLong(double value)
IntFunction<R>	R	apply(int value)
IntToDoubleFunction	double	applyAsDouble(int value)
IntToLongFunction	long	applyAsLong(int value)
LongFunction<R>	R	apply(long value)
LongToDoubleFunction	double	applyAsDouble(long value)

Functional-type interfaces	Return type	Functional method
`LongToIntFunction`	`int`	`applyAsInt(long value)`
`ToDoubleBiFunction<T,U>`	`double`	`applyAsDouble(T t, U u)`
`ToDoubleFunction<T>`	`double`	`applyAsDouble(T value)`
`ToIntBiFunction<T,U>`	`int`	`applyAsInt(T t, U u)`
`ToIntFunction<T>`	`int`	`applyAsInt(T value)`
`ToLongBiFunction<T,U>`	`long`	`applyAsLong(T t, U u)`
`ToLongFunction<T>`	`long`	`applyAsLong(T value)`

Predicate-type functional interfaces

The predicate-type interface is designed for use in situations where a test needs to be performed and a Boolean value needs to be returned. The `Predicate` interface functional `test` method is shown here:

```
boolean test(T t)
```

This is useful when the functionality needed simply returns a Boolean value based on some input value. This is demonstrated next where we determine whether a value is too large to process:

```
Predicate<Integer> tooLarge = s -> s>100;
System.out.println(tooLarge.test(45));
```

We can also use it with a stream as shown here, along with its output:

```
List<Integer> list = Arrays.asList(230, 45, 13, 563, 4);
Stream<Integer> stream = list.stream();
stream.forEach(s->System.out.println(tooLarge.test(s)));
```

true

false

false

true

false

There is a `BiPredicate` functional interface, which accepts two parameters. Three other predicates are defined for double, integer, and long values. We could have defined our `tooLarge` variable using the `IntPredicate` interface as shown here:

```
IntPredicate tooLarge = s -> s>100;
```

There are six predicate-type functional interfaces. They all return a Boolean value, but differ in the number and types of their parameters as shown in the next table:

Predicate-type interfaces	Return type	Functional method
Predicate<T>	boolean	test(T t)
BiPredicate<T,U>	boolean	test(T t, U u)
DoublePredicate	boolean	boolean test(double value)
IntPredicate	boolean	boolean test(int value)
LongPredicate	boolean	boolean test(long value)

Consumer-type functional interfaces

The consumer-type functional interface is intended to accept input, but not return a value. It this sense, it consumes its input. It is typified by the Consumer interface whose accept method's signature is shown here:

```
void accept(T t)
```

We have seen this type of interface used with the earlier forEach method as shown next:

```
list.forEach(s ->System.out.println(
    processString(t->t.toLowerCase(), s)));
```

There are seven functional style interfaces all of which return void. They differ in terms of the number and types of parameters. These are listed next:

Consumer-type interfaces	Return type	Functional method
Consumer<T>	void	accept(T t)
BiConsumer<T,U>	void	void accept(T t, U u)
DoubleConsumer	void	void accept(double value)
IntConsumer	void	void accept(int value)
LongConsumer	void	void accept(long value)
ObjDoubleConsumer<T>	void	void accept(T t, double value)
ObjIntConsumer<T>	void	void accept(T t, int value)

Supplier-type functional interfaces

The supplier-type functional interfaces are intended to return a data type, but no input is provided. It is like a source of information. The `Supplier` interface typifies this style and its `get` method's signature is as follows:

```
T get()
```

The following illustrates the use of the `Supplier` interface to generate a random number between 0 and 9 excluding the numbers, 5, 6, 7, and 8:

```
Supplier<Integer> randomIntegers = () -> {
    Random random = new Random();
    int number = random.nextInt(10);
    while (number >= 5 && number <= 8) {
        number = random.nextInt(10);
    }
    return number;
};
for (int i = 0; i < 10; i++) {
    System.out.print(randomIntegers.get() + " ");
}
System.out.println();
```

The output of this sequence is as follows:

```
9 9 3 1 2 3 9 0 0 9
```

The other supplier-type interfaces use specific data types as shown in the following table:

Supplier-type interfaces	Return type	Functional method
Supplier<T>	T	get()
BooleanSupplier	Boolean	getAsBoolean()
DoubleSupplier	double	getAsDouble()
IntSupplier<R>	R	getAsInt()
LongSupplier	long	getAsLong()

Operator-type functional interfaces

The operator-type functional interfaces are used to apply some operation against one or two operands. It corresponds to unary or binary type operators. The `BinaryOperator` interface typifies the operator type. Its `apply` method's signature is as follows:

```
R apply(T t1, T t2)
```

We could have used this interface instead of the `Concatenation` interface we developed in the Java 8 type inference section. This interface is duplicated here, followed by one possible use:

```
public interface Concatenation<T> {
    public String concatenate(T u, T v);
}


...

Concatenation<String> stringConcatenate = (s,t) -> s+":"+t;
```

Instead, we can define `stringConcatenate` as shown next:

```
BinaryOperator<String> stringConcatenate = (s,t) -> s+":"+t;
System.out.println(stringConcatenate.apply("Cat", "Dog"));
```

The output is identical to the previous example.

Several other operator-type interfaces are available and differ in the number of parameters. The return type as shown in this table:

Operator-type interfaces	Return type	Functional method
`BinaryOperator<T>`	R	`apply(T t1, T t2)`
`DoubleBinaryOperator`	double	`applyAsDouble(double left, double right)`
`DoubleUnaryOperator`	double	`applyAsDouble(double operand)`
`IntBinaryOperator`	int	`applyAsInt(int left, int right)`
`IntUnaryOperator`	int	`applyAsInt(int operand)`
`LongBinaryOperator`	long	`applyAsLong(long left, long right)`
`LongUnaryOperator`	long	`applyAsLong(long operand)`
`UnaryOperator<T>`	R	`apply(T t)`

Summary

In this chapter, we investigated the use of lambda expressions and how they support the functional style of programming in Java 8. When possible, we used examples to contrast the use of classes and methods against the use of functions. This frequently led to simpler and more maintainable functional implementations.

We illustrated how lambda expressions support the functional concepts of high-order, first-class, and pure functions. Examples were used to help clarify the concept of referential transparency. The concepts of closure and currying are found in most functional programming languages. We provide examples of how they are supported in Java 8.

Lambda expressions have a specific syntax, which we examined in more detail. Also, there are several ways of expressing a lambda expression which we illustrated. Lambda expressions are based on functional interfaces using type inference. It is important to understand how to create functional interfaces and to know what standard functional interfaces are available in Java 8. This was covered in the latter part of the chapter.

Having gained a solid foundation in the creation and use of lambda expression, we are ready to explore more advanced use of these expressions. In the next chapter, we will examine function composition and how this is achieved in Java 8.

3
Function Composition and Fluent Interfaces

Having discussed the nature of functions in Java 8, we will now focus on the various ways in which functions can be composed. By compose, we mean how they can be combined in interesting and powerful ways. These techniques include basic function composition and the use of fluent interfaces.

Function composition is concerned with combining two functions to form a third one. Using the output of one function as the input to another one is a common practice. By combining two such functions, we are able to create more complex functions, which can be reused.

We will examine the basic approach for composing functions and then move on to the use of the Function interface and its compose and andThen methods. These methods make it easier to compose functions and use them.

We will also cover the topic of fluent interfaces. This programming style is frequently associated with functional programming languages. Java has used method chaining, which shares attributes with fluent interfaces. However, with Java 8 there has been more of a concerted effort to add fluent interfaces to Java.

In this chapter, you will cover:

- Function composition in Java
- The creation and use of fluent interfaces
- How default methods work in Java 8

Fluent interfaces do not refer to an actual Java interface declaration. Rather, it implies a style of programming that flows easily and is more readable than the typical use of methods. It applies the output of one method directly to another method without using intermediate variables. It also incorporates a naming convention that makes its use more natural than method chaining.

We will examine the use of method chaining in Java prior to Java 8. This will help contrast this approach to that of fluent interfaces. Java 8 fluent interfaces are demonstrated to give the reader a better idea of where they can be used. However, it is equally important to understand how they can be created so that fluent interfaces can be incorporated into new application interfaces and act as a facade for older interfaces.

A summary of default functions will also be presented. This brief coverage will increase your knowledge of Java 8 and help explain how the functional style of programming has been added to Java without breaking the existing classes and interfaces.

Introduction to function composition

Function composition is concerned with combining two functions into one. For example, assume that we have two functions: `f(x)` and `g(x)`. The result of composition is the creation of a third function, let's call *c*, such that:

```
c(x) = f(g(x))
```

That is, the effect of calling `c(x)` is the same as using the output of `g(x)` as the input to the function `f`. To illustrate this approach, let's use the following definitions:

```
f(x) = -x
g(x) = 2*x
c(5) = f(g(5)) = f(2*x) = -(2*5) = -10
```

The effect is that the `g(x)` function is called first. Its results are then used as input to the `f(x)` function. This capability allows more complex functions to be created in a more flexible and useful manner.

Creating composite functions prior to Java 8

Prior to Java 8 it was possible to affect this type of operation using a specialized library such as `http://www.functionaljava.org/` or by creating a class and interface first. We will demonstrate the latter approach here.

The interface will permit two methods to be combined. To illustrate this approach, we will declare a class called Compose. Within the class, we will declare a CompositionFunction interface, containing a single call method along with a compose method. The compose method returns an instance of the CompositionFunction interface using two CompositionFunction interface instances passed to it. The call method does the actual work.

The first part of the Compose class and the CompositionFunction interface are shown next. This interface uses generics to declare a single method, call, that is passed a single value and returns a value:

```
public class Compose {
    public interface CompositionFunction<T, R> {
        R call(T x);
    }
    ...

}
```

The Compose class's static compose method follows. It is passed two objects that implement the CompositionFunction interface, f and g. It uses an anonymous inner class to return a CompositionFunction interface instance. In the call method, the g function is invoked first followed by the f function:

```
public static <T, U, R> CompositionFunction<T, R> compose(
        final CompositionFunction<U, R> f,
        final CompositionFunction<T, U> g) {
    return new CompositionFunction<T, R>() {
        public R call(T x) {
            return f.call(g.call(x));
        }
    };
}
```

We are now ready to use this class. To duplicate the earlier definitions of the f and g functions, anonymous inner classes are created and assigned to the doubleNumber and negateNumber CompositionFunction interface variables as shown here:

```
CompositionFunction<Double, Double> doubleNumber =
        new CompositionFunction<Double, Double>() {
    public Double call(Double x) {
        return 2*x;
    }
};
```

```
CompositionFunction<Double, Double> negateNumber =
        new CompositionFunction<Double, Double>() {
    public Double call(Double x) {
        return -x;
    }
};
```

A doubleThenNegate variable is declared. This will hold the composed function and is invoked as shown here:

```
CompositionFunction<Double, Double> doubleThenNegate;
doubleThenNegate = Compose.compose(doubleNumber,
negateNumber);
System.out.println(doubleThenNegate.call(5.0));
```

This will output a -10.0.

Creating composite functions in Java 8

In Java 8, we can use the Function interface's compose method along with lambda expressions instead to achieve the same results with a lot less effort as shown next. The output will still be -10:

```
Function<Double, Double> doubleFunction = x -> 2 * x;
Function<Double, Double> second
        = doubleFunction.compose(x -> -x);
```

The Function interface is found in the java.util.function package. The source code for this interface is shown next. The default compose method is passed a single function and returns a function encapsulating the passed function. The requireNonNull method is used to support null values, and will be discussed in *Chapter 6, Optional and Monads*. The andThen method will be discussed shortly.

> The compose method uses a parameter named, before, and the andThen method uses a parameter named, after. These names indicate the order that the functions will be evaluated on.

```
@FunctionalInterface
public interface Function<T, R> {
    R apply(T t);

    default <V> Function<V, R> compose(
            Function<? super V, ? extends T> before) {
        Objects.requireNonNull(before);
```

Chapter 3

```
            return (V v) -> apply(before.apply(v));
    }

    default <V> Function<T, V> andThen(
            Function<? super R, ? extends V> after) {
        Objects.requireNonNull(after);
        return (T t) -> after.apply(apply(t));
    }

    static <T> Function<T, T> identity() {
        return t -> t;
    }
}
```

The default methods mean that objects that implement the interface do not have to implement these methods. However, if necessary, they can be overridden. We will elaborate on default methods in the *Default methods and functions* section.

Using the Function interface for function composition

The previous example of the `Function` interface does not demonstrate how the `andThen` method provides support for function composition. Consider these function definitions:

$$f(x) = (2+x)*3;$$

$$g(x) = 2+(x*3);$$

In the first function, we add 2 to x and the multiply it by 3. In the second function, we multiply it by 3 and then add 2. If we apply these functions using a value of 5, we get the following results, respectively:

$$f(5) = 21$$

$$g(5) = 17$$

We can illustrate this set of operations using a series of `Function` declarations. A base function is declared first:

```
Function<Integer, Integer> baseFunction = t -> t + 2;
```

If we desire to duplicate the functionality of *f(x)* using composition, we use the Function interface's andThen method:

```
Function<Integer, Integer> afterFunction =
        baseFunction.andThen(t -> t * 3);
System.out.println(afterFunction.apply(5));
```

This will display a 21. This is like saying, add 2 to the parameter and then multiply it by 3.

To duplicate the functionality of g(x), we use the compose method:

```
Function<Integer, Integer> beforeFunction =
        baseFunction.compose(t -> t * 3);
System.out.println(beforeFunction.apply(5));
```

This will display 17. Here, we are saying multiply the parameter by 3 before you add 2 to it.

In each of these lambda expression's declarations, the lambda expression was matched against the Function interface's functional method. This method is the apply method. This means that when the apply method is executed, the corresponding lambda expression is executed.

Using the Functional interface to supplement methods

However, the previous example does not convey the full power of this approach. In the next example, a Customer and Salesman class are defined, which we will use to get the e-mail address of a specific salesman's best customer:

```
public class Customer {
    private String emailAddress;

    public Customer(String emailAddress) {
        this.emailAddress = emailAddress;
    }

    public String getEmailAddress() {
        return emailAddress;
    }
}

public class Salesman {
```

```
    private Customer bestCustomer;

    Salesman(Customer bestCustomer) {
        this.bestCustomer = bestCustomer;
    }

    public Customer getBestCustomer() {
        return bestCustomer;
    }
}
```

To get the e-mail address of a specific salesman's best customer, we can use an object-oriented approach as shown here:

```
Customer customer = new
    Customer("bestcustomer@thebestcustomer.com");
Salesman salesman = new Salesman(customer);
System.out.println(salesman.getBestCustomer()
    .getEmailAddress());
```

It will return:

```
bestcustomer@thebestcustomer.com
```

Passing instances of the Functional interface

However, this approach does not possess the flexibility of a functional solution. Such a solution starts with three functional expressions:

- `customerToEmailAddress`: This expression returns an e-mail address given a `Customer` instance

- `salesmanToBestCustomer`: This expression returns a `Customer` instance given a `Salesman` instance

- `toEmailAddress`: This is the composite function that returns the e-mail address of the salesman's best customer

These functions are declared here and use method references:

```
Function<Customer, String> customerToEmailAddress =
        Customer::getEmailAddress;
Function<Salesman, Customer> salesmanToBestCustomer =
        Salesman::getBestCustomer;
Function<Salesman, String> toEmailAddress =
        salesmanToBestCustomer.andThen
        (customerToEmailAddress);
```

The following s displays the previous e-mail address using these functions:

```
System.out.println(toEmailAddress.apply(salesman));
```

The effort required to setup the functions requires more effort than the previous object-oriented approach. However, we can use these lambda expressions in many places where the invocation chaining approach cannot be used.

The real power of this approach lies in the ability to pass these functions around, which is not possible using the object-oriented approach. To illustrate this approach, we will create a Manager class which parallels that of the Customer class. A salesman is associated with a manager who possesses an e-mail address. The Manager class is as follows:

```
public class Manager {
    private String emailAddress;

    public Manager(String emailAddress) {
        this.emailAddress = emailAddress;
    }

    public String getEmailAddress() {
        return emailAddress;
    }
}
```

We will need to add the following code to the Salesman class. This will tie a manager to a salesman:

```
private Manager manager
...
public Salesman(Manager manager) {
    this.manager = manager;
}
public Manager getManager() {
    return manager;
}
```

A series of lambda expressions are then declared that parallel the previous customer's e-mail related declarations:

```
Function<Manager, String> managerToEmailAddress =
        Manager::getEmailAddress;
```

```
Function<Salesman, Manager> salesmanToManager =
        Salesman::getManager;
Function<Salesman, String> toManagerEmailAddress =
        salesmanToManager.andThen(managerToEmailAddress);
```

To demonstrate the use of these functions, a `Manager` object is created along with a new salesman. The `toManagerEmailAddress` function is then applied:

```
Manager manager = new Manager("manager@thecompany.com");
Salesman salesman2 = new Salesman(manager);
System.out.println(toManagerEmailAddress.apply(salesman2));
System.out.println(salesman2.getManager().getEmailAddress());
```

The output follows:

manager@thecompany.com

manager@thecompany.com

So far, we have merely duplicated the approach. However, we can declare a method such as the following that is passed a `Salesman` instance and a function. This simple function displays an e-mail address associated with the salesman.

```
public void processEmailAddress(
        Salesman salesman,
        Function<Salesman, String> toEmailAddress) {
    System.out.println(toEmailAddress.apply(salesman));
}
```

The method can be invoked using either of the two functions that return an e-mail address as shown here:

```
processEmailAddress(salesman,toEmailAddress);
processEmailAddress(salesman2,toManagerEmailAddress);
```

The output follows:

bestcustomer@thebestcustomer.com

manager@thecompany.com

The flexibility to pass composite functions around allows their execution to be delayed until it is needed. This flexibility is not available using the object-oriented approach.

Fluent interfaces

Fluent interfaces provide a convenient and easy-to-use technique for expressing solutions to many different types of problems. They are similar to method chaining but are more natural to use. It is a form of function composition where the method invocations are chained together. In this section, we will discuss the difference and similarities between method chaining, method cascading, and fluent interfaces.

Java supported fluent styles before Java 8 though their use was not common. For example, in JavaFX 2 the IntegerProperty class possesses a number of numerical methods that return the NumberBinding instances. These methods are used in a fluent style as shown here:

```
IntegerProperty n1 = new SimpleIntegerProperty(5);
IntegerProperty n2 = new SimpleIntegerProperty(2);
IntegerProperty n3 = new SimpleIntegerProperty(3);
NumberBinding sum = n1
        .add(n2)
        .multiply(n3);
System.out.println(sum.getValue());
```

A value of 21 is displayed. The use of methods on individual lines and their indention is a common way of coding, chaining, cascading, and using fluent interfaces.

As an aside, the term, binding, refers to the ability of these objects to be "re-evaluated" as one of their elements changes. This is demonstrated here:

```
n1.set(2);
System.out.println(sum.getValue());
```

The output will be a 12.

Fluent interfaces in Java 8

In Java 8, the use of fluent interfaces is most visible with the Stream class and the new Date and Time API. We have seen the Stream class used in the previous chapters. The following is a simple example, which sums the integers in a stream that are greater than 6:

```
int hoursWorked[] = {8, 12, 8, 6, 6, 5, 6, 0};
int totalHoursWorked = Arrays.stream(hoursWorked)
        .filter(n -> n > 6)
        .sum();
System.out.println(totalHoursWorked);
```

The sum displayed will be a 28. The `stream` method generates the stream, the `filter` method removes those that are larger than 6, and the `sum` method computes their total.

The Date and Time API uses fluent interfaces to make it easier to construct date and time-type objects. In the following example, a date in the future is computed using method names that clearly convey their intent:

```
LocalDateTime timeInstance = LocalDateTime.now()
        .plusDays(3)
        .minusHours(4)
        .plusWeeks(1)
        .plusYears(2);
System.out.println(timeInstance);
```

One possible output follows:

```
2017-04-28T10:39:43.691
```

There are many other places in Java 8 where fluent interfaces are used.

Method chaining and cascading

Method chaining consists of a series of method calls that are invoked against each other. This technique is used in many Java classes. Method chaining eliminates the need to introduce temporary variables.

Let's assume that we want to convert a string to lower case and then determine the length of the string. In this example, we use intermediate variables to perform this task:

```
String animal = "Cat";
String concat = animal.concat("Dog");
String lower = concat.toLowerCase();
int length = lower.length();
System.out.println(lower);
System.out.println(length);
```

This results in the following output:

```
catdog
6
```

However, this approach is verbose and not as easy to read.

The following illustrates the same process, but uses method chaining:

```
String animal = "Cat";
System.out.println(animal
    .concat("Dog")
    .toLowerCase());
System.out.println(animal
    .concat("Dog")
    .toLowerCase()
    .length());
```

The previous example also illustrates cascading. With cascading, each of the methods in a chain returns an object that subsequent methods execute against. With chaining, the object may not necessarily be the same object the method acted upon.

Cascading is similar to chaining, but the returned object is the current object. Multiple methods are applied to the same object. It can be implemented in Java using chaining where the method always returns `this`.

We will use the following class to contrast these two techniques. The class possesses two methods: `chainedMethod` and `cascadedMethod`. They differ in the objects they return.

```
public class Number {
    public Number chainedMethod(int num) {
        Number newTest = new Number();
        // use num
        return newTest;
    }
    public Number cascadedMethod(int num) {
        // use num
        return this;
    }
}
```

There are two aspects to cascading:

- The return value will return the original object
- This object must be mutable

If it was not mutable, then it would be of limited value.

Sometimes, the terms chaining and cascading are used interchangeably. For our purposes, we will define method chaining as a technique that may return the same or a different object. We define cascading as a technique, which always returns the same object—the original object. The exception to this rule would be a method that returns void. Frequently, it is called a **terminating** method. We will see examples of a terminating method shortly.

Contrasting method cascading and fluent interfaces

Method cascading and fluent interfaces are similar. The methods of both techniques return the original object the method was executed against. They differ in the style of the method names. Cascading is the foundation of fluent interfaces.

Fluent interfaces:

- Make the resulting code more readable and maintainable
- Are typically used to convey domain information

By domain information, we are referring to the use of method names that convey the meaning of the method in a more natural and easier to understand style. For example, we can use a `Book` class using a fluent interface as follows:

```
Book book = new Book();
Book.setTitle("Twenty Thousand Leagues Under the Sea")
    .setPages(129)
    .setAuthor("Jules Verne");
```

Alternatively, it can be expressed as:

```
Book.title("Twenty Thousand Leagues Under the Sea")
    .pageCount(129)
    .author("Jules Verne ");
```

The latter approach is arguably better.

> The key difference between method cascading and fluent interfaces is that fluent interfaces are designed to be more readable and convey more domain-specific information about its target.

Creating and using fluent interfaces

A fluent interface is implemented using method cascading. The critical part of this process is to return the context of the method invocation so that it can be reused. Specifically, it needs to:

- Return the method's context
- Reference itself
- Optionally terminate with a call that returns void

We will use several classes to demonstrate the creation and use of fluent interfaces. Let's start with a simple class called `Boat` as shown here:

```java
public class Boat {
    private String name;
    private String country;
    private int tonnage;
    private int draft;

    public String getName() {
        return name;
    }

    public void setName(String name) {
        this.name = name;
    }

    public String getCountry() {
        return country;
    }

    public void setCountry(String country) {
        this.country = country;
    }

    public int getTonnage() {
        return tonnage;
    }

    public void setTonnage(int tonnage) {
        this.tonnage = tonnage;
    }

    public int getDraft() {
        return draft;
```

```
        }

        public void setDraft(int draft) {
            this.draft = draft;
        }

        public String toString() {
            return "Name: " + this.name + " Country: " + this.country
                    + " Tonnage: " + this.tonnage + " Draft: " +
                    this.draft;
        }

    }
```

The use of this class is demonstrated here where a simple instance of a Boat class is created:

```
        Boat boat = new Boat();
        boat.setName("Albatross");
        boat.setCountry("Panama");
        boat.setTonnage(12000);
        boat.setDraft(25);
```

Next, we will replace the setter methods with new versions that return this. It is necessary to replace the methods as opposed to adding them since their signatures are identical. The only difference is the return data type, which is not part of a method's signature. These declarations are as follows:

```
        public Boat setName(String name) {
            this.name = name;
            return this;
        }

        public Boat setCountry(String country) {
            this.country = country;
            return this;
        }

        public Boat setTonnage(int tonnage) {
            this.tonnage = tonnage;
            return this;
        }

        public Boat setDraft(int draft) {
            this.draft = draft;
            return this;
        }
```

They can then be used with a cascading style as shown here:

```
boat.setName("Albatross")
        .setCountry("Panama")
        .setTonnage(12000)
        .setDraft(25);
```

To create a fluent interface, we need to rename the setter methods. One possible version is shown here:

```
public Boat named(String name) {
    this.name = name;
    return this;
}
public Boat country(String country) {
    this.country = country;
    return this;
}
public Boat tonnage(int tonnage) {
    this.tonnage = tonnage;
    return this;
}
public Boat draft(int draft) {
    this.draft = draft;
    return this;
}
```

They are used to create the same Boat instance as follows:

```
boat.named("Albatross")
        .country("Panama")
        .tonnage(12000)
        .draft(25);
```

These fluent methods are essentially setter methods that violate the standard Java naming convention. Set type methods should be passed a single value and should return void. However, as the term implies, it is a convention and is not cast in stone. Such conventions should only be violated when the results outweigh the benefits of following the convention.

To further illustrate the use of fluent interfaces, a Port class is declared next to hold a list of Boat instances. The class overloads the add method. The first version accepts the name of a boat, creates a new instance of the Boat class, adds it to the list, and then returns this instance.

The second version accepts a `Boat` instance, adds it to the list, and returns the same `Boat` instance:

```
public class Port {
    private List<Boat> boats = new ArrayList();

    public Boat add(String name) {
        Boat boat = new Boat().named(name);
        boats.add(boat);
        return boat;
    }

    public Boat add(Boat boat) {
        boats.add(boat);
        return boat;
    }
}
```

The use of the method's first version is illustrated here:

```
Port port = new Port();
Boat newBoat = port.add("Cloud");
```

The use of the method's second version is as follows:

```
boat.named("Albatross")
        .country("Panama")
        .tonnage(12000)
        .draft(25);
port.add(boat);
```

This leads to an interesting technique where the fluent style is used as part of an anonymous inner class. The previous example is duplicated here using a fluent style:

```
port.add(new Boat() {
    {
        named("Albatross");
        country("Panama");
        tonnage(1500);
        draft(35);
    }
});
```

The double set of curly braces forming the nested blocks can be confusing initially. The inner block statement is the anonymous inner class's initializer block. This sequence of statements is displayed using a fluent style.

In contrast, we could have used the following more explicit version:

```
port.add(new Boat() {
    {
        this.named("Albatross");
        this.country("Panama");
        this.tonnage(1500);
        this.draft(35);
    }
});
```

This example demonstrates that the fluent can be used and encountered in unexpected situations.

Using fluent interfaces to hide older interfaces/classes

As languages mature, they tend to find better ways of doing things. The evolution of Java over the years attests to the changes that can occur. Older techniques are often marked as deprecated to indicate that in the future they will not be supported. However, the actual removal of the feature may not always be practical in some situations.

An alternative is to provide a new interface that hides the older technique. When this need arises, providing a fluent style interface can be a good implementation choice. For example, a class may possess a series of getter and setter methods that can be tedious to use. Supplementing this class with one that uses a fluent interface will result in more readable solutions to problems. We will illustrate how this can be accomplished by hiding the java.util.Random class within another class and providing it with a fluent interface.

A class called FluentRandom is created, which provides a simple implementation. It is limited to generating integers. One of the problems with the Random class is that it does not readily provide a means to set the lower bound on the range of integers that its nextInt method returns. There is an overloaded nextInt version that accepts an integer argument to specify the upper bound. While it is not hard to modify the return value to accommodate a lower bound, it is not always convenient. The FluentRandom class addresses this concern.

The class maintains lower and upper instance variables that are used with the nextInt method as shown next. These variables are set to 0 and Integer.MAX_VALUE, respectively, reflecting the Random class's default range of integers. Methods are provided permitting these values to change. Also, the useAsSeed method controls the seed used for the random number generator:

```
public class FluentRandom extends Random {
    private int lower = 0;
    private int upper = Integer.MAX_VALUE;

    public FluentRandom useAsSeed(long seed) {
        this.setSeed(seed);
        return this;
    }

    public FluentRandom asLower(int lower) {
        this.lower = lower;
        return this;
    }

    public FluentRandom asUpper(int upper) {
        this.upper = upper;
        return this;
    }

    @Override
    public int nextInt() {
        return lower + this.nextInt(upper - lower);
    }
}
```

Here, only the nextInt method is used:

```
FluentRandom fr = new FluentRandom();
for(int i=0; i<5; i++) {
    System.out.println(fr. nextInt());
}
```

One possible output follows:

```
1598703823
802097941
718536822
796766539
803170706
```

In this next example, several of its fluent methods are used. The methods' order is not important and can be changed.

```
fr = new FluentRandom()
        .asLower(5)
        .asUpper(25)
        .useAsSeed(35);
for(int i=0; i<5; i++) {
    System.out.println(fr. nextInt());
}
```

The example will always generate the following sequence, since a seed was provided:

```
17
8
11
20
17
```

Using this approach, we can simplify the use of existing classes and interfaces. However, since these implementations are not standard, they may not be as portable.

Using fluent interfaces with the Properties class

The `Properties` class is used in many applications to provide a common means of declaring a set of properties or attributes of an entity. For example, it is often used to specify the configuration of a database connection as shown next. This has been adapted from `https://docs.oracle.com/javase/tutorial/jdbc/basics/connecting.html`. The `Properties` instance is used to specify the user name and password for a database.

```
Connection conn = null;
Properties connectionProps = new Properties();
connectionProps.put("user", this.userName);
```

```
connectionProps.put("password", this.password);

...

conn = DriverManager.getConnection(
    "jdbc:" + this.dbms + "://" + this.serverName +
    ":" + this.portNumber + "/", connectionProps);
```

This approach can be verbose and non-intuitive. However, older classes may require the use of the `Properties` class. We can hide its usage by introducing a class to encapsulate the entities properties.

In the following code sequence, the `ConnectionProperties` class is declared that encapsulates these properties and provides a `properties` method to return the equivalent `Properties` object:

```
public class ConnectionProperties {
    private String user;
    private String password;
    Properties properties = new Properties();

    public ConnectionProperties user(String user) {
        this.user = user;
        properties.setProperty("user", this.user);
        return this;
    }

    public ConnectionProperties password(String password) {
        this.password = password;
        properties.setProperty("password", this.password);
        return this;
    }

    public Properties properties() {
        return properties;
    }
}
```

We can now use the following sequence to establish a connection using a fluent approach:

```
Connection conn = null;
ConnectionProperties cp = new ConnectionProperties();
cp.user("user")
    .password("password");
...
```

```
conn = DriverManager.getConnection(
    "jdbc:" + this.dbms + "://" + this.serverName +
    ":" + this.portNumber + "/", cp.properties());
```

This shortens the sequence and makes it easier to read and use. Using this technique with a larger list of properties or where the properties are used extensively, will make it even more valuable.

Extending fluent interfaces

Fluent interfaces are elegant and can be extended if needed. However, you have to be careful when you do this. The key to the approach is to use generics. We will illustrate this process by creating a variation of the Boat class called BaseBoat to distinguish it from the Boat class. We will derive a class called SailBoat from the base class.

Let's start with the BaseBoat and SailBoat declarations that do not use generics. The BaseBoat class declaration is shown next, where four private instance variables are declared and supported using fluent style methods:

```java
public class BaseBoat {
    private String name;
    private String country;
    private int tonnage;
    private int draft;

    public String getName() {
        return name;
    }

    public BaseBoat named(String name) {
        this.name = name;
        return this;
    }

    public String getCountry() {
        return country;
    }

    public BaseBoat country(String country) {
        this.country = country;
        return this;
    }

    public BaseBoat tonnage(int tonnage) {
```

```
            this.tonnage = tonnage;
            return this;
        }

        public int getDraft() {
            return draft;
        }

        public BaseBoat draft(int draft) {
            this.draft = draft;
            return this;
        }

        public String toString() {
            return "Name: " + this.name + " Country: " + this.country
                    + " Tonnage: " + this.tonnage + " Draft: "
                    + this.draft;
        }
    }
```

The SailBoat class declaration is shown here. It uses two instance variables:

```
    public class SailBoat extends BaseBoat {
        private int numberOfSails;
        private int numberOfHulls;

        public int getSails() {
            return this.numberOfSails;
        }

        public SailBoat sails(int numberOfSails) {
            this.numberOfSails = numberOfSails;
            return this;
        }

        public int getNumberOfHulls() {
            return this.numberOfHulls;
        }

        public SailBoat hulls(int numberOfHulls) {
            this.numberOfHulls = numberOfHulls;
            return this;
        }

        public String toString() {
```

```
        return super.toString()
                + " Number of sails: " + this.numberOfSails
                + " Number of hulls: " + this.numberOfHulls;
    }
```

Suppose we try to compile this code:

```
SailBoat sailBoat = new SailBoat()
        .named("Endeavour")
        .country("United Kingdom")
        .sails(3)
        .tonnage(15)
        .hulls(2);
```

Then, we will get the following error message:

```
error: cannot find symbol
                .sails(3)
  symbol:    method sails(int)
  location: class BaseBoat
```

This error occurs because the `country` method returns a `BaseBoat` object that does not possess a `sails` method.

The declaration of the `BaseBoat` class methods returns instances of `BaseBoat` and not `SailBoat`. The `country` method is a base class method and thus returns an instance of `BaseBoat`. This class does not have a `sails` method. We can avoid this problem using generics. It will use the derived class to specify the return type for the base class methods.

A new version of the `BaseBoat` class using generics is declared as shown next. It contains the same fields and methods as the `Boat` class. It differs in its use of generics to account for derived classes. The `DERIVED` type forces the derived classes to provide a type that can be incorporated into the base class definition. Otherwise, it is very similar to the original class.

```
public class BaseBoat<DERIVED extends BaseBoat<DERIVED>> {
    private String name;
    private String country;
    private int tonnage;
    private int draft;

    public DERIVED named(String name) {
        this.name = name;
```

```
        return (DERIVED)this;
    }

    public DERIVED country(String country) {
        this.country = country;
        return (DERIVED)this;
    }

    public DERIVED tonnage(int tonnage) {
        this.tonnage = tonnage;
        return (DERIVED)this;
    }

    public DERIVED draft(int draft) {
        this.draft = draft;
        return (DERIVED)this;
    }

    public String toString() {
        return "Name: " + this.name + " Country: " + this.country
                + " Tonnage: " + this.tonnage + " Draft: "
                + this.draft;
    }
}
```

An abbreviated version of the `SailBoat` class follows. The only difference from the first version is the use of generics in its declaration:

```
public class SailBoat extends BaseBoat<SailBoat> {
    ...
}
```

In the following sequence, an instance of `SailBoat` is created and its methods are used:

```
SailBoat sailBoat = new SailBoat()
        .named("Endeavour")
        .country("United Kingdom")
        .sails(3)
        .tonnage(15)
        .hulls(2);
System.out.println(sailBoat);
```

The output follows:

```
Name: Endeavour Country: United Kingdom Tonnage: 15 Draft: 0 Number of
sails: 3 Number of hulls: 2
```

We can use the methods in any order that we desired. The following will produce the equivalent output:

```
sailBoat = new SailBoat()
        .tonnage(15)
        .hulls(2)
        .country("United Kingdom")
        .named("Endeavour")
        .sails(3);
System.out.println(sailBoat);
```

The use of generics allows us to successfully extend a fluent interface. This allows us to use fluent interfaces in many more situations.

Default methods and functions

Default methods can be added to interfaces. They permit existing interfaces to be expanded to include new methods without breaking the older code. It is the default method of an interface that has an implementation. For example, consider a class that implements an interface, and then later a default method is added to the interface. The class has to implement all of the interfaces' abstract methods or the class will be abstract. However, since a default method is not abstract and has an implementation, it does not affect the class.

The addition of functions to Java suggests the need to incorporate their use with older classes and interfaces. After all, it is desirable to take advantage of existing code when possible to avoid rewriting it. Many of the default method additions to existing Java packages have been done with the intent of supporting functions.

Default methods consist of the keyword, default, followed by the declaration of a method and its implementations. This is illustrated in the Saveable interface declared next. It consists of an abstract method, readFile, and a default method, saveFile. The saveFile method constitutes a simplistic implementation:

```
public interface Saveable {
    public Object readFile(String fileName);

    public default void saveFile(String fileName, String content)
            throws IOException {
```

```
FileWriter fileWriter = new FileWriter(new File(fileName));
fileWriter.write(content);
fileWriter.close();
    }
}
```

Any class that implements this interface only needs to implement the `readFile` method.

Since interfaces support multiple inheritance between other interfaces, interesting problems can occur, including the diamond inheritance problem. While we do not cover this topic here, a good reference to these issues is found at `http://examples.javacodegeeks.com/java-basics/java-8-default-methods-tutorial/`.

Static default methods

Java 8 also permits the addition of static methods to an interface. One advantage of this capability is that it is no longer necessary to create a helper class to hold static supporting methods. Prior to Java 8, if we wanted to provide a "standard" method to support an interface, we needed to create a separate class that held these static methods. The ability to add static methods to an interface eliminates the need for these specialized helper classes.

The following code can be added to the `Saveable` interface. This method is treated as a default method:

```
enum FileType {executable, readable, writeable, readWrite};

public static FileType standardFileType() {
    return FileType.readWrite;
}
```

Default methods in Java 8

Default methods have been added to a number of older interfaces. For example, two default methods have been added to the `Iterable` interface: `forEach` and `spliterator`. Their signatures follow:

```
default void forEach(Consumer<? super T> action);
default Spliterator<T> spliterator();
```

The `List` interface implements the `Iterable` interface, which allows us to use these methods immediately. The `forEach` method requires a functional interface for its argument. This means that we can iterate through the elements of a `List` instance using a lambda expression as follows:

```
List<String> list = Arrays.asList(
        "Io", "Europa", "Ganymede", "Callisto");
list.forEach(s->System.out.println(s + " "));
```

The output follows:

Io

Europa

Ganymede

Callisto

To better understand the addition of default methods, let's re-examine the `Function` interface since it includes an abstract method, two default methods, and a static method as follows:

```
@FunctionalInterface
public interface Function<T, R> {
    R apply(T t);

    default <V> Function<V, R> compose(
            Function<? super V, ? extends T> before) {…}

    default <V> Function<T, V> andThen(
            Function<? super R, ? extends V> after) {…}

    static <T> Function<T, T> identity() {…}
}
```

The default methods constitute a means of providing a standard implementation of the intent of the functional interface. It avoids requiring the developer to implement these methods. All the developer needs to do is to implement the `apply` method. This is frequently accomplished using lambda expressions.

There are differences and similarities between an interface and an abstract class. These are summarized in the following table:

	Abstract class	Interface
Can instantiate	No	No
Supports multiple inheritance	No	Yes, between interfaces

	Abstract class	Interface
Fields	Flexible	Are public, static, and final by default
Methods	Flexible	All public

The fields and methods of a class are more flexible than those of an interface. They can be declared as public, private, or protected.

Multiple inheritance in Java 8

Consider the situation where we have two interfaces, both possessing a default display method, and a class that implements both of these interfaces. This situation is illustrated in the following set of declarations:

```java
interface FirstBaseInterface {
    default void display() {
        System.out.println("From FirstBaseInterface");
    }
}

interface SecondBaseInterface {
    default void display() {
        System.out.println("From SecondBaseInterface");
    }
}

public class DerivedClass implements SecondBaseInterface,
        FirstBaseInterface {

    public void display() {
        FirstBaseInterface.super.display();
    }

    public static void main(String... args) {
        new DerivedClass().display();
    }
}
```

The DerivedClass class explicitly declared that it prefers the FirstBaseInterface interface's display method using the following statement:

```java
FirstBaseInterface.super.display();
```

It could have used the other interface, both interfaces' method, or neither. However, it cannot use the following:

```
super.display();
```

This will generate an error indicating that the display cannot be found.

There is also the situation where the diamond inheritance problem occurs. This is where you have one base interface, which possesses a default method. Two other interfaces will then extends this base interface with their own version of the default method. No problem so far, since they are overriding the base interface method. When a fourth interface extends both of the intermediate interfaces, then the fourth interface will need to state its preference as was done in the `DerivedClass` display method.

Summary

Method composition provides a flexible way of combining two or more functions into a single function. This offers flexibility that will otherwise not be present. We illustrate how this technique can be implemented using the `Function` interface. Its `compose` and `andThen` methods support the execution of functions before or after another function. We also demonstrated the usefulness of this technique by passing the composite functions to other methods allowing it be executed when needed.

Fluent interfaces are common in functional programming languages. We discussed the difference between this type of interface and the chaining and cascading techniques. While similar, chaining methods do not necessarily return the same object each time. Cascading does return the same object, and fluent interfaces add a more natural set of method names.

Given the importance of fluent interfaces in a class's design, we demonstrated how to create fluent interfaces. We followed up by showing how it can be used to hide older classes and interfaces. This allows us to make older code more readable and useful.

Default methods are critical in bridging the gap between older Java libraries and the new functional programming approach. It permits the addition of new methods to old interfaces without breaking existing code. Java 8 uses default methods extensively to allow older classes and interfaces to work with and use lambda expressions.

Now that you have a good understanding of function composition and fluent interfaces, we can explore how they are used in the support of streams in the next chapter. Streams are composed of a sequence of elements that offer a more flexible technique for processing data.

4
Streams and the Evaluation of Expressions

In this chapter, we will examine how Java 8 supports the concept of streams. A **stream** can be thought of as a sequence of elements processed by a series of methods using a fluent interface. The stream concept is supported by the Stream class.

We will begin with a brief overview of the Stream class and its methods. After conveying the essence of the stream technique, we will examine how streams are created and show how they can replace imperative and object-oriented approaches to solve similar problems. The intent is to provide an overview of the Stream class and its methods. A detailed coverage of each method is not possible here.

The topics you will cover include the following:

- Creating fixed and infinite length streams
- Filtering a stream
- Sorting streams
- Mapping elements of a stream

How stream methods are evaluated is also of interest — either in a lazy or eager manner. How they are evaluated affects when their methods are executed. The uses and advantages of each approach are explained.

One of the useful features of streams is how they support concurrent behavior. Streams are executed concurrently using the parallel method. While this is easy to achieve, care must be taken use it correctly.

The Stream class and its use

The `Stream` class provides the primary support for the stream concept in Java. However, there are specialized classes, such as the `DoubleStream`, `IntStream`, and `LongStream` classes, that handle numbers. In addition, the `Collection` interface supports the creation of streams.

A stream will support either a finite or an infinite sequence of elements. The methods of a stream can be classified in a number of ways such as mapping, filtering, and sorting type methods. We will start with a simple example of a stream, and then follow up with a discussion of how they are created and several of their methods.

Let's assume that we need to process an array of numbers by summing the values of each unique element. For example, in the following array, there are six distinct numbers whose sum is 35:

```
int[] numbers = {3,6,8,8,4,6,3,3,5,6,9,4,3,6};
```

One approach to solve the problem involves:

1. Finding the distinct numbers in the array.
2. Summing these numbers.

Finding the distinct numbers is an instance of the count-distinct problem as explained at http://en.wikipedia.org/wiki/Count-distinct_problem. The summation is relatively straightforward.

First, we will examine an imperative solution to the problem. We will use the `HashSet` class to hold the distinct elements of the array and a simple loop to compute their sum. The following sequence adds each distinct number in the array to the set:

```
Set<Integer> numberSet = new HashSet<>();
for (int number : numbers) {
    numberSet.add(number);
}
```

Next, we iterate through each element of the set, adding them to the `total` variable:

```
int total = 0;
for(int number : numberSet) {
    total += number;
}
```

However, using streams will greatly simplify this process. In the next sequence, a `Stream` object is created using the `Arrays` class's `stream` method followed by the use of the `distinct` and `sum` methods. The `stream` method takes the `numbers` array and returns a `Stream` instance representing the array. The `distinct` and `sum` methods perform the operations suggested by their names:

```
total = Arrays.stream(numbers)
          .distinct()
          .sum();
```

This is much shorter and easier to follow than the equivalent iterative approach.

We can visualize the typical stream process using the following figure. A data source is converted to a stream. A series of operations are executed against the stream followed by a terminating operation. In the previous example, we used one intermediate method, `distinct`, and then the terminal method, `sum`. The stream operations are effected by methods. Refer to the following diagram:

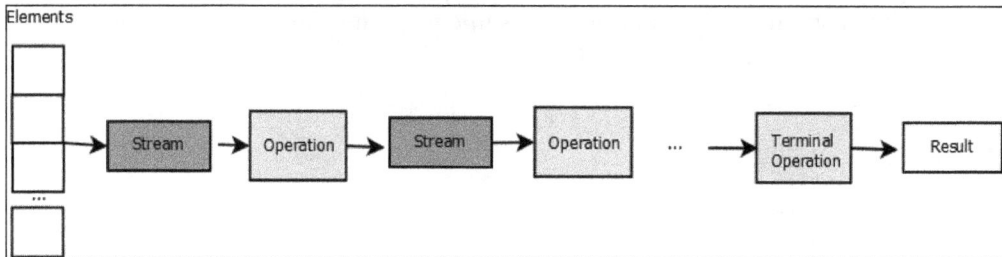

Figure 1: The Stream process

Java 8's stream concept is often a better design and performance choice than many equivalent imperative approaches. It helps separate the "what to do" from "how to do". The implementation details are left to Java. In this sense, it represents a declarative style of programming. In Java, a stream is not a data structure. We can simply think of it as a potentially unbounded sequence of elements.

Collections and streams both represent a series of elements. They differ in a number of ways. A collection holds the entire set of elements in memory. Elements are added and deleted from a collection. A stream is not complete in the same sense. Only part of the stream will be present at any time. Its elements are computed as needed. In addition, a collection requires the programmer to explicitly iterate over its elements using one of several techniques such as the for-each statement. With a stream, the iteration is implicit in its operation.

Intermediate and terminal methods

Most stream methods will perform some operation on the elements of the stream and then return the stream. These are called **intermediate** methods. This includes the distinct method used earlier. There are also **terminal** methods that do not return the stream and effectively end the processing sequence. The sum method is a terminal method.

Intermediate methods always return a stream and do not actually modify the stream, but create a new stream instead. The processing of a stream starts when the terminal operation starts and stops when the terminal method completes. This will be clearer as we work through this chapter's examples.

Terminal methods may produce a result as the sum method did, or it can produce a side effect. After a terminal method has been executed, the stream is said to have been consumed. This means the stream cannot be used again.

For example, we can rewrite the previous example using the IntStream class. This is a specialized stream class that only holds integers. Since our stream consists of integers, this is an appropriate class to use:

```
IntStream stream = Arrays.stream(numbers);
total = stream
        .distinct()
        .sum();
```

This will produce the same results as before. However, if we add the following statement that sums all of the elements of the array, immediately following the previous code sequence, the program will terminate.

```
total = stream.sum();
```

This will generate the following exception:

Exception in thread "main" java.lang.IllegalStateException: stream has already been operated upon or closed

Once a stream has been used, it cannot be reused. We will need to create new stream if we want to perform additional processing. In the next section, we will focus on how steams are created.

Creating streams

Streams can be of fixed or infinite length. In the previous example, we used an array of integers to create a fixed length stream. However, if we want to process data arriving through a network connection, this stream of data may appear to be infinite. We can create both types of streams in Java 8.

We will use a `Rectangle` class to demonstrate the use of streams in several sections of this chapter. The class possesses position and dimension variables and three methods:

- `scale`: This changes the size of a rectangle
- `getArea`: This returns its area
- `toString`: This displays its values

The class declaration follows:

```
public class Rectangle {
    private int x;
    private int y;
    private int height;
    private int width;

    public Rectangle(int x, int y, int height, int width) {
        this.x = x;
        this.y = y;
        this.height = height;
        this.width = width;
    }

    public Rectangle scale(double percent) {
        height = (int) (height * (1.0 + percent));
        width = (int) (width * (1.0 + percent));
        return this;
    }

    public int getArea() {
        return height*width;
    }

    public String toString() {
```

```
            return "X: " + x + " Y: " + y
                + " Height: " + height + " Width: " + width;
    }
}
```

Fixed length streams

We have already seen how a finite stream of integers is created using the `Arrays` class's static `stream` method:

```
int[] numbers = {3,6,8,8,4,6,3,3,5,6,9,4,3,6};
IntStream stream = Arrays.stream(numbers);
```

The `stream` method is not limited to work with integers. It can also be used with objects such as the ones shown here:

```
Rectangle[] rectangles = {
    new Rectangle(10, 10, 50, 75),
    new Rectangle(30, 40, 30, 45),
    new Rectangle(110, 70, 70, 15),
    new Rectangle(50, 10, 45, 35)
};
Stream<Rectangle> stream = Arrays.stream(rectangles);
```

The `stream` method also exists as a default method in the `Collection` interface. This implies that the method can be used with classes such as `ArrayList`, `Hashset`, and `TreeSet`. The following illustrates its use with an `ArrayList` instance:

```
List<String> cities = new ArrayList<>();
cities.add("London");
cities.add("Paris");
cities.add("Cairo");
cities.add("Manila");
Stream<String> cityStream = cities.stream();
```

However, some streams may be conceptually unlimited in length. These are discussed next.

Infinite streams

An infinite stream may be a video or audio feed of indeterminate length. Data from a sensor device may be effectively infinite, at least until the device stops sending information. These types of streams can be represented by the `Stream` class.

The following code illustrates an imperative approach for generating an infinite series of random numbers:

```
Random random = new Random();
while (true) {
    int number = random.nextInt();
    // process number
}
```

There are two Stream methods used to create infinite streams:

- The iterate method
- The generate method

The values returned by these methods are not generated until they are needed. Otherwise, this will require that all of the values be generated before the stream is created. Since there are infinite values, the stream will never be created. Also, the length of an infinite stream is frequently restricted using the limit method. This method will be demonstrated shortly.

Using the iterate method to create an infinite stream

The iterate method uses a seed and a UnaryOperator instance. The method is declared as follows:

```
static <T> Stream<T> iterate(T seed, UnaryOperator<T> f)
```

The seed is the initial value used. The UnaryOperator instance, frequently implemented using a lambda expression, uses the seed value to create a new value. This value is used in the next iteration.

In the following example, a simple series of numbers is displayed. An initial value of zero is returned first. The value is incremented by one each time the iterate method is invoked. The limit method will restrict the output to 10 elements:

```
IntStream.iterate(0, n -> n + 1)
    .limit(10)
    .forEach(n -> System.out.print(n + " "));
```

The following output is produced:

```
0 1 2 3 4 5 6 7 8 9
```

We can create an infinite stream of strings as easily:

```
Stream.iterate("Going",m -> m + "...")
        .limit(5)
        .forEach(System.out::println);
```

The output of this statement follows:

```
Going
Going...
Going......
Going.........
Going............
```

The `limit` method provides simple way of controlling the number of elements produced by a stream.

The `filter` method, which will be detailed in the *Using the filter method* section, will also restrict the numbers generated. In the following sequence, only the numbers 11 through 20 are displayed:

```
IntStream.iterate(0, n -> n + 1)
        .filter(n -> n>10 && n<100)
        .limit(10)
        .forEach(n -> System.out.print(n + " "));
```

We need to be careful when creating our streams. If we reverse the order of the `filter` and `limit` methods, no output is generated. This is because we limit the output to the first 10 numbers, 0 through 9, and these are filtered out.

We can also accidentally create infinite streams. In the previous example, if we had not used the `limit` method, then the numbers 11 through 99 will be displayed, but the stream will never terminate. The program will behave as if it was stuck in an infinite loop.

In the following example, the modulo division means that only 0's and 1's will be generated. The `distinct` method eliminates duplicates, and the `limit` method restricts the output to 10 numbers. Since only two numbers are created, the limit of 10 numbers is never reached and the stream runs forever.

```
IntStream.iterate(0, n -> (n+1)%2)
        .distinct()
        .limit(10)
        .forEach(System.out::println);
```

The problem is compounded when we use a parallel stream. These types of streams are covered in the *Stream and concurrent processing* section.

Generating a stream of random text is useful for testing purposes. It eliminates the need to create a test file containing test data. Instead, a possible random set of strings can be used.

One approach to create such a stream is to use the `Scanner` class to get the input from the keyboard. Another approach uses the `iterate` method. We will demonstrate both the techniques.

The `Scanner` class example is as follows:

```
Scanner scanner = new Scanner(System.in);
Stream.iterate(scanner.next(), s -> scanner.next())
      .forEach(System.out::println);
```

The output will simply display the text entered. We can use the `limit` method to control the number if input values processed.

The next example will create a series of simple sentences based on a random combination of words. Three arrays are created representing the subject, verb, and objects of a sentence. The `Random` class will randomly select among the possible combinations:

```
String[] subject = {"cat", "dog", "monkey", "bat"};
String[] verb = {"chased", "ate", "lost", "swatted"};
String[] object = {"ball", "rat", "doughnut", "tamale"};
Random random = new Random();
```

The `iterate` method is shown next where the three words are combined in a random order:

```
Stream.iterate("", m -> subject[random.nextInt(3)]
            + " " + verb[random.nextInt(3)]
            + " the " + object[random.nextInt(3)])
      .limit(5)
      .forEach(System.out::println);
```

One possible output follows:

```
dog lost the ball
monkey lost the rat
monkey ate the rat
cat lost the rat
```

Only four sentences appear to be generated. This is because we used an empty string for the initial value. This can be corrected using the following expression as the first argument of the `iterate` method instead:

```
subject[random.nextInt(3)]
    + " " + verb[random.nextInt(3)]
    + " the " + object[random.nextInt(3)]
```

Using the generate method to create an infinite stream

The `generate` method uses a `Supplier` interface instance as its argument. Each time a new value is needed, the instance's `get` method is invoked. The declaration of the `generate` method follows:

```
static <T> Stream<T> generate(Supplier<T> s)
```

To generate an infinite stream of repeating values, use a simple lambda expression to return the same value each time. In the following example, a series of five zeros are displayed:

```
Supplier intSupplier = () -> 0;
Stream.generate(intSupplier)
        .limit(5)
        .forEach(System.out::println);
```

To generate a stream based on the previous value, we will need to use a method that allows us to increment a number. We will use the following method that increments a static variable each time it is called:

```
static int number = 0;
public int nextInt() {
    return number++;
}
```

If we use it with the following stream, it will display the numbers from 0 to 4:

```
Stream.generate(()->nextInt())
    .limit(5)
    .forEach(System.out::println);
```

We are unable to use a lambda expression in place of the `nextInt` method. If we try to use the following stream, it will generate a syntax error:

```
int number = 0;
Stream.generate(()->number++)
        .limit(5)
        .forEach(System.out::println);
```

The error message will be:

local variables referenced from a lambda expression must be final or effectively final

We cannot access external variables unless they are effectively final. We violated this rule when we tried to modify the local variable, `number`.

However, we can use a method reference to generate random numbers as shown here.

```
Supplier<Double> randomSupplier = Math::random;
System.out.println();
Stream.generate(randomSupplier)
        .limit(4)
        .forEach(System.out::println);
```

One possible output follows:

`0.3865760805523275`

`0.3560223160363011`

`0.14676285607241135`

`0.46249744143226224`

Infinite streams can also be created using recursion, but this is a rather expensive technique.

Using the Stream class methods

In this section, we will explore how the `Stream` class methods are used to solve various types of problems. Streams are useful for transforming stream elements, filtering elements, and reducing elements. They can mimic SQL-type processing and implement the map-reduce paradigm, which we will illustrate in the *Implementing the map-reduce paradigm* section.

Filter methods

The process of filtering involves iterating over a sequence and eliminating those elements that are no longer needed. We will examine how this is accomplished using an imperative loop and then how it is performed using streams.

Assume that we want to filter out the plural names in an animal list. We start with an array of strings containing animal names. Each element of the array will be matched against a regular expression to determine if ends with an "s". If it is not plural, it will be added to a list as shown here:

```
String[] animals = {"cats", "dog", "ox", "bats"
    , "horses", "mule"};
List<String> list = new ArrayList<>();
for(String name : animals) {
    if(!name.matches(".*s$")) {
        list.add(name);
    }
}
```

The list is then sorted and displayed:

```
list.sort(null);
for(String name : list) {
        System.out.println(name);
}
```

The output follows:

dog

mule

ox

The `list` object was necessary because we wanted to display the animal names in alphabetical order. The iterative approach works, but is verbose compared to the `filter` method that we will demonstrate shortly. In addition, it is harder to perform this operation concurrently. As we will demonstrate in the *Stream and concurrent processing* section using parallel streams that simplifies this task.

We will demonstrate three filter type methods:

- `filter`: This leaves out elements
- `distinct`: This leaves out duplicates
- `skip`: This skips over elements

Each of these removes elements from the stream. Actually, elements are not removed, but rather select certain elements for further processing. We will not demonstrate the `distinct` method since we illustrated its use previously.

Using the filter method

We will duplicate the previous example using a `stream` and the `filter` method. It is simpler and avoids creating an explicit intermediate variable to perform the sorting operation.

The `filter` method takes an argument that implements the `Predicate` interface. This argument must implement the interface's `test` method. It is passed a single value and returns a Boolean result. If the method returns true, then the `filter` method forwards the element, otherwise it is effectively removed from the stream.

In the next code sequence, the previous example is duplicated using the `filter` method. In this case, the `String` class's `matches` method uses a regular expression to determine if its argument is plural.

```
Stream<String> animalStream = Arrays.stream(animals);
animalStream
        .filter(x->!x.matches(".*s$"))
        .sorted()
        .forEach(x->System.out.println(x));
```

The `filter` method can also mimic SQL-type statements. The following SQL select statement will return a set of record from the `Customer` table where `salesman` is "Ralph":

```
Select * from Customer where salesman = "Ralph"
```

We can mimic this behavior easily. Let's assume that we want to perform a select statement similar to the following:

```
Select * from Rectangles where x>10
```

Instead of using a database, we will use the array of `Rectangle` objects created earlier. To support this example, we added a `getX` method to the `Rectangle` class. The following demonstrates the process where the array is converted to a stream, and then the `filter` and `forEach` methods are applied to it:

```
Stream<Rectangle> stream = Arrays.stream(rectangles);
stream.filter(r -> r.getX() > 10)
        .forEach(r -> System.out.println(r));
```

The output follows:

```
X: 30 Y: 40 Height: 30 Width: 45

X: 110 Y: 70 Height: 70 Width: 15

X: 50 Y: 10 Height: 45 Width: 35
```

This illustrates that the SQL paradigm of processing is easily supported by streams. If the nature of the problem lends itself to this technique, then streams can be applied readily.

Using the skip method

The `skip` method acts similar to the `filter` method except that the number of elements, to ignore, are specified by a `long` argument. To demonstrate this method, we will create the following stream containing 14 numbers:

```
int[] numbers = {3, 6, 8, 8, 4, 6, 3, 3, 5, 6, 9, 4, 3, 6};
IntStream stream = Arrays.stream(numbers);
```

Before we demonstrate the `skip` method, let's re-examine the `IntStream` class and its associated `IntSummaryStatistics` class. Streams of numbers can be generated and used for a variety of purposes. They can be used to represent payroll data, grades, a package's dimensions, and any number of other uses. As such, statistics like average and largest numbers are often of interest. The `IntSummaryStatistics` class serves to collect and generate these types of statistics.

In the following sequence, the integer stream is processed by first skipping the first five elements and then using the terminal stream method, `summaryStatistics`, to return an instance of the `IntSummaryStatistics` class:

```
IntSummaryStatistics stats =
    stream.skip(5).summaryStatistics();
```

The `stats` variable is used as shown here:

```
System.out.println("Average: " + stats.getAverage());
System.out.println("Count: " + stats.getCount());
System.out.println("Min: " + stats.getMin());
System.out.println("Max: " + stats.getMax());
System.out.println("Sum: " + stats.getSum());
```

The following output is produced:

```
Average: 5.0
Count: 9
Min: 3
Max: 9
Sum: 45
```

Sorting streams

Sorting is a very common and useful technique. To sort the elements of a stream, the overload `sorted` method is used. There is a no argument version that sorts according the natural ordering of the data stream and a single argument version that uses an object that implements the `Comparator` interface.

Let's continue with our number stream:

```
int[] numbers = {3, 6, 8, 8, 4, 6, 3, 3, 5, 6, 9, 4, 3, 6};
IntStream stream = Arrays.stream(numbers);
```

A simple use of the `sorted` method is as follows:

```
stream.sorted().
    forEach(n->System.out.print(n + " "));
System.out.println();
```

The output will appear as the following:

```
3 3 3 3 4 4 5 6 6 6 6 8 8 9
```

To get distinct values, we can use the following code sequence:

```
stream = Arrays.stream(numbers);
stream
    .sorted()
    .distinct()
    .forEach(n->System.out.print(n + " "));
System.out.println();
```

The output follows:

```
3 4 5 6 8 9
```

Mapping methods

Mapping operations transform an element of a stream. For example, we may want to increase all employees' salaries by five percent or convert a string to lowercase. The map and flatMap methods perform this type of operation.

The map method transforms an element into a different value. The flatMap method can also transform an element, but it is intended to collapse a series of streams into one stream. We will demonstrate the map method first.

We will also explore how the map-reduce process is supported using streams. These techniques perform a mapping operation against each element of a stream, and then it combines these transformations into a terminal value. For example, we can use this technique to give all of our employees the five percent raise and then total these values.

Understanding the mapping operation

To demonstrate these techniques, we start by creating an array of Rectangle objects:

```
Rectangle[] rectangles = {
    new Rectangle(10, 10, 50, 75),
    new Rectangle(30, 40, 30, 45),
    new Rectangle(110, 70, 70, 15),
    new Rectangle(50, 10, 45, 35)
};
```

We will use the following imperative example to apply the scale method to each element and to total their new areas. While the code can be rewritten to use a single loop, two loops are used to clearly separate the mapping and summation operations. The first loop maps the elements of the area to new values. The second loop performs a summation operation:

```
System.out.println("Iterative mapping");
for (Rectangle rectangle : rectangles) {
    rectangle.scale(0.25);
}
int total = 0;
for (Rectangle rectangle : rectangles) {
    total += rectangle.getArea();
}
System.out.println(total);
```

When executed, it will display a total area of 11,812. This is essentially an imperative version of the map-reduce paradigm. In the next sections, we will demonstrate various streaming techniques to accomplish the same task.

Implementing the map-reduce paradigm

The **map-reduce** paradigm is a popular technique for transforming data and then performing a reduction type operation where the data is *condensed* in some way. We will examine several stream techniques that support this operation. The process consists of using the map method followed by the reduce method.

To illustrate the process, instances of the Rectangle class developed in the previous section will be scaled, and then their total area will be computed. The scaling process is the mapping operations, and the total sum represents the reduction operation.

There are several ways of performing the map-reduce operation using a stream. The first technique will use two mapping methods and a sum method. As shown next, a stream of rectangles is created. The first map method applies the scale method against each stream element. The mapToInt method maps a Rectangle instance to an integer using the getArea method. The sum method computes a cumulative total.

```
Stream<Rectangle> stream = Arrays.stream(rectangles);
total = stream
        .map(r -> r.scale(0.25))
        .mapToInt(Rectangle::getArea)
        .sum();
System.out.println(total);
```

The scale method modifies the Rectangle instance, which is not desirable from a pure functional programming approach. Alternatively, we can develop and use a scale method that returns a new instance of a Rectangle instance. In addition, we could have used a second map method instead of the mapToInt method to achieve the same effect as shown next. However, the mapToInt method is more explicit.

```
.map(Rectangle::getArea)
```

The stream approach is easier to follow and more concise than the iterative approach.

The second approach uses two map methods and then the reduce method. The map methods are applied as before. The reduce method takes two parameters: an initial total value of zero and a lambda expression to perform the summation.

```
stream = Arrays.stream(rectangles);
total = stream
        .map(r -> r.scale(0.25))
        .mapToInt(Rectangle::getArea)
        .reduce(0, (r, s) -> r + s);
```

The lambda expression matches the `apply` method of the `BiFunction` interface. This implementation will compute a cumulative sum. The first parameter represents a sum, while the second parameter is the current rectangle's area. While this approach is more verbose than the earlier use of the `sum` method, it provides more flexibility if we need to perform a more sophisticated reduction operation.

To better understand how this works, let's go back and consider this imperative implementation:

```
for (Rectangle rectangle : rectangles) {
    rectangle.scale(0.25);
    System.out.println(total + " - " + rectangle.getArea());
    total += rectangle.getArea();
}
System.out.println(total);
```

It will display each rectangle's area along with a cumulative sum. When executed, we get the following output:

```
0 - 5766
5766 - 2072
7838 - 1566
9404 - 2408
11812
```

Next, let's modify the stream implementation. Instead of using the following:

```
.reduce(0,(r, s) -> r + s);
```

Let's use the following more verbose versions where the values of `r` and `s` are displayed:

```
.reduce(0, (r, s) -> {
    System.out.println(r + " - " + s);
    return r + s;
});
```

The following output is produced, which is identical to the imperative solution:

```
0 - 5766
5766 - 2072
7838 - 1566
9404 - 2408
11812
```

We can see that the r variable holds the cumulative sum, while the s variable holds the area for a specific rectangle.

Using the flatmap method

To understand the flatMap method, it is useful to consider the concat method first. This method simply concatenates two streams together. In the following example, two streams are created from two lists of Rectangle objects:

```
List<Rectangle> list1 = Arrays.asList(
    new Rectangle(10, 10, 20, 20),
    new Rectangle(10, 20, 30, 40),
    new Rectangle(40, 30, 20, 20));
List<Rectangle> list2 = Arrays.asList(
    new Rectangle(50, 50, 30, 30),
    new Rectangle(60, 60, 20, 20));
Stream<Rectangle> list1Stream = list1.stream();
Stream<Rectangle> list2Stream = list2.stream();
```

The concat method is used here:

```
Stream<Rectangle> concatenatedStream =
        Stream.concat(list1Stream, list2Stream);
concatenatedStream.forEach(System.out::println);
```

The output is as follows:

X: 10 Y: 10 Height: 20 Width: 20

X: 10 Y: 20 Height: 30 Width: 40

X: 40 Y: 30 Height: 20 Width: 20

X: 50 Y: 50 Height: 30 Width: 30

X: 60 Y: 60 Height: 20 Width: 20

The concat method simply combined the two streams, but did not modify elements of either stream. Similar to the concat method, the flatMap method also performs a concatenation type operation. Like the concat method, it returns a Stream object. However, it can also modify the stream.

The flatMap method is passed a Function instance, which accepts a value and returns a Stream object. The flatMap method's declaration follows:

```
<R> Stream<R> flatMap(Function<? super T,
                    ? extends Stream<? extends R>> mapper)
```

The `Function` instance's `apply` method's declaration is shown next:

```
R apply(T t)
```

It will be passed an argument of type: `? super T`, as defined by the `mapper` data type. It will return an instance of type: `? extends Stream<? extends R>`. The `Function` interface's `apply` method is executed against each element and then returns a stream. It will be called repeatedly with each invocation returning a stream. That is, each invocation of the `apply` method will return a stream. The `flatMap` method returns a `Stream` object that has "flattened" these multiple argument streams.

We will illustrate how we can combine several lists using an imperative approach. As we will see, this can be done with less effort using streams. First, we declare a list where each element is a list of `Rectangle` objects. This is a list of lists of `Rectangle` objects:

```
List<List<Rectangle>> rectangleLists = Arrays.asList(
        Arrays.asList(new Rectangle(10, 10, 20, 20),
                new Rectangle(10, 20, 30, 40),
                new Rectangle(40, 30, 20, 20)),
        Arrays.asList(new Rectangle(50, 50, 30, 30),
                new Rectangle(60, 60, 20, 20)),
        Arrays.asList(new Rectangle(100, 100, 30, 40),
                new Rectangle(110, 10, 20, 20),
                new Rectangle(120, 10, 50, 60))
);
```

Another list is created that will hold the combined elements of these lists. The `ArrayList` class's `addAll` method adds these to the new list:

```
List<Rectangle> flatList = new ArrayList<>();
for (List<Rectangle> rectangleList : rectangleLists) {
    flatList.addAll(rectangleList);
}
```

The content of the new list is displayed as follows:

```
for (Rectangle rectangle : flatList) {
    System.out.println(rectangle);
}
```

The output for this example is shown here:

```
X: 10 Y: 10 Height: 20 Width: 20
X: 10 Y: 20 Height: 30 Width: 40
X: 40 Y: 30 Height: 20 Width: 20
X: 50 Y: 50 Height: 30 Width: 30
X: 60 Y: 60 Height: 20 Width: 20
X: 100 Y: 100 Height: 30 Width: 40
X: 110 Y: 10 Height: 20 Width: 20
X: 120 Y: 10 Height: 50 Width: 60
```

The lists have been combined and flattened. Instead of a list of lists, we have a single list.

We can achieve the same results using a stream as shown next. A stream of rectangle lists is created. The `flatMap` method is then applied against the list, using a lambda expression. This expression uses the `stream` method to convert each list to a stream and then returns the stream. The `forEach` method then displays the elements of the new stream:

```
Stream<List<Rectangle>> rectangleListStream =
    rectangleLists.stream();
Stream<Rectangle> rectangleStream = rectangleListStream
        .flatMap((list) -> list.stream());
rectangleStream.forEach(System.out::println);
```

The output will be the same one we obtained using the imperative approach. While the `stream` method appears to use a bit more code, its real power comes from its ability to more elegantly express solutions to problem. The previous example can be rewritten to get the same results as follows:

```
rectangleLists.stream()
        .flatMap((list) -> list.stream())
        .forEach(System.out::println);
```

In the previous example, we did not modify any elements of the initial lists. However, we can use the `flatMap` method to modify the stream elements. For example, in the next code sequence, the height of each rectangle is set to 30 and the distinct areas greater than 900 are displayed:

```
rectangleLists
        .stream()
        .flatMap(
```

```
            (list) -> list.stream()
            .map(r -> {
                r.setHeight(30);
                return r;
            })
            .filter(r -> r.getArea() > 900)
        )
        .map(r -> r.getArea())
        .distinct()
        .forEach(System.out::println);
```

The output is as follows:

1200

1800

The `flatMap` method can be useful when multiple streams need to be combined.

Lazy and eager evaluation

There are three terms dealing with this topic: lazy loading, lazy evaluation, and eager evaluation. They are all present in most functional programming languages. These terms are defined as follows:

- **Lazy loading**: Delaying an expensive loading operation until needed.
- **Lazy evaluation**: Refers to the delaying of the evaluation of an operation until it is needed. Lazy evaluation support infinite streams.
- **Eager evaluation**: An operation is executed as soon as it is encountered.

We will discuss lazy and eager evaluation in this section. Lazy loading can occur when a line of a file is not read until it needs to be processed. This can occur in a stream when a line is read depending on the operations performed. Streams are sometimes called lazy sequences because they are often evaluated in a lazy manner.

The following demonstrates lazy evaluation. A part of this example first appeared in *Chapter 1, Getting Started with Functional Programming*. Here, we clearly show that the stream is not evaluated until the terminal operation is introduced. A lambda expression is declared that displays each number as it is processed:

```
IntUnaryOperator sampleMap = num -> {
    System.out.println("number: " + num);
    return num;
```

```
        };
        Random random = new Random();
        IntStream randomStream = random.ints()
                .limit(5)
                .map(sampleMap)
                .sorted();
        System.out.println(randomStream);
        randomStream.forEach(System.out::println);
```

The first line of the following output displays the IntStream class's toString method representation of the random stream. The next five lines are produced by the println method in the lambda expression. The last five lines are the result of the forEach method being called:

```
java.util.stream.SortedOps$OfInt@85ede7b

number: -1920271154

number: -316602508

number: -1274637426

number: 683544337

number: 1482205327

-1920271154

-1274637426

-316602508

683544337

1482205327
```

The map method is not executed when the stream is declared, but rather when the forEach method is used. This is lazy evaluation - the expression is not evaluated until it is needed.

The following example illustrates how even arithmetic expressions are not evaluated until needed. Four lambda expressions are defined. In the first one, we try to divide by zero which, when executed, will abort the program.

```
        Function<Integer,Integer> divide = n->1/0;
        Function<Integer,Integer> add = n->n+3;
        Function<Integer,Integer> multiply = n->n*5;
        Function<Integer,Integer> subtract = n->n-4;
```

These expressions are assigned to an array, which is then converted to a stream:

```
Function[] arr = {divide,add,multiply,subtract};
Stream<Function> stream = Arrays.stream(arr);
```

These expressions are not evaluated until they are needed. Here the first element is skipped and the remaining elements are processed:

```
stream.skip(1)
    .forEach(operation->System.out.println(operation.apply(2)));
```

The output is as follows:

5

10

-2

If we had not skipped the divide operation, the following exception would have been generated:

Java.lang.ArithmeticException: / by zero

If streams were evaluated eagerly, then every stream element would be processed and then the stream would be returned.

There is a `findFirst` method that truncates the stream when an element that meets a specific condition occurs. If we used a method such as `findFirst`, then lazy evaluation avoids processing elements that are never used. This is critical for infinite streams. An infinite stream would never terminate if eager evaluation were used. Lazy evaluation makes it possible to have infinite streams.

Methods such as `findFirst` are called **short-circuiting** methods. When they are used with an infinite stream, they will return a finite stream. Other short-circuiting methods are listed in the following table:

Method	Returns when
anyMatch	Any element matches
allMatch	All of the elements match. For an infinite stream, a limit-type method will restrict its length
noneMatch	None of the elements match
findAny	Finds any element that matches
limit	Restrict the number of elements
subStream	Creates a substream

Stream and concurrent processing

All stream operations execute either sequentially or in parallel. They execute sequentially by default. To execute concurrently, a parallel stream must be created. The `Stream` class uses a `parallel` method, and the `Collection` interface uses a `parallelStream` method to create parallel streams.

The typical iterative loop in Java (such as the `for` or `while` loops) are serial in nature. That is, they are designed to execute sequentially and are not able to easily incorporate concurrent behavior.

Over the years, Java has introduced a number of improvements in how parallel behavior can be achieved. Each of these improvements has built upon the thread concept and frequently addresses specific concurrent approaches such as thread pools. However, these approaches required the developer to deal with possible data corruption and deadlock situations.

To parallelize a stream on the surface, all you need to do is to use the `parallel` method instead of the `stream` method and the system will handle all of the details for you. Ideally, it will produce the same results as if executed serially and execute faster.

However, it is not as simple as this. There are several factors you need to take into consideration before making a stream parallel. We will not be able to address all of these issues, but will address many of them including:

- **Non-inference**: During the processing of the stream, the stream's data source must not be modified.

- **Stateless operations**: A lambda expression whose outcome might vary during its execution are called **state full**. This is potentially a problem, because as the stream's operations are executed, the results can differ each time it is executed. Instead, lambda expressions should be written to not use a state.

- **Side effects**: A stream operation can affect other parts of a program. They should be avoided if possible.

- **Ordering**: The ordering of elements produced by a parallel stream may be important. If so, care must be taken to address the ordering issue.

We will examine each of these issues next.

Understanding non-inference

This type of problem occurs when the stream's data source is modified, while the stream is executing. This can be a problem with non-concurrent data sources whether or not the stream is executed in parallel. There is always the possibility that some other thread may be accessing the data source. Inaccurate results or exceptions can occur.

In the next example, a stream of integers representing hours worked is created from an `ArrayList` instance. In the `map` method, the lambda expression will attempt to modify the underlying `ArrayList`:

```
List<Integer> hours = new ArrayList(
    Arrays.asList(32, 40, 54, 23, 35, 48, 40, 40, 23,
        54, 45, 44, 45, 65, 34, 35, 42, 42, 50, 45,
        35, 45, 35, 31, 12, 56));
Stream<Integer> hoursStream;
hoursStream = hours.parallelStream();
int totalHours = hoursStream
        .map(h -> {
            int amount =h*30;
            if(amount>40) {
                hours.add(h+10);
            }
            return amount;
        })
        .reduce(0, (r, s) -> r + s);
System.out.println(totalHours);
```

This will generate a `ConcurrentModificationException` exception, since we are trying to modify an `ArrayList` instance, which is not thread safe. We can avoid this problem using the `CopyOnWriteArrayList` class instead, which permits concurrent modifications of the list as shown here:

```
CopyOnWriteArrayList<Integer> concurrentHours =
    new CopyOnWriteArrayList(
    Arrays.asList(32, 40, 54, 23, 35, 48, 40, 40, 23,
        54, 45, 44, 45, 65, 34, 35, 42, 42, 50, 45,
        35, 45, 35, 31, 12, 56));
Stream<Integer> hoursStream;
hoursStream = concurrentHours.parallelStream();
int totalHours = hoursStream
        .map(h -> {
```

```
            int amount =h*30;
            if(amount>40) {
                concurrentHours.add(h+10);
            }
            return amount;
        })
        .reduce(0, (r, s) -> r + s);
System.out.println(totalHours);
```

The general rule is to avoid modifying the stream's data source.

Understanding stateless operations

Ideally, lambda expressions should be stateless and not be dependent on external factors. This will ensure that the stream's operations will produce the same result each time it is executed.

To demonstrate such operations, we will use a lambda expression that uses a getPay method. The method is passed the number of hours worked and returns the pay based on a rate variable. However, the rate changes depending on the number of hours. If it exceeds 40 hours, then the current thread is delayed for half of a second. This delay is introduced to highlight the effect of potentially different processing times and the rate values used. The getPay method is as follows:

```
int rate = 30;

public int getPay(int hours) {
    if (hours > 40) {
        rate = 25;
        try {
            Thread.sleep(500);
        } catch (InterruptedException ex) {
            // Handle exception
        }
    } else {
        rate = 30;
    }
    return rate * hours;
}
```

In the following sequence, a series of hours is transformed into a parallel stream and used to compute the total pay. A new stream is created twice to demonstrate various outputs:

```
List<Integer> hours
        = Arrays.asList(32, 40, 24, 23, 35, 18, 40, 30, 23,
               54, 35, 34, 25, 15, 34, 35, 42, 44, 40, 35,
               35, 45, 35, 31, 12, 56); 31, 12, 56);
               Stream<Integer> hoursStream;
for(int i=0; i<2; i++) {
    rate = 30;
    int total = hours
            .parallelStream()
            .map(h -> getPay(h))
            .reduce(0, (r, s) -> r + s);
    System.out.println(total);
}
```

When executed using the `stream` method, we will always obtain a result of 24955. However, if we use a parallel stream, the result will differ. One possible set of results follow:

25175

25450

The output value depends on how the stream is parallelized. We cannot readily predict where the stream will be split, and it will appear to be random. The stream operations should not be dependent on external values.

Understanding side effects

A stateless operation will not be affected by external program elements. In a similar manner, operations should not modify other data elements of a program unless absolutely necessary. If the operation has side effects, then this can have unintended consequences.

In the following example, we use a stream to add overtime hours to a separate list:

```
List<Integer> overtimeList = new ArrayList<>();
hours.parallelStream()
        .filter(s -> s > 40)
```

```
            .forEach(s -> overtimeList.add(s));
    for (Integer hour : overtimeList) {
        System.out.print(hour + " ");
    }
    System.out.println();
```

Since the array list is not thread safe, concurrent modification of the list may produce errors. When this example is executed repeatedly, null values may creep in or an `ArrayIndexOutOfBoundsException` exception may be generated. This is more pronounced when many of the hours exceed 40.

An alternative approach to solve this problem is to use the `collect` method with the `Collectors` class's `toList` method. This will safely create a new list as shown here:

```
    overtimeList =  hours
            .parallelStream()
            .filter(s -> s > 40)
            .collect(Collectors.toList());
```

Some side effects such as displaying intermediate results can be tolerated. However, side effects should be avoided when using a functional style of programming.

Understanding the ordering

The ordering of a stream's elements can be important. For example, sorting the stream's elements is often a task requirement. When we parallelize a stream, we affect the order the elements that are processed. Consider the following example where we sort those hours that are greater than 40 using a parallel stream:

```
    hours
        .parallelStream()
        .filter(s -> s > 40)
        .sorted()
        .forEach(h -> System.out.print(h + " "));
    System.out.println();
```

One possible output follows. However, the list is not sorted.

```
48 54 56 45 65 45 42 45 54 50 45 42 44
```

The order will vary with each execution because each parallel stream sorted its elements, but when the streams merge they are not sorted. Instead, use the forEachOrdered method, which forces the stream to process the stream elements in the encountered order as shown next. However, this method can distract from the efficiency gained from parallel streams:

```
hours
    .parallelStream()
    .filter(s -> s > 40)
    .sorted()
    .forEachOrdered(s -> System.out.print(s + " "));
System.out.println();
```

The output is as follows:

42 44 45 54 56

Parallel operations can significantly improve the performance of an application allowing us to take full advantage of multiple processors. However, care must be taken when working with parallel streams to avoid unintended consequences. We provided an introduction to several of the issues that can affect parallel streams. You are encouraged to carefully consider the consequences of using these types of operations.

Summary

The use of streams is considered to be one aspect of functional programming languages. In this chapter, we addressed the use of streams as supported by Java 8. We demonstrated the creation and use of finite and infinite streams. These depend on some data source, which might be bounded in length as with arrays or indefinite if derived from a source such as a network connection.

The Stream class supports the stream concept in Java. While it possesses many methods, we covered only a few with the goal of imparting a feel for the use and power of streams. We examined the filter, skip, and sorted methods and used them in several examples. We demonstrated the popular map-reduce technique, which potentially modifies a set of data and then combines these values into a result.

The concepts of lazy and eager evaluation were examined and illustrated. Lazy evaluation makes possible the use of infinite streams. You also learned that a stream execution begins when the terminal method starts and ends when the terminal method completes.

In the last section, we examined the nature of parallel streams and the issues that need to be considered when using them. Ideally, the stream's operations should be stateless and not be dependent on external values. Conversely, these operations should not modify external values. Care should also be taken when the order of a stream's elements is important.

In the next chapter, we will examine the use of recursion, its functional implications, and its use in Java 8.

5
Recursion Techniques in Java 8

Recursion is a powerful functional programming technique that lends itself to more elegant and succinct solutions than an iterative approach. Recursion is the technique where a method, either directly or indirectly, calls itself. A lambda expression can also call itself recursively. The discussion in this chapter will focus on method recursion. However, keep in mind that the ideas and concepts apply equally to recursive lambda expressions.

In this chapter, we will:

- Introduce recursion terminology
- Contrast iterative and recursion techniques
- Demonstrate recursive lambda expressions
- Explore common recursion strategies
- Provide guidance as to when to use recursion

Recursion is not new to Java 8. To illustrate recursion using a method, let's examine what is probably the most commonly used problem to illustrate recursion—the factorial problem. It is defined as follows:

```
f(1) = 1
f(n) = n * f(n-1)
where n > 0
```

The following is an iterative solution for the factorial of 5. It will return `120`:

```
long fact = 1;
for(int i=1; i<=5; i++) {
    fact *= i;
}
```

A recursive solution is implemented using the following factorial method, which produces equivalent results:

```
public long factorial(long n) {
    if(n==1) {
        return 1;
    } else {
        return n * factorial(n-1);
    }
}
```

The factorial implementation provided is simplistic. It does not verify that the values passed to it are greater than zero as required by the factorial definition. In addition, even though it uses long data types, eventually a number will be generated that exceeds the maximum long number possible, which will result in overflow and incorrect results. This happens very quickly.

In this chapter, we will start with a discussion of recursive data structures and the types of recursion techniques in common use. We will be using a binary tree to illustrate many of these techniques, including head and tail recursion.

We will discuss common problems encountered when using recursion to help the reader avoid these types of mistakes. Also, recursion implementation issues and how the recursion process can be optimized will be discussed.

It is not always clear when recursion should be used. We will discuss those situations where it is the preferred technique and when iteration is better. A short section concludes the chapter by discussing how recursion has evoked various humorous responses.

Recursive data structures

A recursive data structure contains references to itself, such as a list or tree. These types of structures are dynamic data structures where the structure can theoretically grow to an infinite length.

The recursive nature of this data structure lends itself to recursive algorithms. Examples of recursive data structures include:

- Linked lists
- Trees
- Filesystems
- Graph

It is sometimes thought that recursive methods work differently from regular methods. They don't. They both simply return when they are completed. A problem that can be solved using iteration can be solved using recursion. A problem that can be solved using recursion can be solved using iteration.

A recursive solution will typically take more space than an iterative solution. Each time a method is called, an activation record is created for the method. This activation record will contain its parameters and any local variables as is detailed in *Understanding the program stack*. An iterative solution will require a fixed amount of memory, the memory for the data being processed. Recursive solutions require memory for each activation record. They frequently require at least $O(n)$ memory versus the $O(1)$ for an iterative solution unless optimization such as tail recursion is performed as detailed in *Converting to a tail call*. The $O(n)$ notation classifies how an algorithm responds to increases in input size. It established an upper bound on how the growth rate of an algorithm. A $O(n)$ is linear, while $O(1)$ is constant.

With the iterative factorial solution, memory is only needed for the code and data. For the recursive version, memory needs to be allocated for each invocation of the method for its supporting activation record. The larger the number of recursive calls, the more activation records are needed.

Some problems that can be quite difficult to solve using an iterative approach can be implemented very nicely using recursion. For example, the **N-Queens** problem is concerned with the placement of N queens on an N by N chess board such that no two queens can capture each other. An iterative solution can be found at `http://course.wilkes.edu/Java2Labs/stories/storyReader$9`. A much simpler recursive solution can be found at `http://www.javawithus.com/programs/towers-of-hanoi`. **Tower of Hanoi** is another example of where the iterative solution is more difficult than the recursive version.

Types of recursion

There are several different recursion types and terms. These include:

- **Direct recursion**: This is typified by the factorial implementation where the methods call itself.

- **Mutual recursion**: This happens where one method, say method A, calls another method B, which then calls method A. This involves two or more methods that eventually create a circular call sequence.

- **Multi-recursion**: Multiple recursive calls are made in the method.

- **Head recursion**: The recursive call is made at the beginning of the method.

- **Tail recursion**: The recursive call is the last statement.

Direct recursion is the most common form of recursion. Head and tail recursion are specialized terms for direct and mutual recursion.

Mutual recursion is not as common as other forms of recursion. However, it can be quite useful in the implementations of recursive descent parsers. The reader is referred to `http://en.wikipedia.org/wiki/Recursive_descent_parser` for details on how to use mutual recursion with a recursive descent parser.

There are several other recursion terms that you may encounter but these are generally formal language related such as left and right recursion. These terms are used to describe certain attributes of a language definition.

Using direct recursion

Direct recursion occurs when a method calls itself directly. In the earlier `factorial` method, it called itself if the number passed was not 1. It is the simplest type of recursion. When a method calls itself, it must encounter some condition where it stops calling itself. If a method calls itself again and again without encountering such a case, it will never terminate. This is called **unbounded recursion**. This is not a good form of recursion. It will eventually result in the application terminating abnormally.

To prevent unbounded recursion, at least one condition must exist where the method does not call itself. In addition, it is necessary for the value passed to the method to eventually meet this condition. When this happens, we say that we have **bounded recursion**. This is the useful form of recursion.

In the `factorial` method, when the parameter n is a 1, the method stops calling itself. This eventually becomes possible because in the recursive call the value passed to the method is decreased by one each time.

Every useful recursive solution possesses two types of cases:

- **Base case**: Where the problem is solved directly and the method does not call itself
- **Recursive case**: Where the recursive call is made

The base case represents a solution to a simple, smaller part of the problem. There may be more than one base case. One or more recursive cases must be present. A recursive method requires at least one parameter to be passed to it. It often uses few or no local variables.

The iteration and recursion process works because they perform similar tasks with each iteration. If the tasks change, then either technique is not easy to use. The recursion case needs to perform three steps:

1. Split the problem into simpler parts.
2. Perform the recursive call.
3. Combine the results.

This is a version of the divide-and-conquer strategy. The basic idea of recursion is to reduce a problem to a smaller version of the same type. Each recursive call will convert the problem to a yet a smaller version. When the problem becomes small enough you reach a base case. From here the results are "combined."

Head and tail recursion

A simple illustration of the difference between head and tail recursion is shown with the following two recursive methods. They are both passed a string. The head method will display the string in reverse, while the tail method will display the string normally.

A string is passed to each method. If its length is zero, the method returns. With the head method, a recursive call is made and then the first character of the phrase is displayed. In the tail method, the first character is displayed followed by the recursive call:

```
public void head(String phrase) {
    if (phrase.length() == 0) {
        return;
    }
    head(phrase.substring(1));
    System.out.print(phrase.charAt(0));
}
```

```
public void tail(String phrase) {
    if (phrase.length() == 0) {
        return;
    }
    System.out.print(phrase.charAt(0));
    tail(phrase.substring(1));
}
```

The following statements demonstrate their use:

```
head("Recursion");
System.out.println();
tail("Recursion");
System.out.println();
```

The output is as follows:

noisruceR

Recursion

It is helpful to use other statements to assist in understanding recursion. Try replacing the following statement:

```
System.out.print(phrase.charAt(0));
```

With this one in both of the methods:

```
System.out.println(phrase);
```

This will produce the following output. Each line shows the phrase for each invocation of the method. The first sequence shows head recursion where the first display of the phrase occurs once the stack has grown to its largest size. The second sequence shows tail recursion, where the phrase is displayed before the recursive call. The phrase is shortened each time until there is nothing left to display:

n

on

ion

sion

rsion

ursion

cursion

```
ecursion
Recursion

Recursion
ecursion
cursion
ursion
rsion
sion
ion
on
n
```

In the *Understanding the program stack* section, we will examine the use of the program stack, which will provide further insight into how recursion works.

As a functional programming technique, its use becomes more prominent and important in Java 8. It is now possible to use recursion with other functional programming techniques previously not available in Java such as lambda expressions.

Understanding recursion

Recursion can be understood at several different levels. A simplistic understanding involves knowing the definition of recursion. A method that calls itself is recursive. This understanding is not particularly useful.

Another level of understanding is being able to take a recursive algorithm and implement it using recursion. This is often a fairly direct process, and can be performed without truly understanding recursion.

A mathematical understanding occurs when one can clearly see how the recursive invocation works at a functional level and how local variables are handled. This is an important level of understanding to achieve where one is better able to create and maintain recursive application.

A more complete understanding involves being able to explain how the program stack implements recursive programs. This level, which is closely tied to the previous level, will enable the programmer to fully understand how recursion works and assist in debugging the more difficult recursive programming errors.

The intent of this chapter is to convey these levels of understanding and provide the reader with the ability to develop useful recursive solutions to appropriate problems. In the next section, we will explore the creation of a recursive solution using direct recursion. It will illustrate the essential steps in a recursive solution, which can be applied to mutual or other types of recursion.

The Node class

We will be using the Node class to illustrate recursion as shown next. It supports the creation of binary trees where each element will contain a numerical value and has references to left and right subtrees. A fluent method style is used. We will perform a number of operations against binary trees including **preorder**, **inorder**, and **postorder** traversal.

```java
public class Node {
    private int value;
    private Node left;
    private Node right;

    public Node(int value) {
        this.value = value;
        this.left = null;
        this.right = null;
    }

    public Node(Node node) {
        this.value = node.value;
        this.left = null;
        this.right = null;
    }

    public int getValue() {
        return value;
    }

    public Node left() {
        return this.left;
    }

    public Node addLeft(int value) {
        Node node = new Node(value);
        this.left = node;
```

```
        return node;
    }

    public Node addLeft(Node node) {
        this.left = node;
        return this;
    }

    public Node right() {
        return this.right;
    }

    public Node addRight(int value) {
        Node node = new Node(value);
        this.right = node;
        return node;
    }

    public Node addRight(Node node) {
        this.right = node;
        return this;
    }}
```

Preorder, inorder, and postorder are techniques for traversing a binary tree. They are similar in nature consisting of three basic operations. They differ in the order they are followed as shown in the following table. Going left or right means to traverse the left or right subtree, respectively. To visit a node is to perform some operation on the node:

Technique	Steps
Preorder	Visit the node
	Go left
	Go right
Inorder	Go left
	Visit the node
	Go right
Postorder	Go left
	Go right
	Visit the node

The tree we will use for our examples is initialized with the following code sequence:

```
Node root = new Node(12);
root.addLeft(8).addRight(9);
root.addRight(18).addLeft(14).addRight(17);
```

This represents a tree that appears as follows:

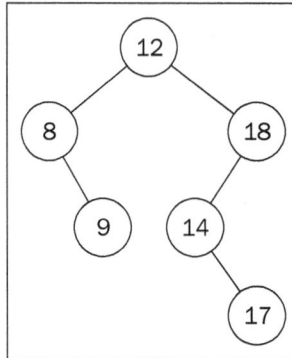

The effect of traversing this tree with each algorithm is shown in the next table:

Algorithm	Output
Preorder	12 8 9 18 14 17
Inorder	8 9 12 14 17 18
Postorder	9 8 17 14 18 12

Using head recursion

Head recursion occurs when the recursive call occurs at the beginning of the method. It cannot actually be the first statement because this will lead to unbounded recursion. The first statement is typically a base case.

We can illustrate head recursion using the following postOrder method, where the left and right nodes are traversed before the node's value is displayed:

```
public void postOrder(Node node) {
    if (node != null) {
        postOrder(node.left());
        postOrder(node.right());
        System.out.print(node.getValue() + " ");
    }
}
```

The output of this code sequence is as follows:

```
9 8 17 14 18 12
```

Head recursion can also be used to implement the power function, which raises a base value to an exponent. In the pow method that follows, a base and exponent are passed to the method. There are three cases:

- **An exponent of 0**: This returns one

- **An exponent of 1**: This returns the base

- **An exponent greater than 1**: The recursive call is made using half the value of the exponent with even and odd exponents being treated differently

```
private static long pow(long base, long exponent) {
    if (exponent == 0) {
        return 1;
    } else if (exponent == 1) {
        return base;
    } else {
        long intermediate = pow(base, exponent / 2);
        if (exponent % 2 == 0) {
            return intermediate * intermediate;
        } else {
            return intermediate * intermediate * base;
        }
    }
}
```

Invoking the method as shown here will return a value of 59049:

```
System.out.println(pow(9,5));
```

Using tail recursion

The preorder traversal of binary tree illustrates tail recursion. The method is called twice at the end as shown in the following implementation:

```
public void preOrder(Node node) {
    if (node == null) {
        return;
    } else {
        System.out.print(node.getValue() + " ");
        preOrder(node.left());
        preOrder(node.right());
    }
}
```

The output of this code sequence follows:

```
12  8  9  18  14  17
```

This type of traversal is often used to create a prefix expression based on a binary tree, where the internal nodes are operators and the leaves are values.

Tail recursion is also useful for copying a tree. The following method demonstrates how this is accomplished. A new copy of a tree node is created. A recursive call is made for the left and right branches of the node, which are added to the new node fluently. The new node is returned allowing it to be added to parent nodes:

```java
public Node copyTree(Node node) {
    if (node == null) {
        return null;
    } else {
        return (new Node(node))
                    .addLeft(copyTree(node.left()))
                    .addRight(copyTree(node.right()));
    }
}
```

The use of the method is shown next:

```java
Node tree = copyTree(root);
```

Using the head and tail recursion

The different types of recursion can be mixed. For example, the following implementation of an inorder traversal of a tree uses both head and tail recursion:

```java
public void inOrder(Node node) {
    if (node == null) {
        return;
    } else {
        inOrder(node.left());
        System.out.print(node.getValue() + " ");
        inOrder(node.right());
    }
}
```

The output of this code sequence is as follows:

```
8  9  12  14  17  18
```

A **Binary Search Tree (BST)** is a binary tree whose node values are ordered. All nodes in a left subtree are less than the base node. All nodes in the right subtree are greater than the base node. The tree we have been using is a BST. A useful characteristic of a BST is when the tree is traversed in an inorder manner. The result will be sorted as demonstrated with the previous results.

Creating a recursive solution based on a formula

When a problem is stated in a formal manner, such as with a formula, it is easy to create a recursive solution. Consider the following definition of finding the greatest common denominator of two numbers:

If $y=0$ then $gcd(x,y) = x$

If $y>0$ then $gcd(x,y) = gcd(y,x \% y)$

In the following implementation, the two conditions are specified using the then and else clauses of an if statement. In the then clause, we simply return x. In the else clause, we perform the recursive call:

```java
public int gcd(int x, int y) {
    if (y == 0) {
        return x;
    } else {
        return gcd(y, x % y);
    }
}
```

We can test this method with the following statements:

```java
System.out.println(gcd(48,72));
System.out.println(gcd(182,154));
```

The results are as follows:

24

14

The implementation of this type of definition simply maps the operations to the matching conditions. For a definition with more than two conditions, a series of elseif type clauses can be used.

When a problem is defined in a recursive manner, it lends itself to a recursive solution. However, that does not necessarily mean it is the best solution. The Fibonacci sequence definition is a classic example. Its definition is as follows:

```
fib(0) = 0
fib(1) = 1
fib(n) = fib(n-1) + fib(n-2)
```

The method can be implemented as follows:

```
public int fib(int n) {
    if(n == 0) {
        return 0;
    } else if(n == 1) {
        return 1;
    } else {
        return fib(n-1) + fib(n-2);
    }
}
```

The next statement will display the Fibonacci of 11:

```
System.out.println(fib(11));
```

It will display 89 as the answer. The reason this implementation is not a good choice is because it involves an excessive number of method invocations. Adding a simple counter to total the number of times it is called will determine that the method was called 287 times for the fib(11).

A more efficient iterative solution follows. The first two elements of the array are initialized to 0 and 1, respectively. The for loop will then set the remaining elements to the sum of their previous two elements:

```
int arr[] = new int[15];
arr[0] = 0;
arr[1] = 1;
for (int i = 2; i < 15; i++) {
    arr[i] = arr[i - 1] + arr[i - 2];
}
System.out.println(arr[11]);
```

This will display 89 as expected.

A more detailed discussion of computing the Fibonacci of a number is found at `http://jlordiales.me/2014/02/20/dynamic-programming-introduction/`. In *Chapter 2*, *Putting the Function in Functional Programming*, we examined the memoization technique. The post also uses this technique as part of a recursive Fibonacci solution.

Converting an iterative loop to a recursive solution

While it is not necessary, or necessarily desirable, to convert iterative loops to a recursive method, it is useful to examine this process to help you better understand how to develop recursive solutions.

Let's use the following iterative approach to compute the sum of the even numbers from 2 to 20. The output of the code sequence will be 110:

```
int sum = 0;
for(int i=2; i<=20; i+=2) {
    sum += i;
}
System.out.println(sum);
```

A recursive solution follows. It is passed an integer, n, which is checked to determine if it is equal to a 2. If so, it simply returns a 2. Otherwise, a recursive call is made where n is added to the return value of the recursive call. To add only even numbers, the value passed is n-2:

```
private static int recursiveSum(int n) {
    if(n == 2) {
        return 2;
    } else {
        return n + recursiveSum(n-2);
    }
}
```

This solution will work for any positive, even number greater than or equal to 2. However, it does not verify that the number passed is an even number. When the number is odd or less than 2, a stack overflow occurs. This can be corrected by checking for evenness as we will demonstrate in *Using a wrapper method*.

Merging two lists

Lists are an example of a recursive data structure. Here, we will illustrate how recursion can be used to merge two lists as implemented using the `ArrayList` class. This method has been adapted from http://stackoverflow.com/ questions/14912835/how-to-create-recursive-merge-of-2-sorted-lists-resulting-in-sorted-merged-list.

Two sorted lists are merged. The `mergeList` method is passed two lists and returns a merged list. A test is made for empty lists in the base cases. Otherwise, a new `ArrayList` is created and the smaller of two elements are added to the list. A recursive call is made and the list returned. One of the lists is reduced in size with each call:

```
public ArrayList<Integer> mergeList(
        ArrayList<Integer> list1,
        ArrayList<Integer> list2) {
    if (list1.isEmpty()) {
        return list2;
    }
    if (list2.isEmpty()) {
        return list1;
    }
    ArrayList list = new ArrayList<>();
    if (list1.get(0) < list2.get(0)) {
        list.add(list1.remove(0));
    } else {
        list.add(list2.remove(0));
    }
    list.addAll(mergeList(list1, list2));
    return list;
}
```

Here two lists are created, and the `mergeList` method is called:

```
Integer arr1[] = {2, 6, 9, 10, 14};
ArrayList<Integer> list1 = new ArrayList<>();
list1.addAll(Arrays.asList(arr1));

Integer arr2[] = {3, 5, 7, 12, 13};
ArrayList<Integer> list2 = new ArrayList<>();
list2.addAll(Arrays.asList(arr2));
```

```
ArrayList<Integer> list3;
list3 = mergeList(list1,list2);
list3.stream().forEach(n -> System.out.print(n + " "));
System.out.println();
```

The output of this sequence is as follows:

```
2  3  5  6  7  9  10  12  13  14
```

Understanding the program stack

A solid understanding of recursion is one where the programmer understands how the program stack works. This is a fundamental data structure used to support method and function invocation in most languages. Most hardware has specialized instructions to help maintain a program stack.

Whenever a method is called, an activation record is created for that method, and it is pushed onto a stack—the program stack. When a method returns, the activation record is popped off the program stack. The activation record consists of several elements, but the only ones of interest to us are the parameters and local variables. It does not contain any of the method's code. The code is located elsewhere in the program.

For example, let's reexamine the `factorial` function duplicated here for your convenience:

```
public long factorial(long n) {
    if(n==1) {
        return 1;
    } else {
        return n * factorial(n-1);
    }
}
```

For the method, there is one parameter, n, and no local variables. We can graphically depict the program stack as shown in the next figure, where the method is invoked with a value of 5. The state of the stack reflects that the method has only been called once and before any of the method's code has been executed.

The names on the left side of the stack are the names of the methods. We are assuming that the factorial method is called from the main method. The boxes to the right of the method's names in the stack correspond to the methods. Parameters and local variables are drawn as boxes inside of the method boxes. For the main method, we have not shown any parameters or local variables to keep it simple. For the factorial method, we show the single parameter n:

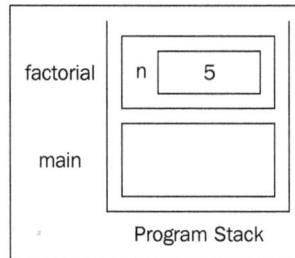

When the factorial method is executed with a value of 5, the else clause of the if statement is executed. This means that a new activation record is created and pushed onto the stack with a new value of 4 for the parameter. There are now two activation records for the factorial method with their own unique parameters. This is the key to understanding how recursion is implemented:

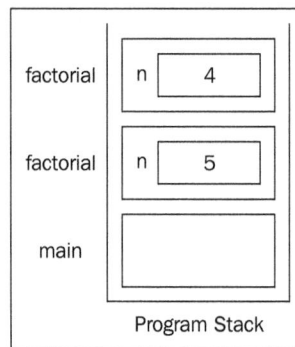

Continuing with the example, the `factorial` function is called three more times until the parameter is 1. This is shown here:

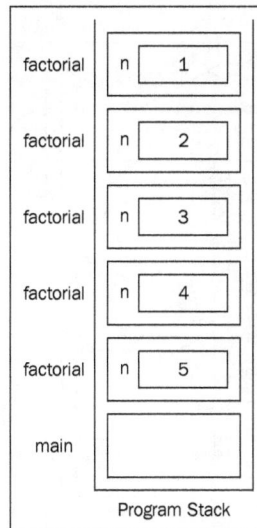

Program Stack

At this point, the base case is selected and the method will return 1. The top `factorial` activation record is popped off of the stack, and 1 is returned to the previous activation record. This is illustrated here where an X is used to depict the removal of the top activation record and 1 being returned:

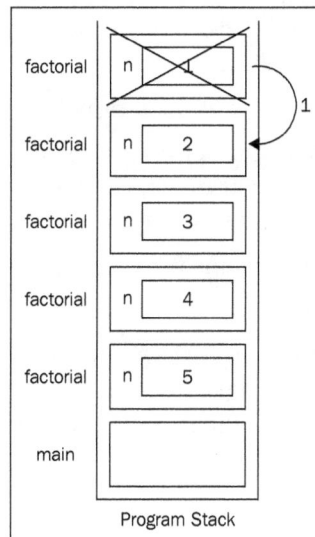

Program Stack

The returned value of 1 is multiplied by 2, and then the method will return. The next activation is popped off the stack, and a 2 is returned. Eventually, a 120 is returned to the main method as shown here:

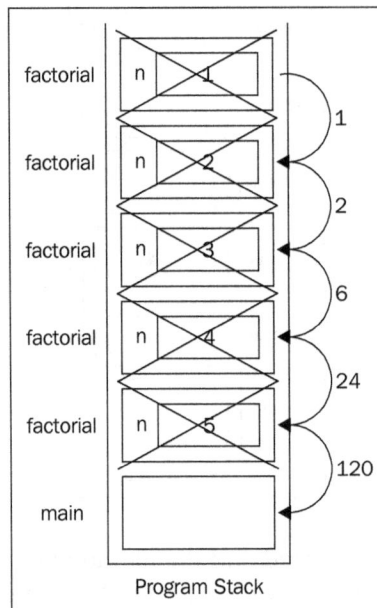

Program Stack

The key points to remember are as follows:

- Each time a method is invoked, an activation record is created for it and is pushed onto the program stack.
- The activation record consists of its parameters and local variables.
- When the method returns, the activation record is popped off the stack and no longer exists. Any of its parameters or local variables are lost. Only the return value is returned to the calling method.
- Each activation record maintains its own copies of its parameters and local variables.

As we will see in *Chapter 8, Refactoring, Debugging, and Testing*, most IDEs provide some support for visualizing the program stack. This visualization helps the programmer understand how a specific recursive method behaves.

Recursive lambda expressions

While we have been focusing on recursion using methods, these techniques are applicable to lambda expressions. To create a recursive lambda expression, we will duplicate the inorder recursion technique using a `Consumer` functional interface and the tree developed in the `Node` class.

As shown next, the `inorder` variable is declared. A lambda expression is assigned to the variable using essentially the same code as used in the method implementation. The `root` tree is created and the `accept` method is called, which results in the lambda expression's execution:

```
Consumer<Node> inorder; // Instance variable
...
inorder = (Node node) -> {
    if (node == null) {
        return;
    } else {
        inorder.accept(node.left());
        System.out.print(node.getValue() +  " ");
        inorder.accept(node.right());
    }
};
Node root = new Node(12);
root.addLeft(8).addRight(9);
root.addRight(18).addLeft(14).addRight(17);
inorder.accept(root);
```

The output follows:

```
8  9  12  14  17  18
```

The process is straightforward. We can use recursive lambda expression as easily as recursive methods.

Common problems found in recursive solutions

Sometimes, there are several problems encountered in recursive solutions, including:

- Absence of a base case
- The use of static or instance variables
- The use of the pre/post increment/decrement operators

The absence of a base case will lead to infinite recursion and stack overflow. Static and instances variable are to be avoided so that the function or method will be pure. Use of these variables can complicate the solution. As we will see, pre- and post-operators can complicate recursion.

Absence of a base case

This is not a common problem. It may manifest itself in complex case selection process, where the criteria needed to meet the base case is never achieved. More likely, this happens due to mistakes made by the programmer.

For example, the `recursiveSum` method, developed in *Converting an iterative loop to a recursive solution*, does not handle odd numbers or numbers less than 2. When called with these values a runtime `StackOverflowError` exception will be thrown because the condition for the base case, n==2, never occurs.

Using static or instance variables

Static and instance variables can be misused in a recursive method. In the following example, the method's purpose is to sum the specified number of elements of an array. It does this using, incorrectly, either an instance or local variable, `total`, to keep a cumulative sum. Both declarations have been included though only one is needed. The approach is loosely based on an iterative solution, where each element of the array is added to a total variable:

```java
public int total = 0;
public int arrayTotal(int numbers[], int index) {
    int total = 0;
    if (index == 0) {
        return numbers[0];
    } else {
        total += numbers[index];
        return arrayTotal(numbers, index - 1);
    }
}
```

When this code is executed, it displays 2 which is not the correct value. There are a couple of problems with this approach. The variable `total` is not incorporated into the return value, and the local variable is not actually needed. They are a distraction from a recursive technique. An additional problem is that if the `total` variable is declared locally, it will result in its re-initialization each time the method is called. Making it an instance or static variable will insure that it is initialized only once.

A better approach will be to replace the second return statement with the following:

```
return numbers[index] + arrayTotal(numbers, index - 1);
```

This will produce the correct output of 20. However, we are no longer using the `total` variable. A simplified version of the method is shown here:

```
public int arrayTotal(int numbers[], int index) {
    if (index == 0) {
        return numbers[0];
    } else {
        return numbers[index] + arrayTotal(numbers, index -
        1);
    }
}
```

Frequently, recursive methods can be avoided, and don't need local variables.

Using the pre- and post-increment operators

Care should be taken when using the pre/post increment/decrement operators in general. For example, in the `arrayTotal` method instead of using the minus operator as shown here:

```
return numbers[index] + arrayTotal(numbers, index - 1);
```

We can use the post-decrement operator instead:

```
return numbers[index] + arrayTotal(numbers, index--);
```

However, this results in unbounded recursion and stack overflow since `index` is passed first and then decremented. The effect is `index` passed never changes. Instead, we should use the pre-decrement operator, which decrements `index` and then passes it:

```
return numbers[index] + arrayTotal(numbers, --index);
```

This will produce the correct answer.

Recursion implementation techniques

There are a few implementation issues that should be addressed. These include the use of wrapper methods and short-circuiting the base case. These techniques can assist in the use of recursion.

Using a wrapper method

A wrapper method is used to support recursion. This method will not actually perform recursion but will call one that does. The wrapper method may:

- Validate parameters
- Perform initialization
- Handle exceptions as errors are generated

The following is an example of a wrapper method for the `arrayTotal` method, which is duplicated here for your convenience:

```java
public int arrayTotal(int numbers[], int index) {
    if (index == 0) {
        return numbers[0];
    } else {
        return numbers[index] + arrayTotal(numbers, index -
        1);
    }
}
```

In the `arrayTotalHelper` method, the `index` variable is checked to see if it is within the bounds of the array. If it is not, then the exception needs to be handled:

```java
public int arrayTotalHelper(int numbers[], int index) {
    if (index >= 0 && index <= numbers.length - 1) {
        return arrayTotal(numbers, index);
    } else {
        // Handle exception
    }
}
```

Using short circuiting

Shorts circuiting occurs when the base case is checked before the recursive call is made. This is an optimization technique. Instead of incurring the expensive method invocation and then checking for the base case, the base case is tested first. This normally requires a wrapper method to handle an initial base case call.

For example, with a tree traversal, a left or right value of null is common. If we check it for a null value before we make the recursive call, the activation record and its associated costs are not incurred. In the following example, the left and right subtrees are tested before the call is made:

```java
public void inOrder(Node node) {
    if (node == null) {
        return;
    } else {
        if(node.left() != null) {
            inOrder(node.left());
        }
        System.out.print(node.getValue() + " ");
        if(node.right() != null) {
            inOrder(node.right());
        }
    }
}
```

This will result in the `inorder` method being invoked 13 times versus 26 times for the earlier implementation and the sample tree.

Tail call optimization

A **tail call** is where the last operation is a "simple" recursive call. Tail call optimization is an optimization technique, which converts the recursive call to one where the activation record is reused. This technique will save space and time.

The `gcd` method, used in the *Creating a recursive solution based on a formula* section, illustrates a tail call and is duplicated here. The last statement of the recursive case is a simple recursive call:

```java
public int gcd(int x, int y) {
    if (y == 0) {
        return x;
    } else {
        return gcd(y, x % y);
    }
}
```

The following factorial method does not use a tail call. Since it uses a deferred multiplication that accumulates, this requires it to be stored on the program stack. The compiler is not able to optimize the call:

```java
public long factorial(long n) {
    if(n==1) {
        return 1;
    } else {
        return n * factorial(n-1);
    }
}
```

Tail calls can be optimized by effectively reusing the current activation record. Without tail call optimization, it is necessary to create a new activation record to hold and process the method's values. However, since the tail call does not involve an additional computation beyond the recursive call, the current activation record and its values can be reused.

Implementing tail call optimization results in a faster program that uses less space and has the ability to express algorithms in a more maintainable and an often easier to read recursion form. However, not all compilers incorporate tail call optimization, including those that support Java 8. In future versions, this optimization technique will be available.

In the meantime, it will be prudent to employee tail calls whenever possible. Thus, when the optimization technique becomes available, your code can take immediate advantage of it instead having to be rewritten.

Converting to a tail call

The previous factorial implementation did not use a tail call. We will provide an alternate version of the method that uses a tail call. The following `factorial` method uses the recursive `factorialHelper` method to do the actual work. In the original `factorial` method, tail recursion was not employed because the recursive return value was multiplied against the variable n. In this implementation, the multiplication has been used as part of the parameter to the recursive call. Since the multiplication occurs before the call, it performs a tail call.

```java
public long factorialHelper(long n, long value) {
    if (n < 2) {
        return value;
    } else {
```

```
            return factorialHelper (n - 1, n * value);
    }
}

public long factorial(long n) {
    return factorialHelper (n, 1);
}
```

When to use recursion

There have been two main criticisms of recursion:

- It takes longer to execute than an iterative version
- It is hard to understand

In the early days of software development, the technique was even barred in some organizations.

While a recursive version may take longer, for many problems this efficiency issue is not a significant concern given the improved processing speed on modern machines. Recursive efficiency issues lie with its typical implementation using a program stack. It is the pushing and popping of the activation record during method invocation that is expensive. This concept was detailed in *Understanding the program stack*.

Not all problems are suited for recursive solutions. Recursion should be used when:

- The problem lends itself to a recursive solution
- The number of recursive calls are not excessive
- Maintainability is important

Some problems are naturally solved by recursion. Most tree problems are of this nature. For some problems, an iterative solution is not always that clear. When this is the case, recursion is the best way to go.

The number of method invocations that can be considered to be excessive depends on the platform used. For a platform with ample amounts of memory, then hundreds of calls should not be a problem. Ultimately, the implementation and platform need to be tested to ensure that adverse effects do not occur. In addition, the efficiency of the program stack's implementation is a factor.

Premature optimization should be avoided. A correctly executing program should be the first consideration. Once it is working correctly, then optimization may be needed. Paramount to the efficiency of a program is its design and the algorithms used. After that, code optimizations should be considered where techniques such as profiling can help. Profiling provides a means of systematically addressing the real performance bottlenecks in a program.

A more important factor than execution time is the maintainability of the code. A complex iterative solution is more difficult to understand and to maintain than a simple recursive version.

Recursion, once understood, is no more difficult to use than iteration. It is frequently shorter and more elegant. When the recursive solution is easier to write and maintain than an iterative solution, then recursion should be used. Recursion frequently uses fewer local variables. Recursion is not any more difficult than most other complex computer science topics. It takes a bit more time to learn, but once mastered, it provides a life-long problem solving skill.

The correct choice depends on the nature of the problem and its implementation environment. The lower the level of programming, the more iterative solutions are favored. The more abstract the level of programming, the more recursion you see. Iteration will often improve the performance of your program. Recursion will often improve your performance as a programmer.

Recursion and humor

It is hard to resist passing on various recursion-related humor. This is a short discussion of recursion and how humor has been applied to it. Sources of recursion humor can be a found at:

- http://en.wikipedia.org/wiki/Recursion#Recursive_humor
- https://recursivelyrecursive.wordpress.com/category/recursive-humour/page/2/
- http://www.newpaltz.k12.ny.us/cms/lib/NY01000611/Centricity/Domain/122/recursion%20humor.html

For example, if you google the term, **recursion**, you can get the following response:

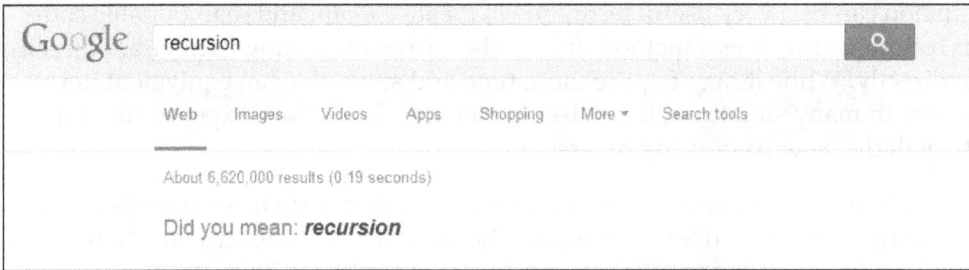

In some books, an index for the term recursion will sometimes include the current page number. You may find an entry for recursion which leads to itself:

Recursion – See Recursion

Found in several places, including some T-shirts, is the following:

Recursive acronyms are fairly common. One list can be found at `http://en.wikipedia.org/wiki/Recursive_acronym`. Perhaps one of the best-known recursive acronyms is for GNU: *GNU's Not Unix*.

From a bumper sticker:

What we learn from history is that we don't learn from history

Summary

Recursion can be a very useful technique to create elegant and maintainable code. This technique involves a method or lambda expression calling itself either directly or indirectly. While it may require more time and space than an equivalent iterative solution, in many situations, it will be a better solution if these expenses do not outweigh the benefits of using recursion.

Many data structures are recursive in nature. Such data structures are self-referencing. They have references within the structure to same structure. For example, a linked list node will have a reference to a linked list node such as to the next node in the list. We used a left and right node reference in our tree examples to illustrate a recursive data structure in several of our examples. Recursive data structures lend themselves to recursive solutions.

The recursion technique involves breaking a problem down into smaller units, making a recursive call and then combining the results. We demonstrated how to create a recursion solution to a problem stated as a formula. We also examined how to convert a loop to a recursion solution.

We illustrated how recursion is supported using the program stack and activation records. When a method is invoked, an activation record for that method is created and pushed onto the program stack. The activation record consists of the parameters and local variables of the method. When the method returns, the activation record is popped off the stack. Understanding how the program stack works gives the programmer a better understanding of recursion and enables him to solve recursion type problems when they occur.

There are several different types of recursion. When the recursive call is made at the beginning of the method, it is called head recursion. When it occurs at the end of the method, it is called tail recursion. Recursive calls can be made at in the middle of a method and more than once within a method.

Wrapper methods and tail calls can be useful when writing recursive solutions. These methods are used to handle special cases and exception handling. When a tail call is used, tail call optimization is possible to avoid excessive method invocations and yet use more readable code.

Recursion is not always the best solution to problems. Sometimes, iteration provides a more efficient approach. We discussed how to decide when recursion should be used.

In the next chapter, you will examine `Optional` class and monads and learn how they contribute to writing code in a functional style.

6
Optional and Monads

In functional languages, there is a data type called the **option** type, also called the maybe type. Its purpose is to encapsulate a value, which is returned from a function. This option return type may indicate that there is no return value. The problem with returning a value such as zero or null is that these may be legitimate return values. With an option type, we can return a good value or indicate that nothing is returned.

In Java 8, the `Optional` class has been added to serve as an option type. It is used to wrap an object and possesses a number of methods that can reflect a non-value and deal with these values. The calls allow us to handle null values and avoid the dreaded null pointer exception. The `Optional` class also plays an important role in supporting fluent interfaces.

We will also examine the nature and use of monads. This is a technique to compose functions using a fluent style. This concept is present in functional programming languages and promotes more maintainable and resilient code.

Java 8 supports monads in the form of the `Optional` and `Stream` class. We will discuss the nature of monads and provide numerous examples of how they are used.

Using the Optional class

In this section, we will examine the use of the `Optional` class to make our programs more robust and maintainable. The `Optional` class is useful for returning values from a method and supporting fluent programming.

We will examine these scenarios and illustrate the creation and use of various `Optional` methods. These examples will illustrate how to handle situations where an empty `Optional` instance is encountered.

The `Optional` class is not intended to avoid all null pointer situations. Rather, it provides a means of defining better API interfaces where the user can clearly see when an empty value is possible.

There are also three classes that support specialized numeric versions of the `Optional` class: `OptionalInt`, `OptionalLong`, and `OptionalDouble`. They possess many of the same methods, but are designed to work with integer, double, and long data types, respectively. However, they do not possess the `map`, `flatMap`, and `filter` methods found in the `Optional` class. In addition, using them can incur the overhead of boxing and unboxing. We will see several uses of these classes in this chapter.

Creating Optional instances

There are two methods used to create an `Optional` instance: `of` and `ofNullable`. The `of` method requires a non-null value. If a null value is used, the method will generate a `NullPointerException` exception.

In the following code sequence, the second use of the `of` method will throw this exception:

```
String animal = "cat";
Optional<String> opt;
opt = Optional.of(animal);
System.out.println(opt);

animal = null;
opt = Optional.of(animal);
System.out.println(opt);
```

The `ofNullable` method will accept a null or non-null value. If null is used, it returns an empty `Optional` instance. Otherwise, it will return an `Optional` instance with the value wrapped inside of it. The following code illustrates its use:

```
animal = "cat";
opt = Optional.ofNullable(animal);
System.out.println(opt);

animal = null;
opt = Optional.ofNullable(animal);
System.out.println(opt);
```

The output of this sequence is as follows:

```
Optional[cat]
Optional.empty
```

Using the Optional class to support return values

The use of the Optional class will reduce the number of null pointer exceptions and promote fluent interfaces. Its use helps clarify the intent of the code. There is nothing inherent in an Optional return value that indicates the meaning of the absent value. The appropriate documentation needs to be consulted to determine its meaning.

So, why not use null? If the programmer has not read the method's documentation carefully or has forgotten how it is intended to be used, returning a null value can result in a null pointer exception. In addition, a null value may be a legitimate return value.

We will use the Customer and Customers classes to demonstrate the use of the Optional class. The Customer class represents a simple customer. As shown here, it uses an ID and name along with a few standard methods:

```java
public class Customer {
    private int id;
    private String name;

    public Customer(int id, String name) {
        this.id = id;
        this.name = name;
    }

    public int getId() {
        return id;
    }

    public String getName() {
        return name;
    }

    @Override
    public String toString() {
        return "Customer{" + "id=" + id + ", name=" + name + '}';
    }
}
```

The Customers class contains a collection of Customer instances. A HashMap instance is used to maintain the collection. An addCustomer method will add a Customer instance to the HashMap. Two methods are used to find a customer in the collection given an ID:

- findCustomerWithID: This returns a Customer instance
- findOptionalCustomerWithID: This returns an Optional<Customer> instance

This class is shown here:

```java
public class Customers {
    private HashMap<Integer,Customer> customers;

    public Customers() {
        customers = new HashMap<>();
    }

    public void addCustomer(int id, Customer customer) {
        customers.put(id, customer);
    }

    public Customer findCustomerWithID(int id) {
        if(customers.containsKey(id)) {
            return customers.get(id);
        } else {
            return null;
        }
    }

    public Optional<Customer> findOptionalCustomerWithID(int id) {
        if(customers.containsKey(id)) {
            return Optional.of(customers.get(id));
        } else {
            return Optional.empty();
        }
    }
}
```

In the findOptionalCustomerWithID method, the Optional class's static of method is used to wrap a Customer instance inside of an Optional instance. Its static empty method is used to indicate that there was no customer with the specified ID.

An alternate shorter implementation of the `findOptionalCustomerWithID` method follows using the `ofNullable` method:

```
public Optional<Customer> findOptionalCustomerWithID(int id) {
    return Optional.ofNullable(customers.get(id));
}
```

We will use the following set of statements to initialize an instance of these classes:

```
Customer customer1 = new Customer(123, "Sue");
Customer customer2 = new Customer(456, "Bob");
Customer customer3 = new Customer(789, "Mary");
Customer defaultCustomer = new Customer(0, "Default");

Customers customers = new Customers();

customers.addCustomer(defaultCustomer.getId(),
defaultCustomer);
customers.addCustomer(customer1.getId(), customer1);
customers.addCustomer(customer2.getId(), customer2);
customers.addCustomer(customer3.getId(), customer3);
```

The `id` and `customer` variables are used to return a `Customer` instance using the `findCustomerWithID` method:

```
int id = 234;
Customer customer = customers.findCustomerWithID(id);
```

The problem with this approach is that we need to verify that null was not returned by the method. In the next code sequence, we fail to perform this test:

```
if (customer.getName().equals("Mary")) {
    System.out.println("Processing Mary");
}
```

With an ID of 234, the method will return `null` and a `NullPointerException` will be thrown. A better approach is shown next where we test for a `null` value. If the method returns `null`, we will use the `defaultCustomer` instance. If we find `Mary`, then we display a line to that effect. If it is not `Mary`, then we display that customer.

```
if (customer != null) {
    if (customer.getName().equals("Mary")) {
        System.out.println("Processing Mary");
    } else {
```

```
      System.out.println(customer);
   }
} else {
   System.out.println(defaultCustomer);
}
```

We can use the `findOptionalCustomerWithID` method instead, as shown here. This uses the identical logic presented in the previous solution, but uses various `Optional` class methods to make the decisions. Its `isPresent` method will return true if the `Optional` instance contains a `Customer` object. Its `get` method will return the `Customer` object:

```
Optional<Customer> optionalCustomer =
   customers.findOptionalCustomerWithID(id);

if (optionalCustomer.isPresent()) {
   if (optionalCustomer.get().getName().equals("Mary")) {
      System.out.println("Processing Mary");
   }else {
      System.out.println(optionalCustomer.get());
   }
} else {
   System.out.println(defaultCustomer);
}
```

This example does not do anything more than the `findCustomerWithID` method. In addition, it takes as much code and appears more complex. While this is true, the `Optional` class provides us with additional methods that can make related tasks more difficult. We will illustrate a more succinct solution to this problem in the *Optional solution of Customer problem* section.

For example, the `ifPresent` method accepts a lambda expression implementing the `Consumer` interface as shown here. This can result in a more concise and reusable code in many situations:

```
Consumer<Customer> consume = o -> {
   if (o.getName().equals("Mary")) {
      System.out.println("Processing Mary");
   } else {
      System.out.println(optionalCustomer.get());
   }
};

optionalCustomer.ifPresent(consume);
```

This approach is not possible with the `findCustomerWithID` method. This example did not handle the case when an empty `Optional` instance is returned. We will address this deficiency shortly.

The `findOptionalCustomerWithID` method could have returned `null`. However, this defeats the purpose of using `Optional`.

Handling missing values

The use of `Optional` allows methods and functions to return a value that indicates there is no return value. When there is no return value, then the three things that can be done are as follows:

- Use a substitute value
- Call a function to return a substitute value
- Throw an exception

The action to take when there is no return value is dependent on the state of the program. Instead of letting the method decide which of the options to use, it is better to let the user of the method make that decision. The `Optional` class supports this capability with three methods: `orElse`, `orElseGet`, or `orElseThrow`. Each of these will be illustrated next.

Using the orElse method to get a substitute value

The earlier imperative approach used an if statement to select the `defaultCustomer` instance if the `findCustomerWithID` method returned null. The `Optional` class's `orElse` method can be used for the same purpose and avoids the if statement.

The following statement is used to return the `defaultCustomer` instance when `findOptionalCustomerWithID` doesn't return a customer:

```
Customer current = customers
        .findOptionalCustomerWithID(id)
        .orElse(defaultCustomer);
```

This is simpler than the previous approaches.

Using the orElseGet method to use a function to get a substitute value

The orElseGet method uses an instance of the Supplier interface to obtain a substitute value. In the following statement, it uses the findOptionalCustomerWithID method a second time using an ID of 0:

```
current = customers
        .findOptionalCustomerWithID(id)
        .orElseGet(()- >
        customers.findOptionalCustomerWithID(0).get());
```

Using the orElseThrow method to throw an exception

Exception handling in Java has been a controversial topic. The way exceptions are handled has evolved from the simple try-catch blocks to the introduction of the more elegant try-with-resources block.

In Java 8, we now have another way to throw an exception. This new approach uses the orElseThrow method allowing us to avoid an if statement. A simple NoCustomerFoundException exception class is defined here:

```
public class NoCustomerFoundException extends Exception {}
```

Its use is shown here where it is thrown when a customer is not returned:

```
try {
    current = customers
            .findOptionalCustomerWithID(id)
            .orElseThrow(NoCustomerFoundException::new);
    System.out.println(current);
} catch(NoCustomerFoundException ex) {
    // Handle exception
}
```

Using the Optional class, in this manner, provides a more succinct and easier-to-use technique. The programmer does not have to potentially throw exceptions from several different places. It makes the intent of code sequences and exceptions clearer.

Filter and transforming values

It is desirable to restrict or transform Optional values. For example, while a method may return an employee, we may want to further restrict the result to an employee that meets a certain set of conditions such as pay grade or location. Having obtained an Optional instance, we may want to transform it.

In this section, we will introduce the filter and map methods. The filter method will limit the results, while the map method performs transformations on an object. There is also a flatMap method, which performs transformations similar to the map method. We will provide more extensive examples of the map and flatMap methods when we discuss monads.

Using the Optional class's filter method

The Optional and Stream classes possess a filter method. Both of these methods work in similar manner to restrict their results. However, most Stream class's methods return a Stream instance, and the Optional class's method returns an Optional instance.

There are several Stream class methods that return Optional values: findAny, findFirst, max, min, and reduce. This means that no result may be present.

In the following example, the Stream class's filter method restricts its result to those values greater than 10. The max method returns an Optional instance containing the largest value, if any. If such a value exists, the ifPresent method will display it:

```
OptionalInt result = IntStream.of(1, 5, 12, 7, 5, 24, 6)
        .filter(n -> n > 10)
        .max();
result.ifPresent(o -> System.out.println(o));
```

In this example, 24 will be displayed.

In contrast, the Optional filter method shown next will restrict its result to a customer with an ID value greater than 400. The single Optional instance returned will be empty or contain a customer. The .orElseGet method will return the defaultCustomer instance if the filter method fails to return a value:

```
id = 456;
current = customers
        .findOptionalCustomerWithID(id)
```

```
        .filter(i -> i.getId() > 400)
        .orElseGet(() ->
            customers.findOptionalCustomerWithID(0).get());
System.out.println(current);
```

When executed, we get the following output:

```
Customer{id=456, name=Bob}
```

Using the Optional class's map method

Sometimes, it is desirable to perform a transformation on the value wrapped in an Optional instance. In the next code sequence, an Optional<Customer> instance is processed. We remove leading and trailing blanks from the Customer class's name field and assign it to the name variable, or we assign a default value to the variable:

```
id = 456;
String name;
Optional<Customer> optCustomer =
    customers.findOptionalCustomerWithID(id);
if (optCustomer.isPresent()) {
    name = optCustomer.get().getName().trim();
} else {
    name = "No Name";
}
System.out.println(name);
```

The output will be Bob.

The map method makes this type of operation easier. The method takes a Function interface instance. This function takes a value, performs an operation on it, and returns the transformed value. The method will return the value wrapped inside of an Optional instance. The previous example is expressed more concisely as implemented here:

```
name = customers
        .findOptionalCustomerWithID(id)
        .map(o->o.getName().trim())
        .orElse("No Name");
System.out.println(name);
```

The map and flatMap methods will be discussed in more detail in the *Monads in Java 8* section.

Optional solution to the Customer problem

With a grasp of the fundamental Optional class's methods, we can reexamine the customer problem described in the *Using the Optional class to support return values.* Here, we will demonstrate a simpler solution to the problem where exceptions are also handled.

We will start with three functional lambda expressions used to process the customer Mary. The processMary and processNotMary expressions handle the situations where a non-empty Optional<Customer> is returned from the findOptionalCustomerWithID method. Two expressions are used to simplify the logic. The third lambda expression, processCustomer, combines the logic into one expression:

```java
Function<? super Customer, Customer> processMary =
    x -> {
        if (x.getName().equals("Mary")) {
            System.out.println("Processing Mary");
        }
        return x;
    };
Function<? super Customer, Customer> processNotMary =
    x -> {
        if (!x.getName().equals("Mary")) {
            System.out.println(x);
        }
        return x;
    };

Function<? super Customer, Customer> processCustomer
    = x -> {
        if (x.getName().equals("Mary")) {
            System.out.println("Processing Mary");
        } else {
            System.out.println(optionalCustomer.get());
        }
        return x;
    };
```

The `try` block that follows contains the `Optional` solution. It uses the `findOptionalCustomerWithID` method in conjunction with two `map` methods and the `orElseThrow` method. In the first `map` method, Mary is processed. In the second `map` method, Mary is effectively ignored:

```
try {
    id = 789;
    current = customers
            .findOptionalCustomerWithID(id)
            .map(processMary)
            .map(processNotMary)
            .orElseThrow(NoCustomerFoundException::new);
    System.out.println(current);
} catch (NoCustomerFoundException ex) {
    ex.printStackTrace();
}
```

The output is as follows:

```
Processing Mary
Customer{id=789, name=Mary}
```

We can replace the two `map` methods with the following one to achieve the same results:

```
.map(processCustomer)
```

If we use an invalid `id` value, a `NoCustomerFoundException` will be thrown. The last situation occurs when the `id` value is valid, but the customer is not named Mary. We can test this scenario with this code sequence:

```
id = 789;
customer3.setName("Mary Sue");
```

The output is as follows:

```
Customer{id=789, name=Mary Sue}
Customer{id=789, name=Mary Sue}
```

This solution allows us to reuse lambda expressions and uses an easier to use fluent style of programming.

Disadvantages of the Optional class

The Optional class does have a few drawbacks. The class will invoke some overhead, since effort is required to wrap a value within it. This is not normally a significant issue.

The Optional class is also not serializable. This is due to the effort that would be required to maintain this feature (http://mail.openjdk.java.net/pipermail/jdk8-dev/2013-September/003276.html). If you need to serialize an Optional instance, then the following link provides a possible solution: http://blog.codefx.org/java/serialize-optional/.

The Optional instances cannot be sorted using the Arrays class's sort method. If used, it throws a java.lang.ClassCastException. This is because an Optional instance cannot be cast to Comparable. However, an array of Optional values can be sorted manually.

The Optional instances should not be used as constructor or method parameters. Null and missing values are better handled using overloaded constructors and methods. Overloaded constructors and methods permit variations in the number and types of parameters. A missing parameter is one possibility. In this situation, one version of the method can process it and the other version will not use the parameter.

To demonstrate why it is not a good idea to pass an Optional instance, consider the use of the following constructors added to the Customer class:

```
public Customer(int id) {
    this.id = id;
    this.name = "Default Name";
}

public Customer(int id, Optional<String> name) {
    this.id = id;
    this.name = name.get();
}
```

The first constructor does not use a name parameter and a default name is provided. This is the preferred approach. In the second constructor, an Optional instance is passed and used to initialize the name field. However, if we used the following statement, we will get a NoSuchElementException exception:

```
customerOptional = new Customer(123, Optional.empty());
```

Instead, we will need to modify the constructor to take into account an empty value as shown here:

```
public Customer(int id, Optional<String> name) {
    this.id = id;
    if(name.isPresent()) {
        this.name = name.get();
    } else {
        this.name = "Default Name";
    }
}
```

The single argument constructor, combined with the original two argument constructor, handles the empty name easier.

These disadvantages of the Optional type are outweighed by the benefits of more maintainable and robust applications.

Monads

A monad structure can be thought of as a chain of operations wrapped around an object. These operations are executed against an object and return some value. In this sense, monads support function composition.

The chaining sequence allows programmers to create **pipelines**, a sequence of operations, to solve their problems. In addition, monads allow operations against the contained values without having to extract them.

To illustrate the use of monads, we will be using a Part class as defined here:

```
public class Part {
    private int partNumber;
    private String partName;
    private boolean outOfStock;

    public Part(int partNumber, String partName) {
        this.partNumber = partNumber;
        this.partName = partName;
    }

    public boolean isOutOfStock() {
        return outOfStock;
    }
}
```

```java
public void setOutOfStock(boolean outOfStock) {
    this.outOfStock = outOfStock;
}

public Optional<Part> outOfStock(boolean outOfStock) {
    this.outOfStock = outOfStock;
    return Optional.of(this);
}

public Part setPartName(String partName) {
    this.partName = partName;
    return this;
}

public Optional<Part> partName(String partName) {
    this.partName = partName;
    return Optional.of(this);
}

public int getPartNumber() {
    return partNumber;
}

public String getPartName() {
    return partName;
}

public Optional<Part> replicatePartMonad() {
    // Replicate part
    System.out.println("Part replicated: " + this);
    return Optional.of(this);
}

@Override
public String toString() {
    return "Part{" + "partNumber=" + partNumber + ",
        partName=" + partName + ", outOfStock=" + outOfStock +
        '}';
}

}
```

Let's assume that we want to obtain a part, mark it as out-of-stock, and then replicate in some potentially distributed system. Consider the following imperative solution to this problem. We use HashMap to store our parts. In a more realistic implementation, both the part ID and the parts will be obtained from another source, such as a database. The Part class's setOutOfStock method marks the part as being unavailable. The part name is augmented with the string "-Out-Of-Stock". The replicatePart method is then called to perform any replication:

```
private static void replicatePart(Part part) {
    // Replicate part
    System.out.println("Part replicated: " + part);
}
...
Map<Integer, Part> parts = new HashMap<>();
parts.put(123, new Part(123,"bolt"));
parts.put(456, new Part(123,"nail"));
parts.put(789, new Part(123,"wire"));

int partId = 123;
Part part = parts.get(partId);
part.setOutOfStock(true);
part.setPartName(part.getPartName()+"-Out-Of-Stock");
replicatePart(part);
```

The output of this sequence is as follows:

Part replicated: Part{partNumber=123, partName=bolt, outOfStock=true}

There are several issues with this implementation. First, numerous exceptions can occur which are not handled. For example, while we obtained a part number using an integer literal, getting from a less reliable source may return one that is invalid. The part may not be in HashMap. If the get method returns null, this will throw a null pointer exception when used with the setOutOfStock method.

Instead, the following illustrates how these operations can be performed using a monad. We will delay a complete explanation of the solution until the *Using monads with the Part class* section. The monad solution is simpler, fluent, and easier to understand:

```
Optional<Part> optPart = Optional.of(parts.get(456));
System.out.println(
    optPart
        .flatMap(x -> x.outOfStock(true))
```

```
        .flatMap(x -> x.partName(x.getPartName()
            + "-Out-of-stock"))
        .flatMap(Part::replicatePartMonad)
        .orElseThrow(() -> new RuntimeException())
    );
```

> The use of monads can result in more resilient code, which does not break as easily.

Monads in Java 8

In Java 8, the Optional class is a monad. The Optional class is an example where we take some value, such as a Part instance, and return an Optional instance that wraps the object inside of it. The Optional class is an example of a **maybe** monad. This is where the monad will contain either a value or nothing.

There are other types of monads besides the maybe monad. These include **state**, **environment**, and **continuation** monads and are discussed at http://en.wikipedia.org/wiki/Monad_%28functional_programming%29#Other_examples.

Monads have their roots in category theory (https://reperiendi.wordpress.com/2007/11/03/category-theory-for-the-java-programmer/). However, it is not necessary for us to understand category theory in order to understand and use monads.

A monad uses two operations:

- **The unit operation**: This takes some values and uses a constructor to place it into a monadic container. A monadic container can be thought of as a class in Java

- **The bind operation**: This uses a monadic value and a function (which converts its argument into a monadic value) and returns a new monadic value

The bind operation achieves chainability by returning an instance of the monadic value.

The Optional class's of method corresponds to the unit operation, and its map and flatMap methods correspond to the bind operation. We will demonstrate uses of these methods and the Optional class's map method using the Integer and String classes first. In the *Using monads with the Part class* section, we will use a Part class to provide a more comprehensive example.

The Stream class is also a monad. Its unit function is the of method, and its bind function is its flatMap method. It differs from an Optional in its return type.

Using the of method as the unit function

While we used the of method many times before, it is worth repeating it here in the context of monads. In addition, the declarations set up other examples to follow:

```
Optional<Integer> one = Optional.of(1);
Optional<String> ostring = Optional.of("go");
```

The integer, 1, has been contained inside of the Optional monad and the string, "go", is contained in the ostring variable.

Using the flatMap method

We can use the flatMap method to transform a monad. The method takes a Function interface instance. This instance is passed an Optional<U> and returns a transformation of it of type Optional<U>. The flatMap method returns this value. If there is no result, then an empty Optional is returned.

In this example, we simply add 1 to the one monad:

```
Optional<Integer> plusOne = one.flatMap(
    n -> Optional.of(n + 1));
System.out.println(plusOne.get());
```

This will display a result of 2. We can rewrite the example to use a variable to hold the lambda expression:

```
Function<? super Integer, Optional<Integer>> plusOneFunction =
        n -> Optional.of(n + 1);
plusOne = one.flatMap(plusOneFunction);
System.out.println(plusOne.get());
```

This produces the same results, but it is more convenient if you need to reuse the lambda expression.

Using the map method

The `Optional` class's `map` method takes a `Function` instance. This instance is passed a `T` object and returns a transformation of it of type `U`. The `map` method will take the function's return value and return it as an instance of `Optional<U>`. That is, the `map` method returns an instance of `<U> Optional<U>` wrapping the mapping function's return value in it. If there is no result, then an empty `Optional` is returned.

Both the `map` and `flatMap` methods may throw `NullPointerException` if:

- The mapping function passed is null
- The mapping function returns a null result

They both return an instance of `<U> Optional<U>` allowing the methods to be chained. They differ in that the `map` method's `Function` instance is passed a `U` while the `flatMap` method's `Function` instance is passed an `Optional<U>`.

The following code sequence defines a function that duplicates the functionality of the previous `flatMap` example. It adds 1 to its integer argument. The argument `x` is implicitly of type `Optional<Integer>`. The `intValue` method is implicitly applied to it returning an integer to which 1 is added. The resulting integer is then encapsulated into an `Optional<Integer>` instance:

```
plusOne = one.map(x->x+1);
System.out.println(plusOne.get());
```

The output will be a 2. We can rewrite this code to use a lambda expression variable:

```
Function<? super Integer, ? extends Integer>
    plusOneMapFunction = n -> n + 1;
plusOne = one.map(plusOneMapFunction);
System.out.println(plusOne.get());
```

The `flatMap` and `map` methods can be used together as demonstrated here:

```
plusOne = one
        .map(x->x.intValue()+1)
        .flatMap(n -> Optional.of(n + 1));
System.out.println(plusOne.get());
```

As expected, this will display a 3.

Using the Optional class with strings

We will use variables of type `Optional<String>` to provide further examples of using monads. Two operations are defined. The first will concatenate the string `"ing"` as a suffix and the second will convert all of the string's characters to upper case.

```
Function<? super String, Optional<String>> toConcatString =
    x -> Optional.of(x + "ing");
Function<? super String, Optional<String>> toUpperString =
    x -> Optional.of(x.toUpperCase());
```

The `flatMap` method is used to transform a string:

```
ostring = Optional.of("go");
result = ostring
         .flatMap(toConcatString)
         .flatMap(toUpperString);
System.out.println(ostring.get());
System.out.println(result.get());
```

The output is as follows. The original `ostring` value has not been modified:

go

GOING

The order of execution of the `flatMap` methods is important. If they are reversed, we get the following output:

go

GOing

The following iterative solution accomplishes the same tasks with less code:

```
String iterative ;
iterative = "go".toUpperCase().concat("ing");
iterative = "go".concat("ing").toUpperCase();
```

However, using lambda expressions with the `Optional` class provides more flexibility in the operations we can use.

Using monads with the Part class

Having illustrated the use of the `Optional` class with integers and strings, we will now examine how to use it with the `Part` class. We will use a `HashMap` instance to store parts as shown here:

```
Map<Integer, Part> parts = new HashMap<>();
parts.put(123, new Part(123, "bolt"));
parts.put(456, new Part(456, "nail"));
parts.put(789, new Part(789, "wire"));
```

We will use the `optPart` variable for these examples:

```
Optional<Part> optPart;
```

The monad solution to the problem posted in the *Using the Optional class* section is repeated here with a try-catch block added. This solution uses the `flatMap` and `orElseThrow` methods to process the part:

```
try {
    optPart = Optional.of(parts.get(456));
    System.out.println(
            optPart
            .flatMap(x -> x.outOfStock(true))
            .flatMap(x -> x.partName(
                x.getPartName() + "-Out-of-stock"))
            .flatMap(Part::replicatePartMonad)
            .orElseThrow(() -> new RuntimeException())
    );
    System.out.println(optPart);
} catch (RuntimeException ex) {
    System.out.println("Exception: " + optPart);
}
```

When executed, we get the following output:

**Part replicated: Part{partNumber=456, partName=nail-Out-of-stock,
outOfStock=true}**

Part{partNumber=456, partName=nail-Out-of-stock, outOfStock=true}

In the following statement, we try to retrieve a non-existent part:

```
optPart = Optional.ofNullable(parts.get(111));
```

This will handle the exception and generate the following output:

Exception: Optional.empty

We can also define variable to hold our lambda expressions as follows:

```
Function<? super Part, Optional<Part>> setOOSState
        = x -> x.outOfStock(true);
Function<? super Part, Optional<Part>> setOOSName
        = x -> x.partName(x.getPartName() + "-Out-of-stock");
Function<? super Part, Part> setOOSNameMap
        = x -> x.setPartName(x.getPartName() + "-Out-of-stock");
```

The next code sequence illustrates their use. However, instead of using the `flatMap` method, the `map` method is used. The output will be identical to earlier example using this part:

```
optPart = Optional.of(parts.get(456));
System.out.println(
        optPart
        .flatMap(x -> x.outOfStock(true))
        .map(setOOSNameMap)
        .flatMap(Part::replicatePartMonad)
        .orElseThrow(() -> new RuntimeException())
);
```

A formal discussion of monads

Monads are containers for values, which allow operations to be performed on these values using chains or pipeline approach. The value is contained within the monad. Operations are performed on the value within the monad without extracting the value first. These operations can be chained together using a fluent style of programming.

A monad needs a unit and a bind operation. A get type of operation to obtain the contained value is also useful.

We can illustrate the concept of a monad using the following class adapted from `http://mttkay.github.io/blog/2014/01/25/your-app-as-a-function/`. This is a parameterized monad accepting a value of type T. The constructor and `unit` method will create an instance of a `Monad` class.

The `flatMap` method is passed a function that is applied against the contained value. The `get` method returns the monad's value:

```java
public class Monad<T> {
  private T value;

  private Monad(T value) {
    this.value = value;
  }

  public static <T> Monad<T> unit(T value) {
    return new Monad<T>(value);
  }

  public <R> Monad<R> flatMap(Function<T, Monad<R>> func) {
    return func.apply(this.value);
  }

  public T get() {
    return value;
  }
}
```

It is not necessary to use this class in order to use monads in Java 8. As mentioned before, the `Optional` class provides similar capabilities. The following are relevant portions of the `Optional` class implementation. It is useful to sometimes examine the implementation of methods from time to time to further one's understanding of Java. The `Optional` class's implementation parallels the `Monad` class implementation:

```java
public final class Optional<T> {
    private static final Optional<?> EMPTY = new Optional<>();
    private final T value;

    private Optional(T value) {
        this.value = Objects.requireNonNull(value);
    }

    public static <T> Optional<T> of(T value) {
        return new Optional<>(value);
    }
```

```java
    public static <T> Optional<T> ofNullable(T value) {
        return value == null ? empty() : of(value);
    }

    public T get() {
        if (value == null) {
            throw new NoSuchElementException("No value present");
        }
        return value;
    }

    public<U> Optional<U> map(Function<? super T, ? extends U>
            mapper) {
        Objects.requireNonNull(mapper);
        if (!isPresent())
            return empty();
        else {
            return Optional.ofNullable(mapper.apply(value));
        }
    }

    public<U> Optional<U> flatMap(
            Function<? super T, Optional<U>> mapper) {
        Objects.requireNonNull(mapper);
        if (!isPresent())
            return empty();
        else {
            return Objects.requireNonNull(mapper.apply(value));
        }
    }

    public static<T> Optional<T> empty() {
        @SuppressWarnings("unchecked")
        Optional<T> t = (Optional<T>) EMPTY;
        return t;
    }

    ...

}
```

In addition, monads support the following rules:

- Associativity
- Left identity
- Right identity

These are explained next.

Associativity

Associativity is concerned about the order of composition of the operations. It implies that two different operations can be composed in either order without affecting the outcome. However, this does not imply that the order of execution is not important. This occurs quite often when the operations have side effects.

Left identity

Left identity means that the value within a monad can be transformed within the monad. That is, it is not necessary to remove an object from a monad, transform it, and then place it back into a monad.

We can see this with the string monad we used in the *Using the Optional class with strings* section. The following creates an instance of monad1 where the toConcatString operation has been applied to the ostring instance. The monad's internal value is extracted using the get method, which is then used as an argument to the apply method to create the monad2 instance:

```
ostring = Optional.of("go");
Optional<String> monad1;
Optional<String> result;
monad1 = ostring.flatMap(toConcatString);
result = toUpperString.apply(monad1.get());
System.out.println(result.get());
```

The output is as follows:

GOING

The extraction operation is not necessary as shown here:

```
Optional<String> result = ostring
        .flatMap(toConcatString)
        .flatMap(toUpperString);
System.out.println(result + " " + result.get());
```

We can invoke operations against a monads value without extracting it.

> Monads are sometimes called programmable semicolons, as the operations between the semicolons are placed into a monad and handled there. You can think of semicolons as operators to chain imperative statements together. The extra code and variables used to connect these statements are eliminated with monads.

Right identity

The right identity law supports the chaining behavior of monads. One way of stating this law is the application of the unit function against a monad has the same effect as if the unit function was never applied.

This is demonstrated with the next code sequence. The flatMap method is applied using a lambda expression that returns an Optional instance of itself. In the series of print statements the equality operator and equals method test the relationship of the variable and the results of the flatMap method:

```
ostring = Optional.of("right");
System.out.println(
    ostring.flatMap(s->Optional.of(s)) == ostring);
System.out.println(
    ostring.flatMap(s->Optional.of(s)).equals(ostring));
System.out.println(
    ostring.flatMap(s->Optional.of(s)) +"==" +  ostring);
```

The output is as follows:

false

true

Optional[right]==Optional[right]

While not the same object, they are equivalent.

A further demonstration of these laws for the Optional class can be found at https://gist.github.com/ms-tg/7420496#file-jdk8_optional_monad_laws-java. While these three laws are important, as a programmer, you will not need to deal with them explicitly. However, having a deeper understanding of basic concepts is important.

Summary

The Optional class provides a better way of dealing with null and missing values. In many situations, it can be used to avoid the dreaded null pointer exceptions. This class supports the fluent style of programming.

We illustrated how to create and use Optional instances. The ability to return default values was illustrated using the or else type of methods. The orElseThrow method, in particular, is useful for dealing gracefully with exceptions. We are able to transform and filter Optional objects as illustrated using the map and filter methods.

Monads were introduced, and are used to chain a series of functions together using a fluent style. A monad encapsulates a value, allows that value to be transformed using operations, and permits these operations to be cascaded together. You learned that monads follow certain laws.

In the next chapter, we will investigate how the functional elements of Java 8 can be used to implement various design patterns. This presents new and exciting ways to construct Java applications.

7
Supporting Design Patterns Using Functional Programming

In this chapter, we will examine several design patterns and their possible implementations. Under each design pattern, we will begin with a short discussion of the pattern and follow it with an imperative solution and a functional solution. This will highlight the differences between the two approaches and provide the reader with additional experience implementing functional solutions in Java. The intent of this chapter is not necessarily to provide a detailed explanation or justification for each pattern, but rather to illustrate how these patterns can be supported in Java 8.

The general approach is to identify a problem and then apply a design pattern against it. However, this is not always easy. One approach to simplify this task is by breaking an application down into smaller pieces, determine if that piece is a good candidate for a specific design pattern, and then apply the pattern.

Overusing design patterns can make the system hard to understand when a simpler solution is obfuscated by a more complex pattern implementation. Design patterns are a good communication tool, but should not be treated as gospel. When the problem doesn't match the proposed pattern, don't use the pattern. Choose the right pattern for the right problem.

You must understand a design pattern before you can apply it. Applying it using functional approach requires experience with the functional programming style. At this point, you have been exposed to many of the techniques Java 8 provides to support functional programming. We will examine several commonly used design patterns and how they can be implemented using a functional programming approach. This will further your understanding and ability to use functional approaches in Java.

We will find that different Java 8 features allow us to enhance the implementation of design patterns. Lambda expressions will allow an alternate means of expression functionality. Streams will allow us to combine operations in a more flexible and succinct way. Functional interfaces and default methods will allow us to reduce the amount of coding required to implement a solution.

Design patterns are often specific to a specific programming paradigm. Some design patterns support Java applications very well. However, many object-oriented design patterns are irrelevant to some functional programming languages. For example, the singleton pattern is not present in pure functional programming languages. Object-oriented design patterns are not always useful when used with some imperative implementations. Object-oriented features such as inheritance and polymorphism are built into object-oriented languages. However, in an imperative language, they can be considered a design pattern.

The introduction of functional features to Java allows you to avoid using some object-oriented design patterns. However, functional languages have a need for their own design patterns. Monads are an example of a functional design pattern aimed at handling global state, which is not a problem when using an object-oriented approach. The key is to use the appropriate paradigm for the problem at hand.

The intent of this chapter is to illustrate how some object-oriented design patterns can be supported using the functional features provided by Java. Writing code that is more terse and expressive will improve your productivity as a programmer. Using lambda expression can result in more succinct ways to express solutions to problems.

In this chapter, we will cover only a few of the many design patterns you may see used. These include the following:

- **Execute-around**: This supports the reuse of boilerplate code
- **Factory**: This assists in the creation of complex objects
- **Command**: This groups operations, so they can be stored and used later
- **Strategy**: This provides a means of using different algorithms over a collection
- **Visitor**: This applies an operation on a common set of elements
- **Template**: This supports implementations based around a common problem structure

Implementing the execute-around-method pattern

The **execute-around-method** pattern is intended to make it easy to reuse boilerplate code. For example, every time we modify a key value, we may want to log the result. Perhaps, we want to make sure resources are cleaned up after particular operations are performed.

Sometimes code needs to be executed before or after a method executes. To illustrate this pattern, we will examine how to determine the time required to perform an operation. We will obtain the time before and after an operation to calculate its execution time.

Object-oriented solution to the execute-around-method pattern

A simplistic approach is to copy and paste the code before and after the method call. Consider the situation where we have a complex computation, which we would like to time. We can use the currentTimeMillis method before and after the computation to determine its duration.

In the following method, we perform this operation. However, to keep the example simple, we will only compute the square of an integer and delay the operation for 500 milliseconds to simulate a more complex operation. All of the code in the method is boilerplate exception for where value passed is squared.

```java
public int executeImperativeSquareSolution(int value) {
    long start = System.currentTimeMillis();
    int result = 0;
    try {
        // Perform computation
        result = value * value;
        Thread.sleep(500);
    } catch (InterruptedException ex) {
        ex.printStackTrace();
    }
    long end = System.currentTimeMillis();
    long duration = end - start;
    System.out.print("Duration: " + duration + " - ");
    return result;
}
```

If we wanted to perform a different computation (such as cubing an integer) we would have to duplicate the method's code with the exception of the actual computation. A method that cubes an integer follows and differs only in the computation of `result`:

```
public int executeImperativeCubeSolution(int value) {
    ...
        result = value * value * value;
    ...
}
```

However, this is not a good approach because it clutters the code making it harder to read. In addition, if the boilerplate code changes we have to remember the location of the code and replace it with the new version. Encapsulating the functionality in two methods will help but we will still need to explicitly insert the method calls.

Functional solution to the execute-around-method pattern

A functional approach uses a method that is passed the computation to be performed and a value to be used with the computation. In the following `executeDuration` method, we pass a `Function` instance and a value to use with the function. The `apply` method executes the function with the data. Otherwise, the code is identical to the imperative solution:

```
public int executeDuration(
        Function<Integer, Integer> computation, int value) {
    long start = System.currentTimeMillis();
    int result = 0;
    try {
        result = computation.apply(value);
        Thread.sleep(500);
    } catch (InterruptedException ex) {
        ex.printStackTrace();
    }
    long end = System.currentTimeMillis();
    long duration = end - start;
    System.out.print("Duration: " + duration + " - ");
    return result;
}
```

The next code sequence uses both the imperative and functional solutions:

```
System.out.println(executeImperativeSquareSolution(5));
System.out.println(executeImperativeCubeSolution(5));
System.out.println(executeDuration(x -> x * x, 5));
System.out.println(executeDuration(x -> x * x * x, 5));
```

The output is as follows:

Duration: 501 - 25

Duration: 501 - 125

Duration: 500 - 25

Duration: 500 - 125

Instead of using lambda expressions as an argument of the functional methods, we can use the variables as defined here:

```
Function<Integer, Integer> computeSquare = x -> x * x;
Function<Integer, Integer> computeCube = x -> x * x * x;
System.out.println(executeDuration(computeSquare, 5));
System.out.println(executeDuration(computeCube, 5));
```

To further illustrate this design pattern, the following methods will perform a logging operation. The withLog method simply performs the logging process, while the executeWithLog method logs the value and performs the desired operation. Having both of these methods will provide flexibility in how functions can be combined to support the execute-around-method pattern:

```
private static int withLog(int value) {
    System.out.print("Operation logged for " + value + " - ");
    return value;
}

private static int executeWithLog(
        Function<Integer, Integer> consumer, int value) {
    System.out.print("Operation logged for " + value + " - ");
    return consumer.apply(value);
}
```

The executeWithLog method will execute the supplied function and perform logging as shown here:

```
System.out.println(executeWithLog(x -> x * x, 5));
System.out.println(executeWithLog(computeSquare, 5));
```

The output of this sequence is as follows:

```
Operation logged for 5 - 25
Operation logged for 5 - 25
```

While the `withLog` method will log a value, it does not perform an operation as illustrated here:

```
System.out.println(withLog(5));
```

It will display the following:

```
Operation logged for 5 - 5
```

However, what if we want to perform the logging operation and the duration operation on the same function? One approach will use an intermediate variable to hold the result of the `executeDuration` method, and then use it with the `withLog` method as shown here:

```
int result = executeDuration(x -> x * x, 5);
System.out.println(withLog(result));
```

This will display:

```
Duration: 500 - Operation logged for 25 - 25
```

There is an easier way. The `withLog` method can use the output of the `executeDuration` method to achieve the same results:

```
System.out.println(withLog(executeDuration(x -> x * x, 5)));
```

An alternative approach that produces the same results is shown here:

```
System.out.println(executeDuration(x -> x * x, withLog(5)));
```

We can use a more generic approach to support the execute-around-method pattern. The following method takes two `Function` instances and a value. One instance represents the function to be executed and the second represents either a before or after operation:

```
public int executeBefore(
        Function<Integer, Integer> beforeFunction,
        Function<Integer, Integer> function,
        Integer value) {
    beforeFunction.apply(value);
    return function.apply(value);
}
```

```
public int executeAfter(
        Function<Integer, Integer> function,
        Function<Integer, Integer> afterFunction,
        Integer value) {
    int result =  function.apply(value);
    afterFunction.apply(result);
    return result;
}
```

These can be used as shown next. The `withLog` method is used as a method reference where the enclosing class is `Chapter7`.

```
System.out.println(
    executeBefore(Chapter7::withLog,computeSquare, 5));
System.out.println(
    executeAfter(computeSquare,Chapter7::withLog, 5));
```

The output of this sequence is shown here:

Operation logged for 5 - 25

Operation logged for 25 - 25

Using the execute-around-method pattern with a stream

We may need to use the pattern with specific steps in a stream. This can be accomplished using the `map` method. In the next example, the `computeDuration` variable's function will perform the duration operation and square a number. It is then used as the `map` method's argument:

```
Function<Integer, Integer> computeDuration =
        x -> executeDuration(computeSquare, x);
Integer arr[] = {1, 2, 3, 4, 5};
Stream<Integer> myStream = Arrays.stream(arr);
myStream
        .map(computeDuration)
        .forEach(x -> System.out.println(x));
```

This code sequence generates the following output:

Duration: 501 - 1

Duration: 500 - 4

Duration: 501 - 9

Duration: 500 - 16

Duration: 501 - 25

Alternatively, we can use the following:

```
.map(x -> executeDuration(v -> v * v, x))
```

We cannot create a `withDuration` type method, which would mirror the previous `withLog` method, because this operation requires code to be executed before and after the function is executed. We need to maintain a duration type variable, but these variables need to be effectively final, meaning that we cannot modify them.

If we need to perform some action other than those handled by the `java.util.function` interface, we can always define our own functional interface.

Implementing the factory pattern

A common way of creating objects is using the `new` keyword with a constructor. However, if this is done repeatedly in many places in a program, the code used to create the object will need to be modified in each location should this process change. Using a factory method will simplify this process. The factory pattern is used to create different instances of different classes of the same base type.

The factory pattern is used to assist in the creation of objects. Where the use of the `new` keyword is not advisable, this technique should be used. This includes situations where context-dependent information is needed to create an instance and where we wish to have more control over the creation process.

In the former case, creating a connection to an external resource such as a database may be dependent on several factors. These can include the availability of the server hosting the database, type of database support required, and potentially legal issues such as whether the license is current or can be used in a specific country.

The life cycle management of objects is frequently concerned with the number and types of objects created. A server will typically have limits on the number of objects it can support at one time. Some objects may be clustered to support common operations against them.

The pattern typically does not support the `new` operation and provides methods such as `getInstance` or `create` instead. Making constructors `private` or `protected`, forces a user to use a `getInstance` type method. This pattern is used in several places in the Java SE SDK. The `DriverManager` class's `getConnection` and the `URL` class's `openConnection` methods are examples of such use.

To illustrate the factory pattern, we will demonstrate how to create instances of a vacuum cleaner. For example, a `VacuumCleaner` factory will create instances of objects that implement a `VacuumCleaner` interface. The details of creating a `VacuumCleaner` instance will be contained within the `getInstance` method.

Object-oriented solution to the factory pattern

We will demonstrate this pattern with two classes that implement the
VacuumCleaner interface. The interface, as shown here, uses two methods:
vacuum and clean. The intent of the clean method is to clean a vacuum cleaner:

```java
public interface VacuumCleaner {
    public void vacuum();
    public void clean();
}
```

Two classes are declared that implement the VacuumCleaner interface:
DirtVacuumCleaner and WaterVacuumCleaner as shown here. While the constructors
are declared as public in this example, to hide them we can use a more restricted
constructor modifier:

```java
public class DirtVacuumCleaner implements VacuumCleaner {

    public DirtVacuumCleaner() {
        System.out.println("Creating DirtVacuumCleaner");
    }

    @Override
    public void vacuum() {
        System.out.println("Vacuuming dirt");
    }

    @Override
    public void clean() {
        System.out.println("Cleaning Dirt Vacuum Cleaner");
    }
}


public class WaterVacuumCleaner implements VacuumCleaner {

    public WaterVacuumCleaner() {
        System.out.println("Creating WaterVacuumCleaner");
    }

    @Override
    public void vacuum() {
        System.out.println("Vacuuming water");
    }
```

```
        @Override
        public void clean() {
            System.out.println("Cleaning Water Vacuum Cleaner");
        }
    }
```

A `VacuumCleanerFactory` class is declared next. It provides a static `getInstance` method that takes a string indicating the type of vacuum cleaner needed. While the creation of the two vacuum cleaner classes is simple, the process of creating an instance for a different class may be more involved:

```
public class VacuumCleanerFactory {
    public static VacuumCleaner getInstance (String type) {
        VacuumCleaner vacuumCleaner = null;
        if("Dirt".equals(type)) {
            vacuumCleaner = new DirtVacuumCleaner();
        } else if("Water".equals(type)) {
            vacuumCleaner = new WaterVacuumCleaner();
        } else {
            // Handle bad type
        }
        return vacuumCleaner;
    }
}
```

The following code sequence demonstrates the creation of the factory:

```
VacuumCleaner dvc =
    VacuumCleanerFactory.getInstance("Dirt");
dvc.vacuum();
dvc.clean();
VacuumCleaner wvc =
    VacuumCleanerFactory.getInstance("Water");
wvc.vacuum();
wvc.clean();
```

The output of this sequence is as follows:

```
Creating WaterVacuumCleaner
Vacuuming water
Cleaning Water Vacuum Cleaner
Creating WaterVacuumCleaner
Vacuuming water
Cleaning Water Vacuum Cleaner
```

Functional solution to the factory pattern

Using lambda expressions provided by Java 8 eliminates the need for an explicit factory class. The next sequence illustrates the definition and use of two `Supplier` lambda expressions to support the creation of the `DirtVacuumCleaner` and `WaterVacuumCleaner` instances. The variable, `dvcSupplier`, represents an object that supports the `Supplier` interface's `get` method, which returns an instance of a `DirtVacuumCleaner`. The constructor reference will return an object of this type. The `wvcSupplier` variable works the same way:

```
Supplier<DirtVacuumCleaner> dvcSupplier =
    DirtVacuumCleaner::new;
dvc = dvcSupplier.get();
dvc.vacuum();
dvc.clean();

Supplier<WaterVacuumCleaner> wvcSupplier =
    WaterVacuumCleaner::new;
wvc = wvcSupplier.get();
wvc.vacuum();
wvc.clean();
```

The use of the lambda expressions avoids creating a new factory class.

Implementing the command pattern

The command pattern is useful for storing an arbitrary set of operations that can be executed at a later time. It has been used to support GUI action controls such as buttons and menus, recording macros, and supporting undo operations.

It is a behavioral design pattern where an object encapsulates the information needed to perform an operation at a later time. We will illustrate this pattern using a macro-like facility where a character can walk, run, or jump. A sequence of these actions can be saved and executed as needed.

Object-oriented solution to the command pattern

We start with the declaration of the Command interface as shown next. It has a single method, execute, whose intent is to execute some command and return whether it was successful or not.

```
public interface Command {
    public boolean execute();
}
```

The Move interface details the actions that will be supported:

```
public interface Move {
    public boolean walk();
    public boolean run();
    public boolean jump();
}
```

The next three classes: WalkCommand, RunCommand, and JumpCommand, implement the Command interface by displaying simple messages. They differ in which Move interface method is used:

```
public class WalkCommand implements Command{
    private final Move move;

    public WalkCommand(Move move) {
        this.move=move;
    }

    @Override
    public boolean execute() {
        return move.walk();
    }
}

public class RunCommand implements Command{
    private final Move move;

    public RunCommand(Move move) {
        this.move=move;
    }

    @Override
    public boolean execute() {
```

```
        return move.run();
    }
}

public class JumpCommand implements Command{
    private final Move move;

    public JumpCommand(Move move){
        this.move=move;
    }

    @Override
    public boolean execute() {
        return move.jump();
    }
}
```

However, it is the Character class that actually implements the moves for a character:

```
public class Character implements Move {
    @Override
    public boolean walk() {
        System.out.println("Walking");
        return true;
    }
    @Override
    public boolean run() {
        System.out.println("Running");
        return true;
    }
    @Override
    public boolean jump() {
        System.out.println("Jumping");
        return true;
    }
}
```

The Commands class supports the macro functionality. It uses an ArrayList instance to hold the commands to be executed as shown next. The addCommand method adds a new command to the list, and the executeCommand method will execute those commands in the order they were added:

```
public class Commands {
    private final List<Command> commands = new ArrayList<>();
```

```
        public void addCommand(Command action) {
            commands.add(action);
        }

        public void executeCommand() {
            commands.forEach(Command::execute);
        }
    }
```

The next code sequence illustrates the use of these classes:

```
        Character character = new Character();
        Commands commands = new Commands();

        commands.addCommand(new WalkCommand(character));
        commands.addCommand(new RunCommand(character));
        commands.addCommand(new JumpCommand(character));
        commands.executeCommand();
```

The output is as follows:

Walking

Running

Jumping

An alternate series of commands can be easily supported.

Functional solution to the command pattern

Here, we will create a better version of this implementation using lambda expressions. We start with a replacement of the Commands class with the FunctionalCommands class as shown next. The primary difference is the use of the Supplier interface instead of the Command interface. This allows us to potentially use the new class with other "commands." We can use any method that matches Supplier<Boolean>:

```
    public class FunctionalCommands {
        private final List<Supplier<Boolean>> commands =
            new ArrayList<>();

        public void addCommand(Supplier<Boolean> action) {
            commands.add(action);
        }
```

```
public void executeCommand() {
    commands.forEach(Supplier::get);
}
}
```

The `WalkCommand`, `RunCommand`, and `JumpCommand` classes are no longer needed. We can replace them with lambda expressions as shown here:

```
Character character = new Character();
FunctionalCommands fc = new FunctionalCommands();
fc.addCommand(() -> character.walk());
fc.addCommand(() -> character.run());
fc.addCommand(() -> character.jump());
fc.executeCommand();
```

The output is as follows and is identical to the previous solution:

Walking

Running

Jumping

We can use method references instead, as shown next to achieve the same results:

```
fc.addCommand(character::walk);
fc.addCommand(character::run);
fc.addCommand(character::jump);
fc.executeCommand();
```

The functional implementation uses fewer classes and is more flexible since it uses the `Supplier` interface and lambda expressions to define a command.

Implementing the strategy pattern

The strategy pattern allows an algorithm to be selected at runtime based on the needs of the application. Instead of using the `if` type statements to select an algorithm, the algorithm's implementation is contained in classes that implement an interface depicting the desired operation. This allows the algorithm executed to vary depending on the client it is applied against.

The pattern does not use inheritance, but rather encapsulates the behavior in another class. This composition approach decouples the behavior from the classes that use the behavior. Changing the behavior does not affect the class that uses it.

Let's assume that a list of tasks needs to be processed. However, there are various task ordering algorithms that can be used. The idea is to associate a list of tasks with a specific algorithm. The algorithm can then be applied to decide which task should be used executed next.

We will illustrate this pattern by showing how to implement scheduling algorithms for tasks. The algorithms are kept simple to focus on the strategy pattern. We will begin with an object-oriented implementation, and then show how to use Java 8 to implement it in a more succinct and elegant manner.

Object-oriented solution to strategy pattern

A `Task` class holds the name and duration of a task. These tasks are managed by a `Tasks` class. This class possesses methods to add tasks, hold a specific scheduling strategy, and return the next task to perform. These two classes are shown next:

```java
public class Task {
    private String name;
    private int duration;

    public Task(String name, int duration) {
        this.name = name;
        this.duration = duration;
    }

    public String getName() {
        return name;
    }

    public void setName(String name) {
        this.name = name;
    }

    public int getDuration() {
        return duration;
    }

    public void setDuration(int duration) {
        this.duration = duration;
    }

    @Override
    public String toString() {
        return "Task{" + "name=" + name + ", duration="
```

```
                + duration + '}';
        }
    }

    public class Tasks {
        private List<Task> tasks;
        private SchedulingStrategy strategy;

        public Tasks() {
            tasks = new ArrayList();
        }

        public void addTask(Task task) {
            tasks.add(task);
        }

        public void setTasks(List<Task> tasks) {
            this.tasks = tasks;
        }

        public void setStrategy(SchedulingStrategy strategy) {
            this.strategy = strategy;
        }

        public Task getNextTask() {
            return strategy.nextTask(tasks);
        }
    }
```

The `SchedulingStrategy` interface shown next will be implemented by the various scheduling algorithms. Each algorithm will use a different approach to select the next task to be performed. The `nextTask` method will return this task:

```
    public interface SchedulingStrategy {
        public Task nextTask(List<Task> tasks);
    }
```

For this example, we will use three different algorithms: **first-come-first-serve**, **shortest-task-first**, and **longest-task-first**. These reflect common approaches to scheduling tasks. These algorithms are implemented in the `FCFSStrategy`, `STFStrategy`, and `LTFStrategy` classes, respectively. Each of these classes implement the `SchedulingStrategy` interface.

For these scheduling implementations, the tasks are not removed from the list. The need for removal depends on the nature of the application. For an operating system, the task may represent processes which may execute for a short interval but are not completed and thus need to remain on the list.

The FCFSStrategy class is shown first. It simply returns the first task in the list:

```java
public class FCFSStrategy implements SchedulingStrategy {

    @Override
    public Task nextTask(List<Task> tasks) {
        return tasks.get(0);
    }
}
```

The STFStrategy class searches for the task with the shortest duration. In this implementation, the shortest task is assumed to be the first task. If this is not the case, then the shortest task will eventually be found:

```java
public class STFStrategy implements SchedulingStrategy {

    @Override
    public Task nextTask(List<Task> tasks) {
        Task shortest = tasks.get(0);
        for(Task task : tasks) {
            if(shortest.getDuration() > task.getDuration()) {
                shortest = task;
            }
        }
        return shortest;
    }
}
```

The LTFStrategy class shown here is very similar to the STFStrategy class. It selects the task with the longest duration instead:

```java
public class LTFStrategy implements SchedulingStrategy {

    @Override
    public Task nextTask(List<Task> tasks) {
        Task longest = tasks.get(0);
        for(Task task : tasks) {
            if(longest.getDuration() < task.getDuration()) {
                longest = task;
            }
        }
```

```
        return longest;
    }
}
```

With all of the pieces of the pattern created, we can now demonstrate its use. We start with the declaration of four tasks as shown here:

```
Task tasks[] = {new Task("Quick",25), new Task("Longest",200),
    new Task("Shortest",2), new Task("Slow",35)};
```

To use the pattern, we create an instance of the `Tasks` class and initialize its list using the `setTasks` method. The `setStrategy` method will specify that the `STFStrategy` class be used to select a task as shown here:

```
Tasks taskList1 = new Tasks();
taskList1.setTasks(Arrays.asList(tasks));
taskList1.setStrategy(new STFStrategy());
System.out.println(taskList1.getNextTask());
```

This code will produce the output shown here where the task with the shortest duration is selected:

Task{name= Shortest, duration=2}

We can use a second `Tasks` instance to select and use the other two scheduling strategies:

```
Tasks taskList2 = new Tasks();
taskList2.setTasks(Arrays.asList(tasks));
taskList2.setStrategy(new FCFSStrategy());
System.out.println(taskList2.getNextTask());
taskList2.setStrategy(new LTFStrategy());
System.out.println(taskList2.getNextTask());
```

These will choose the first and longest tasks as shown here:

Task{name=Quick, duration=25}

Task{name=Longest, duration=200}

Functional solution to the strategy pattern

The functional implementation uses less code and is easier to follow. We will reuse the `Task` and `Tasks` class. The `SchedulingStrategy` interface is the same, except we use the `FunctionalInterface` annotation to explicitly state it is a functional interface as shown here:

```
@FunctionalInterface
public interface SchedulingStrategy {
    Task nextTask(List<Task> tasks);
}
```

The `FCFSStrategy`, `STFStrategy`, and `LTFStrategy` classes are no longer needed. Instead, we will use lambda expressions to implement their functionality. We will reuse the code used to set up the `taskList1` instance as duplicated here:

```
Task tasks[] = {new Task("Quick", 25),
    new Task("Longest", 200), new Task("Shortest", 2),
    new Task("Slow", 35)};
Tasks taskList1 = new Tasks();
taskList1.setTasks(Arrays.asList(tasks));
```

The `SchedulingStrategy` variable, `STF`, is initialized with a lambda expression that is essentially a duplicate of the `STFStrategy` class logic:

```
SchedulingStrategy STF = t -> {
    Task shortest = t.get(0);
    for (Task task : t) {
        if (shortest.getDuration() > task.getDuration()) {
            shortest = task;
        }
    }
    return shortest;
};
```

We then use this variable in the same way we did for the class:

```
taskList1.setStrategy(STFStrategy);
System.out.println(taskList1.getNextTask());
```

This generates the same output:

Task{name= Shortest, duration=2}

However, the lambda expression does not take advantage of the full power of Java 8. We can rewrite it using the `Comparator` interface and a `Stream` class as shown in the following example. Since the `nextTask` method is passed an instance of `List<Task>`, we can use the `List` interface's `stream` method to obtain an instance of type `Steam<Task>`. The `min` method is then used with the `Comparator` interface instance to find the task with the smallest duration. The `get` method will return this instance:

```
Comparator<Task> comparator =
    (x,y) -> x.getDuration()-y.getDuration();
SchedulingStrategy STFStrategy =
    t -> t.stream().min(comparator).get();
```

This is a much simpler implementation than the previous lambda expression. The other two scheduling strategies can be implemented in similar fashion:

```
SchedulingStrategy FCFSStrategy = t -> t.get(0);
SchedulingStrategy LTFStrategy =
    t -> t.stream().max(comparator).get();
```

The following code sequence produces the same output as the object-oriented solution:

```
taskList1.setStrategy(STFStrategy);
System.out.println(taskList1.getNextTask());

Tasks taskList2 = new Tasks();
taskList2.setTasks(Arrays.asList(tasks));
taskList2.setStrategy(FCFSStrategy);
System.out.println(taskList2.getNextTask());

taskList2.setStrategy(LTFStrategy);
System.out.println(taskList2.getNextTask());
```

The functional programming solution eliminated the need for the three strategy classes and facilitated the implementation of simpler strategy algorithms.

Using the Function interface

We can further simplify the solution by eliminating the `SchedulingStrategy` interface all together and using the `Function` interface instead. The signature of the `SchedulingStrategy` interface's `nextTask` method is a variation of the `Function` interface's `apply` method. All we need to do is replace `SchedulingStrategy` with `Function<List<Task>,Task>` and the `nextTask` method with the `apply` method in the `Task` class as shown here:

```
public class Tasks {
    ...
    private Function<List<Task>,Task> strategy;
```

```
    . . .
    public void setStrategy(Function<List<Task>,Task> strategy) {
        this.strategy = strategy;
    }

    public Task getNextTask() {
        return strategy.apply(tasks);
    }
}
```

In the declarations of the `strategy` class's lambda expressions, replace `SchedulingStrategy` with `Function<List<Task>,Task>` as shown here:

```
Function<List<Task>,Task> FCFSStrategy = t -> t.get(0);
Function<List<Task>,Task> STFStrategy =
    t -> t.stream().min(comparator).get();
Function<List<Task>,Task> LTFStrategy =
    t -> t.stream().max(comparator).get();
```

The solution is shorter and uses standard functional interfaces found in the `java.util.function` package. The intent of the `apply` method is not as clear as using the `nextTask` method. This is a small price to pay for losing an interface.

Implementing the visitor pattern

The visitor pattern is useful when you need to use different algorithms to apply to elements of a collection at different times. For example, you may have a collection of components of a train engine. Periodically, maintenance checks will need to be performed against each element. You may also want to occasionally display the status of each component. The collection does not necessarily change, only the operations performed against the components.

The visitor pattern is a way of structuring your data to facilitate the application of different algorithms against the structure without a new algorithm impacting the components.

The structure of the visitor pattern uses a base element interface or collection representing the collection of interest. For the train engine example, this base might represent the engine itself and its derived components will be elements such as wheels, engine, horn, and windows.

A visitor interface is added, which defines a `visit` method that is applied against each potential component of the collection. The argument of the `visit` method is code that implements the desired functionality such as check status. A component may have a method that allows other subcomponents to be added.

We will use a graphic scene used in many game engines to hold the elements that make up a scene. This can include elements such as characters, buildings, plants, and similar elements. Given a scene, we will apply either of two operations against the scene. The first will be to refresh each element. A second operation will print information about each elements. When we implement the functional version of this pattern, we will introduce a third operation.

Object-orient solution to the visitor pattern

We will start with the definition of the base element— ISceneElement. This interface defines two methods. The getName method returns the name of an element and the accept method initiates the application of a visit operation against its elements:

```
public interface ISceneElement {
    public String getName();
    void accept(ISceneElementVisitor visitor);
}
```

The ISceneElementVisitor interface defines a visit method which takes an ISceneElement instance and "visits" it:

```
public interface ISceneElementVisitor {
    public void visit(ISceneElement element);
}
```

We will use three classes that implement the ISceneElement interface: Scene, BuildingElement, and PlantElement. The Scene class represents the scene to be rendered. It maintains an array of ISceneElement elements. Its constructor will supply a name for the scene and initialize the array of scene elements. Its accept method will apply a visitor operation against each element of the scene and the scene itself:

```
public class Scene implements ISceneElement {
    ISceneElement[] elements;
    private String name;

    public Scene(String name) {
        this.name = name;
        this.elements = new ISceneElement[] {
            new BuildingElement("Tool Shed"),
            new BuildingElement("Brick House"),
            new PlantElement("Oak Tree") ,
            new PlantElement("Lawn") };
    }
```

```
        public void accept(ISceneElementVisitor visitor) {
            for(ISceneElement elem : elements) {
                elem.accept(visitor);
            }
            visitor.visit(this);
        }

        @Override
        public String getName() {
            return this.name;
        }
    }
```

The `BuildingElement` and `PlantElement` classes also implement the `ISceneElement` interface and provide similar capabilities. Two distinct classes are defined to clearly differentiate the types of elements that can be added to a scene. Their implementations are as follows:

```
    public class BuildingElement implements ISceneElement {
        private String name;

        public BuildingElement(String name) {
            this.name = name;
        }

        public String getName() {
            return this.name;
        }

        @Override
        public void accept(ISceneElementVisitor visitor) {
            visitor.visit(this);
        }
    }
    public class PlantElement implements ISceneElement {
        private String name;

        public PlantElement(String name) {
            this.name = name;
        }

        public String getName() {
            return this.name;
        }
    }
```

```
        @Override
        public void accept(ISceneElementVisitor visitor) {
            visitor.visit(this);
        }
    }
```

The two visitor algorithms are implemented by the `SceneElementRefreshVisitor` and `SceneElementPrintVisitor` classes as shown here. These are simple implementations that indicate that the element has been refreshed or printed. In a more sophisticated implementation, they will perform more detailed operations. An element is passed to the `visit` method where the operation is performed:

```
    public class SceneElementRefreshVisitor implements
            ISceneElementVisitor {

        @Override
        public void visit(ISceneElement element) {
            System.out.println("Refreshing " + element.getName());
        }
    }
    public class SceneElementPrintVisitor implements
            ISceneElementVisitor {

        @Override
        public void visit(ISceneElement element) {
            System.out.println("Printing " + element.getName());
        }
    }
```

A simple demonstration of this solution follows where a primary scene is created and the two visitors are used as arguments to the `accept` method. The `accept` method will then apply the visitor to each element of the scene:

```
    public class SceneVisitorDemo {
        public static void main(String[] args) {
            ISceneElement scene = new Scene("Primary Scene");
            scene.accept(new SceneElementPrintVisitor());
            scene.accept(new SceneElementRefreshVisitor());
        }
    }
```

The output of this example is shown here:

```
Printing Tool Shed
Printing Brick House
Printing Oak Tree
Printing Lawn
Printing Primary Scene
Refreshing Tool Shed
Refreshing Brick House
Refreshing Oak Tree
Refreshing Lawn
Refreshing Primary Scene
```

Functional solution to the visitor pattern

We will make several modifications to the object-oriented solution. The
ISceneElement interface will be converted to a functional interface. Making the
getName method abstract will allow us to access the name of an element that we will
display in a visitor lambda expression implementation. The accept method is the
same for each element, so we can convert it to a default method:

```java
@FunctionalInterface
public interface ISceneElement {
    public String getName();
    public default void accept(ISceneElementVisitor visitor) {
        visitor.visit(this);
    }
}
```

The interface's implementation is the same, except that we added the
FunctionalInterface annotation to it:

```java
@FunctionalInterface
public interface ISceneElementVisitor {
    public void visit(ISceneElement element);
}
```

The PlantElement class is left as a class to contrast it with the BuildingElement
interface. The original class is duplicated here for your convenience:

```java
public class PlantElement implements ISceneElement {
    private String name;
```

```
    public PlantElement(String name) {
        this.name = name;
    }

    @Override
    public String getName() {
        return this.name;
    }
}
```

We will replace the `BuildingElement` class with the following functional interface. All of its required functionality is provided by the base interface `ISceneElement` and the lambda expression that uses it as we will see in the `Scene` class shortly:

```
@FunctionalInterface
public interface BuildingElement extends ISceneElement {}
```

The `SceneElementPrintVisitor` and `SceneElementRefreshVisitor` classes have not been modified.

The `Scene` class differs in how the element's array is initialized. We use lambda expressions to provide the functionality for several scene elements. The `building` lambda expression variable illustrates how the lambda expression can be reused if needed. The creation of the brick house uses a lambda expression directly:

```
public class Scene implements ISceneElement {
    ISceneElement[] elements;
    private String name;

    public Scene(String name) {
        this.name = name;
        BuildingElement building = ()->"Tool Shed";
        this.elements = new ISceneElement[] {
            building ,
            ()->"Brick House",
            new PlantElement("Oak Tree"),
            new PlantElement("Lawn") };
    }

    @Override
    public void accept(ISceneElementVisitor visitor) {
        for(ISceneElement elem : elements) {
            elem.accept(visitor);
        }
```

```
        visitor.visit(this);
    }


    @Override
    public String getName() {
        return this.name;
    }
}
```

The following example shows how this functional implementation can be used to create a scene. The two visitor classes are used as before:

```
ISceneElement scene = new Scene("Primary Scene");
scene.accept(new SceneElementPrintVisitor());
scene.accept(new SceneElementRefreshVisitor());
```

However, we can add a new visitor operation on the fly using a lambda expression that implements the `ISceneElementVisitor` functional interface. This requires the lambda expression to match the `visit` method, which is a method that is passed an `ISceneElement` instance and returns `void`. Here, the `ISceneElement` interface's `getName` method is called, and like the previous visitors implementations, a message is displayed:

```
scene.accept(t -> System.out.println(
    "Another visitor operation on " + t.getName()));
```

If we need to implement different visitor functionality, we can use a different abstract method other than the `getName` method. The method can easily return an object containing information to be processed.

Implementing the template pattern

The template pattern is based around the idea that certain problems have structures that are reflected in a core method. This method uses the same set of operations to perform a task. This can be seen in a loading task where the basic steps to load a container is essentially the same whether the container is a box or a truck.

The steps are the same, such as prepared item to be loaded, but the specific preparation will vary depending on the container. A box may require that the item be wrapped in paper while the truck may require the application of a plastic wrap.

We will use a game engine to illustrate this template. The basic steps include:

1. Rendering an image.
2. Updating the game.
3. Terminating the game when it is over.

Object-oriented solution to the template pattern

This approach uses an abstract Game class that contains a template method and abstract methods for the initialization, rendering, and updating steps. Its implementation follows where an infinite loop is used to render an image, update the game, and then break out of the loop. The logic for game termination will be more complex than suggested by this implementation:

```
public abstract class Game {
    abstract void initialize(String name);
    abstract String render();
    abstract int update(String name);

    // Template method
    public final void run(String name) {
        initialize(name);
        while (true) {
            String image = render();
            System.out.println("Rendering " + image);
            int status = update(name);
            // Evaluate termination conditions
            System.out.println("...");
            break;
        }
    }
}
```

The run method is declared as final. This is the template method and does not need to be overridden.

Two games are based on the Game class: a first-person shooter game and a strategy game. They override the abstract methods of the Game class and provide similar but slightly different implementations:

```
public class FPSGame extends Game {

    public FPSGame() {
        run("FPS Game");
```

```
        }

        @Override
        void initialize(String name) {
            System.out.println("Starting " + name);}

        @Override
        String render() {
            System.out.println("Generating FPS Image");
            return "FPS Image";}

        @Override
        int update(String name) {
            System.out.println("Updating " + name);
            return 0;
        }
    }

    public class StrategyGame extends Game {

        public StrategyGame() {
            run("Strategy Game");
        }

        @Override
        void initialize(String name) {
            System.out.println("Starting " + name);}

        @Override
        String render() {
            System.out.println("Generating Strategy Image");
            return "Strategy Image";}

        @Override
        int update(String name) {
            System.out.println("Updating " + name);
            return 0;
        }
    }
```

Using the games requires the creation of a new instance of each class as shown here:

```
        FPSGame td = new FPSGame();
        StrategyGame sg = new StrategyGame();
```

This will produce the following output:

```
Starting FPS Game
Generating FPS Image
Rendering FPS Image
Updating FPS Game
...
Starting Strategy Game
Generating Strategy Image
Rendering Strategy Image
Updating Strategy Game
...
```

New games can be added by extending the Game class.

Functional solution to the template pattern

In this functional implementation of this pattern, we use a class that contains functional interface reference variables to hold the implementation of the initialization, rendering, and updating functionality. We cannot replace the Game class with a functional interface because we will have multiple abstract methods in a single class, which is not permitted in a functional interface. Using these reference variables requires a derived class to supply the functionality needed in a constructor or possibly setter methods.

The implementation of the Game class follows, which uses the same logic as the object-oriented solution:

```
public class Game {
    Consumer<String> initialize;
    Supplier<String> render;
    Function<String, Integer> update;

    // Template method
    public final void run(String name) {
        initialize.accept(name);
        while (true) {
            String image = render.get();
            System.out.println("Rendering " + image);
            int status = update.apply(name);
            // Evaluate termination conditions
            System.out.println("...");
```

```
            break;
        }
    }
}
```

The implementation of the FPSGame and StrategyGame classes is identical,
suggesting that they can be combined. The constructor is used to initialize
the abstract methods of the Game class:

```
public class FPSGame extends Game {

    public FPSGame(
            Consumer<String> initialize,
            Supplier<String> render,
            Function<String, Integer> update) {
        this.initialize = initialize;
        this.render = render;
        this.update = update;
        run("FPS Game");
    }
}

public class StrategyGame extends Game {

    public StrategyGame(
            Consumer<String> initialize,
            Supplier<String> render,
            Function<String, Integer> update) {
        this.initialize = initialize;
        this.render = render;
        this.update = update;
        run("Strategy Game");
    }
}
```

To use these classes, we need to develop methods or lambda expressions to provide
the abstract method's functionality. We will illustrate both these approaches. The
following methods that are used support both the games with the exception of the
render method, which is specific to the FPS game:

```
public static void initializeGame(String name) {
    System.out.println("Starting " + name);
}
```

```
public String render() {
    System.out.println("Generating FPS Image");
    return "FPS Image";
}

int update(String name) {
    System.out.println("Updating " + name);
    return 0;
}
```

This code, and the previous methods, are found inside of a driver class called `TemplateDriver`. In the next statements, an instance of the driver and `FPSGame` classes are created. The initialization functionality is provided by a static method reference to the `initializeGame` method. An instance method reference is used for the rendering functionality, and a lambda expression supports the update functionality:

```
TemplateDriver td = new TemplateDriver();
FPSGame fps = new FPSGame(
        TemplateDriver::initializeGame,
        td::render,
        name -> {
            System.out.println("Updating " + name);
            return 0;
        });
```

An instance of the `StrategyGame` is created next. Lambda expressions are used for the initialization and rendering operations. An instance method reference implements the update logic for the game:

```
StrategyGame sg = new StrategyGame(
        n -> System.out.println("Starting " + n),
        () -> {
            System.out.println("Generating Strategy Image");
            return "Strategy Image";
        },
        td::update);
```

The output of this implementation is identical to the object-oriented solution. While the same number of classes is used, functional interfaces provide more implementation flexibility.

Summary

We examined how the functional programming features of Java can simplify the implementation of object-oriented design patterns. Lambda expressions were used as an alternate means of expression functionality. Streams allowed us to combine operations. Functional interfaces and default methods allowed us to reduce the amount of coding required to implement a solution. However, functional interfaces can limit how problems can be addressed since it supports a single abstract method.

We looked specifically at the execute-around-method, factory, command, strategy, visitor, and visitor patterns. Each of these patterns is designed to address a specific problem. An object-oriented approach was presented and then followed up with a functional solution.

In the next chapter, we will discuss how IDEs can provide support for refactoring object-oriented code to a functional approach, how to debug lambda expressions, and how the functional implementations can be tested.

8

Refactoring, Debugging, and Testing

There is more to software development than simply writing code. Among other things, we may need to modify or reuse existing code to correct bugs and enhance the product. As we create code, we will need to uncover errors using various debugging approaches. We will need to test our application at various points in the development process to ensure it meets its business and technical requirements. There are other activities required when developing software, but these are the ones of interest to us in this chapter. Here, we will focus on three major activities: refactoring code, debugging, and testing.

Whether we are writing new code or modifying old code, refactoring is a powerful tool in your programming arsenal. With the support of IDEs, you can quickly and safely transform code to address a particular design concern. There are a number of refactoring operations supported by IDEs, including simple support for consistent and comprehensive renaming variables to extracting methods, classes, and interfaces.

In this chapter, we will examine how to refactor code to convert older code to use lambda expressions and how to refactor lambda expressions. You will learn how particular refactoring operations can be applied to all of the code in a project. These techniques will improve your ability to create readable and maintainable Java 8 code. Specifically, we will cover:

- The IDE support provided by NetBeans and Eclipse to support refactoring
- Techniques for debugging lambda expressions
- Approaches for testing functional programs

As we code, we are bound to introduce errors that will need to remove. While the old school approach of inserting print statements may be sufficient for simple problems, more sophisticated debugging techniques are required for more complex problems. The process of debugging in IDEs has been enhanced to support lambda expression evaluation. In addition, we will demonstrate the use of the `Stream` interface's `peek` method to assist in debugging streams.

Testing is essential to ensure that an application has met its requirements. Not only are we interested in learning how the functional programming techniques added to Java 8 can be tested, but also we will examine the new opportunities to perform testing using Java 8. Much of the testing section will use JUnit to demonstrate testing techniques. We do not assume that you used JUnit and provided introductions to the key aspects of this testing approach.

By exploring the techniques that IDEs provide to support refactoring, debugging, and testing, you will develop new skills that will improve your ability to create robust and maintainable programs in Java.

IDEs, such as NetBeans and Eclipse, provide editor support for refactoring, debugging, and testing code to utilize functional programming techniques. In this chapter, we will show how NetBeans and Eclipse provide such support. We will be using NetBeans IDE 8.0.2 and Eclipse IDE for Java developers, Mars Release Version 4.5.0 in these examples.

Other IDEs also provide support but are not addressed. You are encouraged to explore those IDEs' documentation for specifics regarding their refactoring capabilities.

Refactoring functional code

Refactoring code is the process of reworking the code to improve its readability and the maintainability of the program. In this section, we will examine the refactoring support provided by NetBeans and Eclipse. This support can be categorized as follows:

- Converting anonymous inner classes to lambda expressions
- Refactoring multiple instances of code
- Miscellaneous refactoring support

In *Chapter 2, Putting the Function in Functional Programming,* we demonstrated how to convert the following anonymous inner class to a lambda expression:

```
List<String> list = Arrays.asList("Huey", "Dewey", "Louie");
list.forEach(new Consumer<String>() {
    @Override
    public void accept(String t) {
        System.out.println(t);
    }
});
```

We will use this example to demonstrate refactoring.

NetBeans support for refactoring

We will examine how refactoring can be achieved in NetBeans. This IDE provides the basic functionality needed for most of the common refactoring needs related to lambda expressions.

Converting anonymous inner classes to lambda expressions

Anonymous inner classes can be readily converted to lambda expressions. In NetBeans, the editor will display a yellow lightbulb symbol in the left margin on lines where it supports refactoring among other possible actions. Using the list example, we can either convert the code to a lambda expression or a member reference, as shown next. The menu is brought up with a single click on the lightbulb symbol:

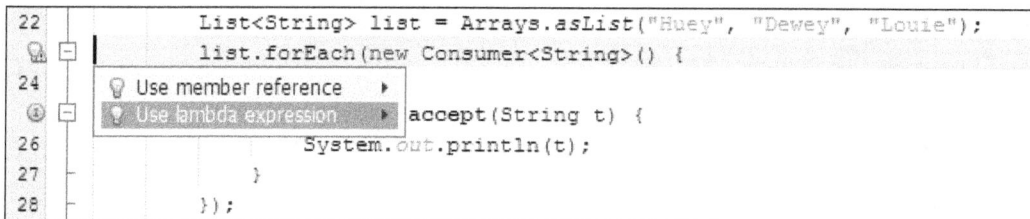

```
22              List<String> list = Arrays.asList("Huey", "Dewey", "Louie");
                list.forEach(new Consumer<String>() {
24      💡 Use member reference      ▶
        💡 Use lambda expression     ▶ accept(String t) {
26                  System.out.println(t);
27                  }
28              });
```

Converting the inner class to a lambda expression will change the code to this sequence:

```
list.forEach((String t) -> {
    System.out.println(t);
});
```

Converting the code to a member reference produces even more succinct code:

```
list.forEach(System.out::println);
```

Another common use of an inner class is in support of button events. In the following code sequence, a JavaFX `Button` class instance is created and the `handle` method of the `EventHandler` class is overridden:

```
Button button = new Button("Ok");
button.setOnAction(new EventHandler<ActionEvent>() {
    @Override
    public void handle(ActionEvent e) {
        System.out.println("Ok button clicked.");
    }
});
```

After conversion, the anonymous inner class is replaced, as shown here:

```
button.setOnAction((ActionEvent e) -> {
    System.out.println("Ok button clicked.");
});
```

This refactoring operation can save time when converting older code to use Java 8.

Refactoring multiple code instances

Refactoring can be applied to multiple code instances at once. If we expand the previous menu, we can select the **Run Inspect& Transform on...** submenu item, as shown here:

Selecting the menu item will bring up this dialog box:

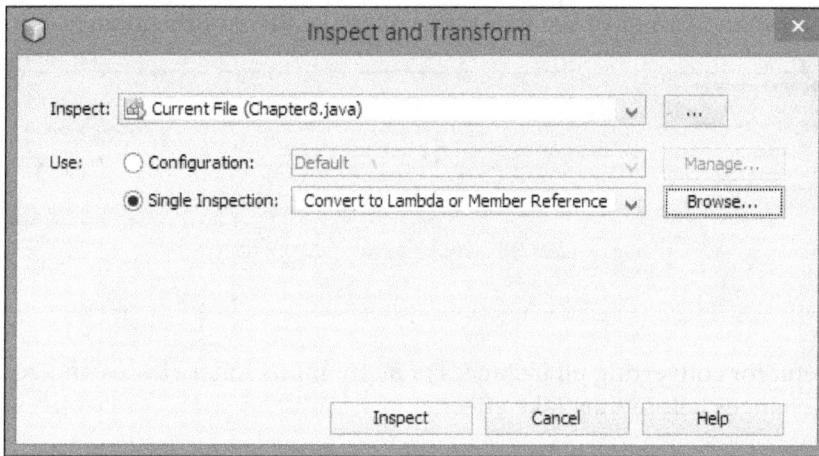

Selecting the **Inspect** button will display an intermediate box:

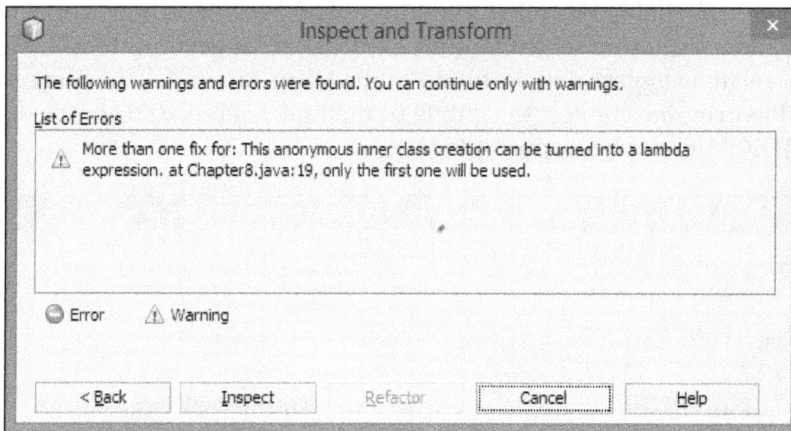

Selecting **Inspect** will display a new tab at the bottom of the window showing the code to be modified and the result. Selecting the **Do Refactoring** button, found in the lower left-hand corner of the window, will make the modifications:

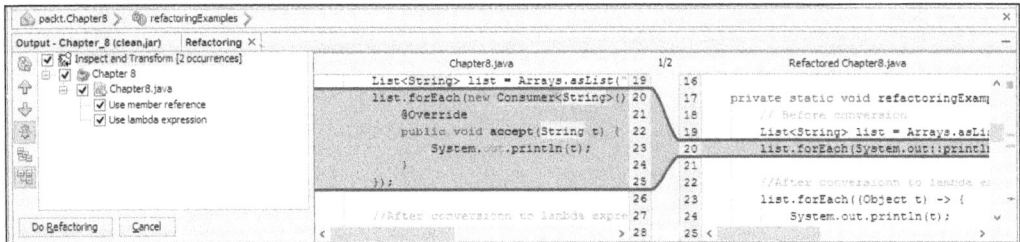

This is useful for converting all instances of anonymous inner classes and being able to see the changes before they take effect.

Support of other refactoring operations

Navigating to the **Tools | Options** menu will bring up the **Options** dialog box, as shown here. The dialog box allows you to control how the editor works with your application, including which lambda expression suggestions to use. Most of the lambda-related suggestions are found in the **Hints** tab under the **Suggestions** category. However, the convert to lambda or method reference support is found under the **JDK Migration Support** category:

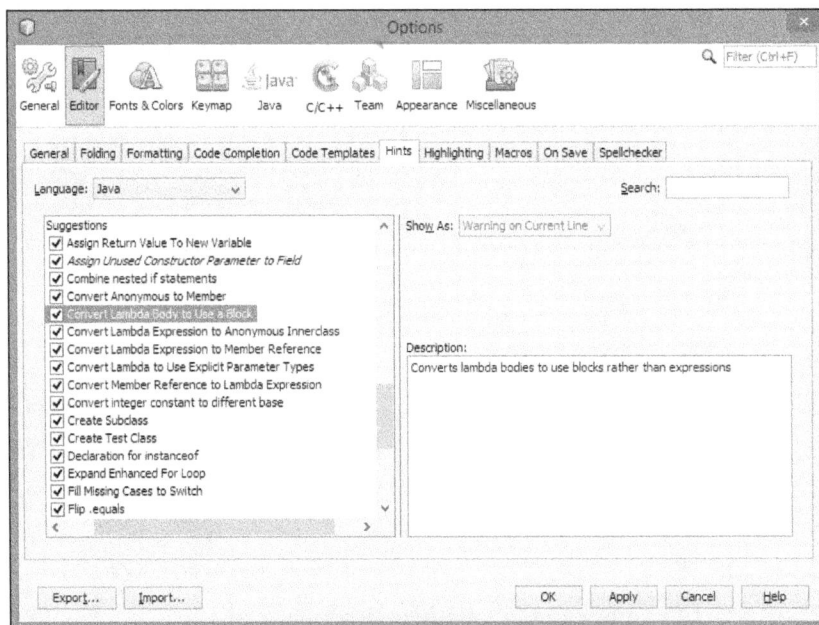

A lambda expression can take on various forms. NetBeans provides support for altering these expressions. Assume that we remove the `String` parameter type from the previous list example, as shown here:

```
list.forEach((t) -> {
    System.out.println(t);
});
```

We are then presented with the **Use explicit parameter types** suggestion:

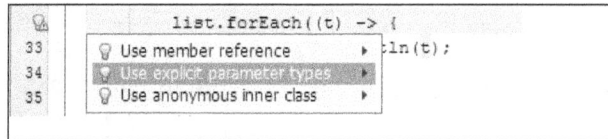

Selecting this option modifies the code to use a `String` parameter:

```
list.forEach((String t) -> {
    System.out.println(t);
});
```

Eclipse support for refactoring

We will examine how refactoring can be achieved in Eclipse. This IDE supports several functional programming refactoring operations.

Converting anonymous inner classes to lambda expressions

We will demonstrate this type of conversion using the list example duplicated here:

```
List<String> list = Arrays.asList("Huey", "Dewey", "Louie");
list.forEach(new Consumer<String>() {
    @Override
    public void accept(String t) {
        System.out.println(t);
    }
});
```

Clicking on the `accept` method and using **Quick Assist**, the *Ctrl + 1* key combination will bring up the menu shown here:

```
20          List<String> list = Arrays.asList("Huey", "Dewey", "Louie");
21          list.forEach(new Consumer<String>() {
22              @Override
23              public void accept(String t) {
24                  System.out.p
25              }                      Rename in file (Ctrl+2, R)
26          });                        Rename in workspace (Alt+Shift+R)
27                                      Convert to lambda expression
28
```

Selecting the **Convert to lambda expression** menu item will transform the code:

```
list.forEach(t -> System.out.println(t));
```

Eclipse also allows you to preview the proposed changes. If we click on the lambda operator (`->`) and use the *Ctrl + 1* keyboard sequence, you will be presented with several menu options. Single clicking on each option will preview the changes in the box to the right of the menu. Here, the option to use a block for the lambda expression body is shown:

```
31          list.forEach(t -> System.out.println(t));
32
33              Change body expression to block               ...
34              Convert to anonymous class creation           list.forEach(t -> {
35              Extract to local variable (replace all occurrences)   System.out.println(t);
36              Extract to local variable                     });
37                                                            ...
38
39
```

Refactoring multiple code instances

When there are a number of potential places in code where lambda expressions are an option, Eclipse's cleanup option is available to simplify this task. Start by right-clicking on the source code and then navigating to the **Source | Clean up...** popup menu item. This will bring up the **Clean Up** dialog box:

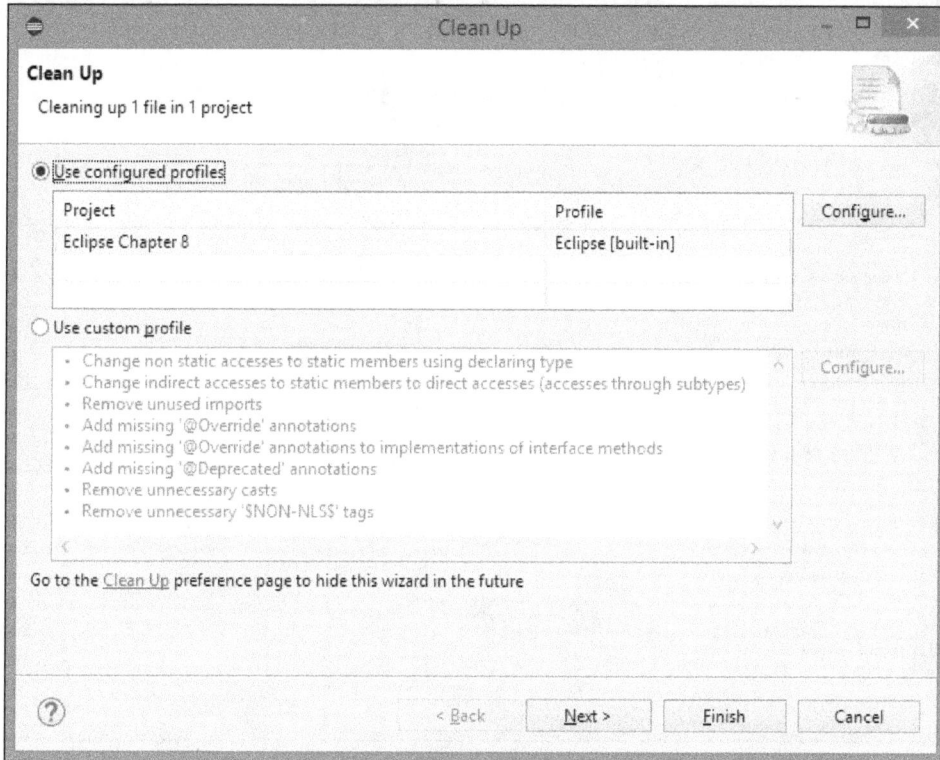

By default, the cleanup process does not support the conversion to lambda expressions. This must be enabled for a profile. In this dialog box, the **Eclipse [built-in]** profile is being used. We can either change this profile, create a new profile, or modify the properties for this project's cleanup profile using the **Use custom profile** radio button option.

Selecting the **Configure...** button enabled in the previous image will start the process of creating a new profile. However, we will select the **Use custom profile** radio button and then its **Configure...** button instead. This will bring up the **Custom Clean Up** dialog box, as shown next. Select the **Code Style** tab and then the **Convert functional interfaces instances** checkbox:

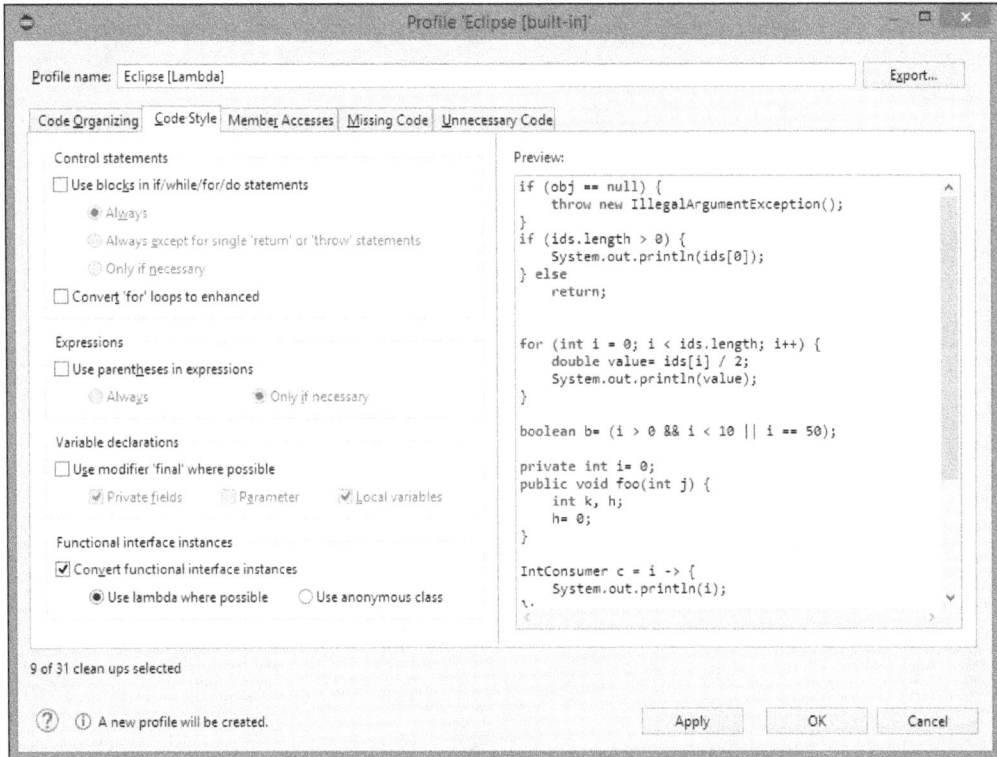

Select **OK**, which brings us back to the **Clean Up** dialog box. Selecting **Next** will show the changes that will be made if the **Finish** button is pressed:

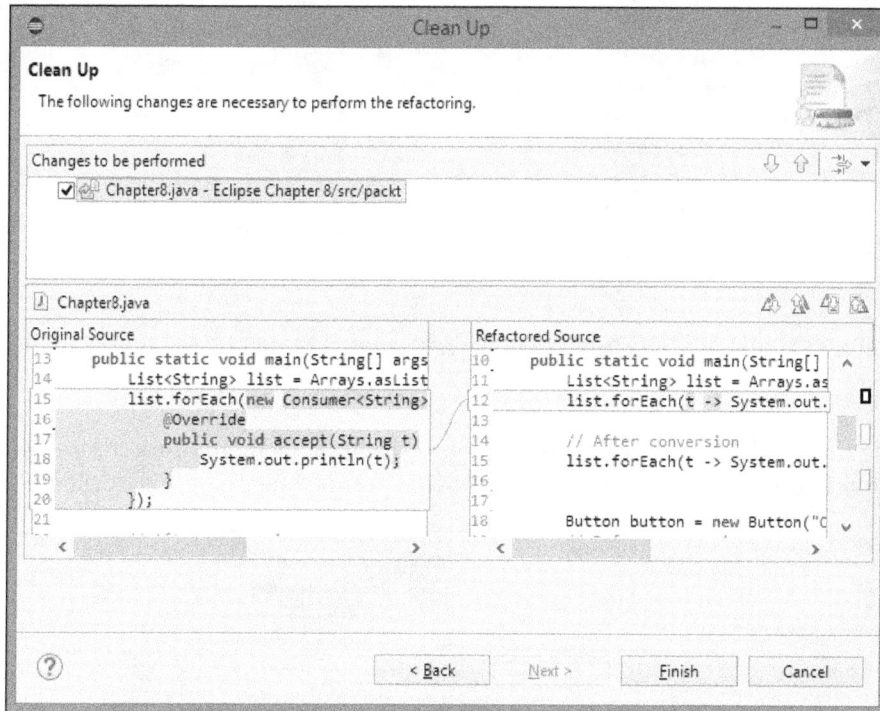

Support of other refactoring operations

We can also hover over a lambda expression to determine which functional interface method is implemented. This can be useful when learning how to use a new method.

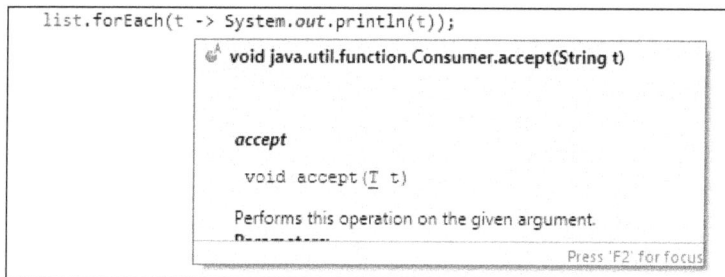

When the lambda expression is highlighted, the **Quick Assist** command will provide other options, as shown here:

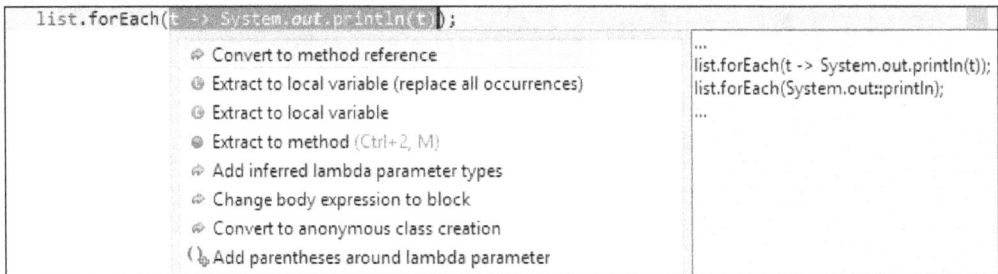

```
list.forEach( -> System.out.println(t));
```

- Convert to method reference
- Extract to local variable (replace all occurrences)
- Extract to local variable
- Extract to method (Ctrl+2, M)
- Add inferred lambda parameter types
- Change body expression to block
- Convert to anonymous class creation
- Add parentheses around lambda parameter

```
...
list.forEach(t -> System.out.println(t));
list.forEach(System.out::println);
...
```

If we convert it to a method reference, we get:

```
list.forEach(System.out::println);
```

Holding the *Ctrl* button and hovering over the lambda or method reference operator will provide options for either showing a method's declaration or its implementation:

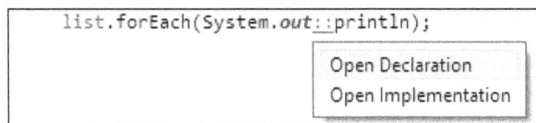

```
list.forEach(System.out::println);
```

Open Declaration
Open Implementation

There are several other Eclipse IDE support options available, including support for controlling how lambda expressions are formatted, searching for method references, and displaying lambda expression that implement a specific functional interface. A more detailed coverage of these topics can be found at https://www.eclipse.org/community/eclipse_newsletter/2014/june/article1.php.

Debugging lambda expressions

Both NetBeans and Eclipse support debugging lambda expressions. While it is always possible to create multiline lambda expressions and use print statements to display the values of variables, it is better to use a debugger when possible. Not only do we have to add additional statements which would have to be removed in the production version of the application, but debuggers also provide additional information about the state of the program and frequently allow some variables to be modified while the debugger is executing.

We will demonstrate how to debug a lambda expression that takes a string and returns the string concatenated with its lowercase equivalent. This operation is shown here:

```
List<String> list = Arrays.asList("Huey", "Dewey", "Louie");
list.stream()
        .map(s -> s + "-" + s.toLowerCase())
        .forEach(s -> System.out.println(s));
```

When this code executes, you will get the following output:

```
Huey-huey
Dewey-dewey
Louie-louie
```

We will use it for the debugging examples in this section.

Using the println method to assist debugging

While not necessarily the best debugging approach, using print statements will be sufficient for some problems. The next code sequence rewrites the previous lambda expression to use println methods before and after the concatenation operation:

```
list.stream()
        .map(s -> {
            System.out.println("Before: " + s);
            s += "-" + s.toLowerCase();
            System.out.println("After: " + s);
            return s;
        })
        .forEach(s -> System.out.println(s));
```

The output of this code sequence behaves as you would expect:

```
Before: Huey
After: Huey-huey
Huey-huey
Before: Dewey
After: Dewey-dewey
Dewey-dewey
Before: Louie
After: Louie-louie
Louie-louie
```

However, this is awkward and requires adding a body to the expression, a return statement, and the print statements. Using a debugger will eliminate the need for this extra work.

Using the peek method to assist debugging

Before we illustrate these debuggers, the use of the `Stream` interface's `peek` method can be useful at times. The `peek` method takes an object that implements the `Consumer` interface. It is similar to using print type statements but is more convenient and is not necessarily limited to displaying information. It could also be used for logging type operations.

In the next code sequence, the `peek` method is used twice. In its second use, the length of the string is also displayed:

```
list.stream()
        .peek(s -> System.out.println("First peek-" + s))
        .map(s -> s + "-" + s.toLowerCase())
        .peek(s -> System.out.println(
                "Second peek-" + s + ":" + s.length()))
        .forEach(s -> System.out.println(s));
```

This method helps provide insight into how a specific stream works.

Debugging lambda expressions using NetBeans

Breakpoints are set in NetBeans by single clicking on the left margin of the code editor. The breakpoint is indicated by the red square. To remove the breakpoint, single click on the left margin of the line a second time:

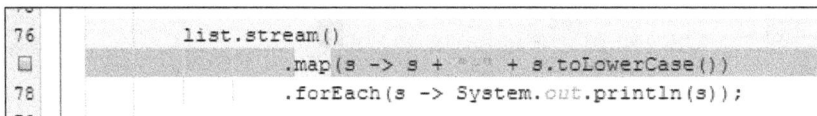

```
76          list.stream()
□               .map(s -> s +    + s.toLowerCase())
78              .forEach(s -> System.out.println(s));
```

To start debugging, select the **Debug Project** toolbar button, as shown next. It is the second button from the right. You can also use the *Ctrl + F5* key combination:

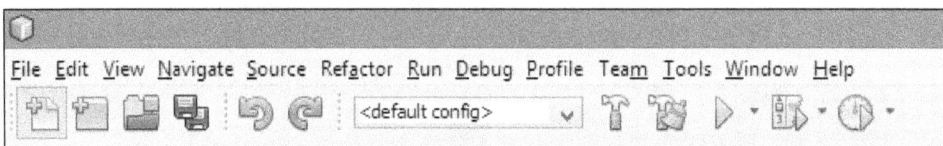

File   Edit   View   Navigate   Source   Refactor   Run   Debug   Profile   Team   Tools   Window   Help

The program will then start and execute up to the breakpoint where it will pause. That statement has not been executed yet. Below the code window you should see a debugging window with several tabs. On the left-hand side is the **Output** window for the program. As shown next, the **Variables** tab has been selected, which shows the variables for the lambda expression. In this case, the **s** variable shows the value **"Huey"** assigned to it:

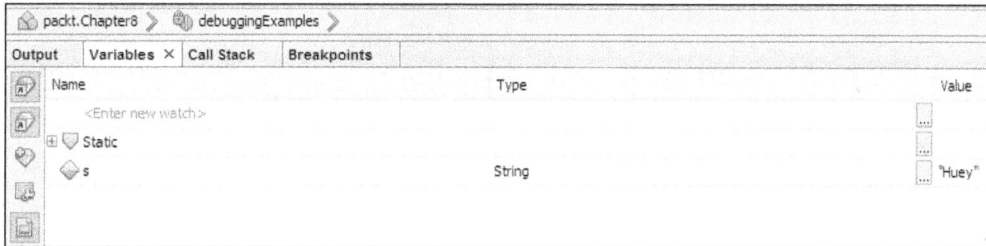

Above the code window a set of toolbar debug buttons are enabled, as shown next. The square red button is used to stop the program. The button with the green circle with the white right arrow is the **Continue** button. Selecting this button will cause the program to continue running until the next breakpoint is encountered:

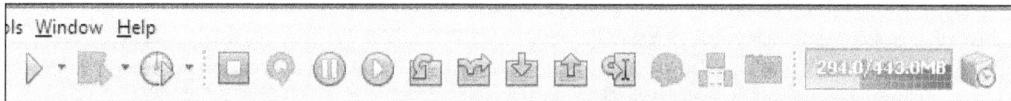

Select the **Continue** button. The program advances to the same breakpoint, but the **s** variable has changed to **"Dewey"**. Each use of the **Continue** button will advance the program. Selecting the green right arrow **Run Project** button will cause the program to run to completion without stopping at breakpoints.

You can also change the values of certain variables while debugging. As shown next, the value of the **s** variable has been changed to **"Donald"** by clicking on the old value and entering the new value:

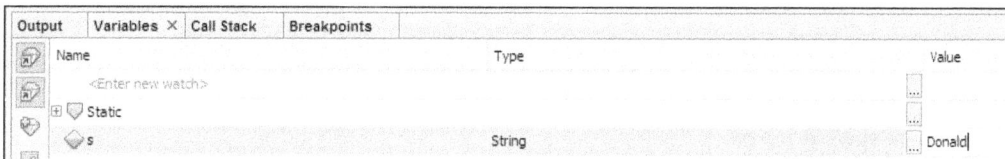

The **Call Stack** tab will display the state of the class stack, as shown next. This shows which methods have been called. For a more sophisticated example, a hierarchy of method calls will be displayed showing how the program arrived at its current position:

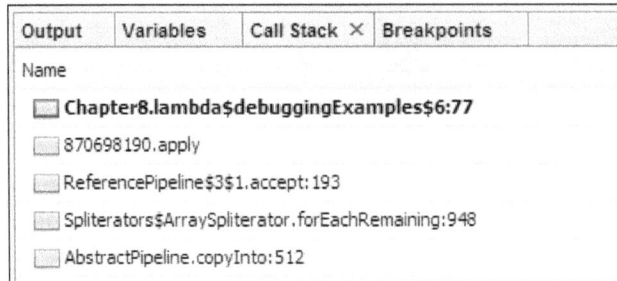

Output	Variables	Call Stack ×	Breakpoints	
Name				
☐ **Chapter8.lambda$debuggingExamples$6:77**				
☐ 870698190.apply				
☐ ReferencePipeline$3$1.accept:193				
☐ Spliterators$ArraySpliterator.forEachRemaining:948				
☐ AbstractPipeline.copyInto:512				

> One of the drawbacks of using streams and lambda expression is the larger call stacks that are frequently generated to support these features.

NetBeans allow you to set breakpoints for lambda expressions. However, it is better if each lambda expression is on a line by itself. For example, if we used the following form of the stream where everything is on one line, the breakpoint may not be as useful. This statement has been split over two lines here for formatting purposes:

```
list.stream().map(s -> s + "-" + s.toLowerCase())
    .forEach(s -> System.out.println(s));
```

Each use of the **Continue** button results in the return value being displayed, as shown here:

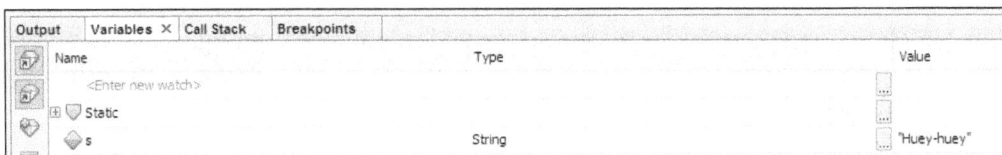

Output	Variables ×	Call Stack	Breakpoints			
	Name		Type			Value
	<Enter new watch>					...
	⊞ ▽ Static					...
	◇ s		String			"Huey-huey"

For more complicated lambda expressions, it can be useful to extract the expression and move it to a method. A static method reference can then be used to invoke the method, as shown here:

```
private static String toLower(String token) {
    String lowerCase;
```

```
            lowerCase = token + "-" + token.toLowerCase();
            return lowerCase;
    }
    ...
    list.stream()
            .map(Chapter8::toLower)
            .forEach(s -> System.out.println(s));
```

Setting a breakpoint within the method can give us a better understanding of how the method works. For this simple lambda expression, it does not help us much. For a more complex lambda expression, using a debugger can make all the difference in the world.

Debugging lambda expressions using Eclipse

Debugging with Eclipse provides similar debugging functionality to NetBeans. One difference is the use of **Debug View**, which presents different sets of windows to those used in **Java View**. The Eclipse toolbar is also different where the **Debug** toolbar button uses a bug icon. In the next image, it is the third button from the right:

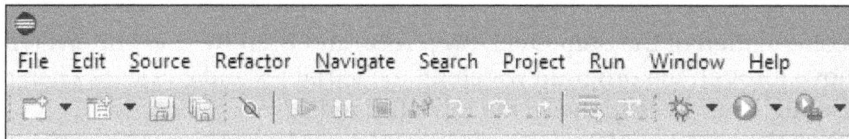

To set a breakpoint, we double-click on the margin to the left of the code window, as shown here:

The debugging buttons are enabled when the debugger starts. These are the set of buttons underneath the **Navigate** and **Project** menu items in the previous toolbar image. The **Resume** button is the left most of these. Selecting this button will cause the program to run until it encounters a breakpoint, as shown here:

The **Step Into** button will move the execution of the program statement by statement. Select this button until the debug line is selected and the **Variables** window in the upper right-hand corner of Eclipse shows the **s** variable. As with NetBeans, it is possible to modify the value of a variable while debugging:

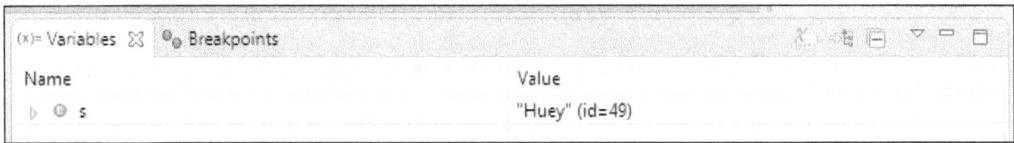

When the **Variables** window is present, hovering over the variable will display the same information:

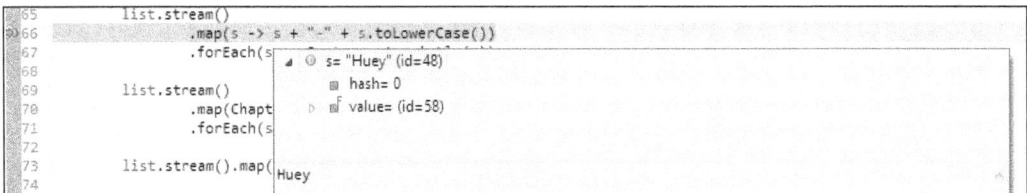

Using a combination of the **Step Over**, **Step Into**, and **Step Return** buttons will allow you to move through the program watching the variables and call stack change. The Eclipse **Debug** window is found in the top left-hand corner of Eclipse:

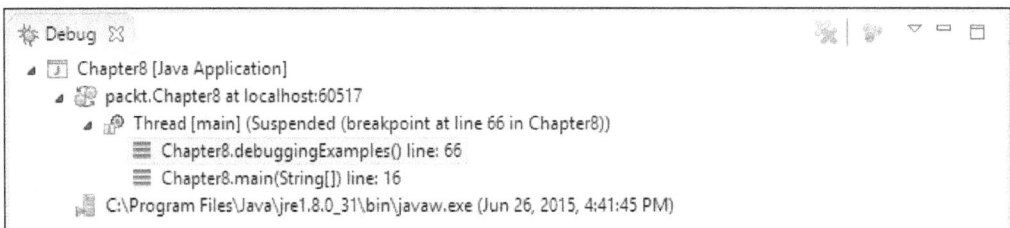

Selecting other frames in the call stack will show their corresponding variables in the **Variables** window. This will permit you to see what other variables hold at that point in the program.

Debugging recursive lambda expressions

Recursion was discussed in detail in *Chapter 5, Recursion Techniques in Java 8*. This can be a confusing topic to programmers who have not used this technique before. Understanding how the program stack is used will improve your ability to debug recursive lambda expressions and methods. In this section, we will use the recursive lambda expression we created in *Chapter 5, Recursion Techniques in Java 8*, to illustrate how it works with the program stack.

The lambda expression was used to perform an inorder traversal of a tree of Node objects. The code for this expression is duplicated here:

```
static Consumer<Node> inorder; // Instance variable
...
inorder = (Node node) -> {
    if (node == null) {
        return;
    } else {
        inorder.accept(node.left());
        System.out.print(node.getValue() + " ");
        inorder.accept(node.right());
    }
};
Node root = new Node(12);
root.addLeft(8).addRight(9);
root.addRight(18).addLeft(14).addRight(17);
inorder.accept(root);
```

We will use NetBeans to illustrate this recursion example. Eclipse works in a very similar manner. Start by setting a breakpoint on the following line:

```
inorder.accept(node.left());
```

Execute the program in debug mode. It will stop at this line. Examine the call stack, and you will see that the program has stopped on this line, as shown in the next image. In this case, the method containing the lambda expression was called `recursionExample` and the statement was on line number 150:

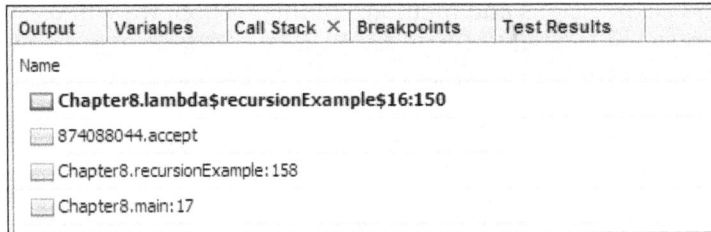

Output	Variables	Call Stack ×	Breakpoints	Test Results	

Name

    Chapter8.lambda$recursionExample$16:150

    874088044.accept

    Chapter8.recursionExample: 158

    Chapter8.main: 17

Next, examine the **Variables** tab. Expand the node variable to examine its contents. As shown next, you can see the values of each node:

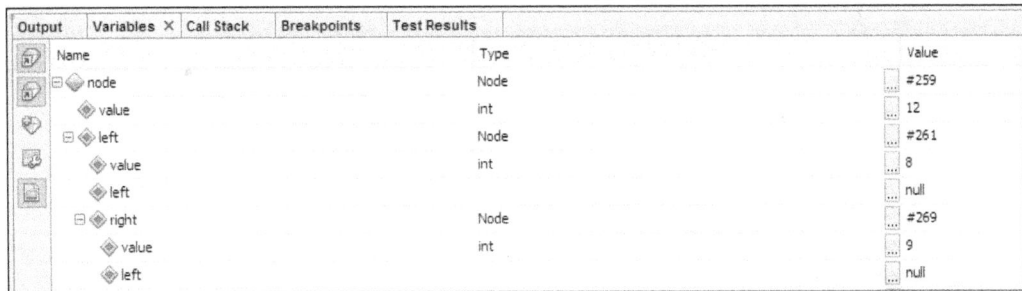

Output	Variables ×	Call Stack	Breakpoints	Test Results	

Name	Type	Value
⊟ node	Node	#259
◈ value	int	12
⊟ ◈ left	Node	#261
◈ value	int	8
◈ left		null
⊟ ◈ right	Node	#269
◈ value	int	9
◈ left		null

Select the **Continue** button. This will advance the program until the statement is reached again. As shown next, the `recursionExample` method has been pushed into the program stack a second time:

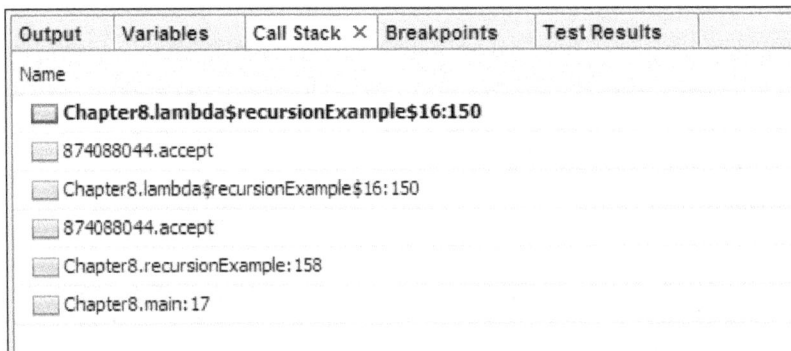

Output	Variables	Call Stack ×	Breakpoints	Test Results	

Name

    Chapter8.lambda$recursionExample$16:150

    874088044.accept

    Chapter8.lambda$recursionExample$16: 150

    874088044.accept

    Chapter8.recursionExample: 158

    Chapter8.main: 17

You can continue executing the program until it completes examining the variables and the content of the program stack as it runs. The call stack and variable windows can be very useful for understanding how recursion works in general and how to solve specific recursive problems when they occur.

Debugging parallel streams

When parallel streams are used, the debugging process becomes more difficult due to the nondeterministic nature of concurrent operations. It is not possible to predict which operation will be executed or which processor will be used. Care must be taken in writing and debugging these types of operations.

There are limited tools for assisting with this debugging task. However, we can always display the current thread in use to provide a clue into how a stream is being processed. In the following statement, a parallel stream is created:

```
list.parallelStream()
        .map(Chapter8::toLower)
        .forEach(s -> System.out.println(s));
```

We can modify the `toLower` method to use the `Thread` class's `currentThread` method to display the thread being used, as shown here:

```
private static String toLower(String token) {
    String lowerCase;
    lowerCase = token + "-" + token.toLowerCase();
    System.out.println("Thread: " + Thread.currentThread()
            + " token: " + token);
    return lowerCase;
}
```

One possible output sequence is shown as follows:

```
Thread: Thread[main,5,main] token: Dewey
Dewey-dewey
Thread: Thread[main,5,main] token: Louie
Louie-louie
Thread: Thread[ForkJoinPool.commonPool-worker-1,5,main] token: Huey
Huey-huey
```

Re-executing the example will generate a potentially different order of execution and thread use.

Testing functional programs

Testing is a complex yet important aspect of software development. Java 8 has impacted how testing can be conducted. The intent of this section is not to explore all of the possible ways of testing Java 8 code, but to provide some insight into possible testing approaches.

JUnit is the standard for testing Java applications and is used to test the functional aspects of Java. Typically, a JUnit test is created to test a method by passing it data and comparing the return value to determine if the method executed properly. In this section, we will examine various testing approaches.

Testing lambda expressions

A significant consideration is whether to test a lambda expression at all. If it is too simple to break, then there is no need to test it. The question is, what is too simple? The answer to this depends on the situation. A simple lambda expression, such as, n -> 2*n, is easy to understand and probably not worth the effort to test it. However, a more complicated multiline expression may need extensive testing.

Some developers suggest you shouldn't test private methods separately but rather test their effects. Lambda expressions can be considered to be a private method, since they are not visible outside of their context. This impacts how they are tested.

Since lambda expression do not have a name, it is not possible to directly call them. To test them you can either:

- Copy the lambda expression into the test case and test it there
- Move the expression into a method and call the method
- Refactor the expression into a simpler one and test it

The first approach doesn't really test the lambda expression in the context of where it is used. It only tests the expression. Potential problems may be missed with this approach. The second approach allows us to test it in its context but requires us to restructure the code. The third approach is a general guideline that should always be followed.

Simplify the expression when possible. While we tend to hang on to old habits, the new features of Java 8 can make our life a lot easier if we let it. Instead of using nested loops, a stream using the `flatMap` method may suffice. A stream and the `filter` method can replace decision statements. If you are dealing with a complex lambda expression, then breaking it apart into smaller chunks can simplify the testing process.

JUnit (`http://junit.org/`) is a technology that assists in the testing of Java applications. Typically, a class is created that consists of test methods that test other methods of an application. These test methods are preceded with the `@Test` annotation. Within these methods, specialized methods are used in the testing process, as we will see shortly. Most IDEs provide support for the creation and management of these tests.

We will place our test methods in the `ExampleTest` class:

```
public class ExampleTest {
    ...
}
```

We will use the `@Test` annotation to designate a test method. The `assertThat` and `equalTo` methods will be used to support the test operation found in the `org.junit.Assert` and `org.hamcrest.CoreMatchers` packages, respectively. For NetBeans and Eclipse, these packages should be available without adding libraries to a project.

The next method demonstrates the essence of the approach. Code is inserted into the method that tests some piece of code. The `assertThat` method will return a failed test if `resultValue` does not match `correctValue`. The `equalTo` method handles testing for equality and is useful for more complex data types:

```
@Test
public void testSomething() {
    // Code to be tested
    assertThat("Bad results", resultValue,
        equalTo(correctValue));
}
```

Should the test fail using NetBeans, we will get results similar to those shown in the next image where one of eight tests failed:

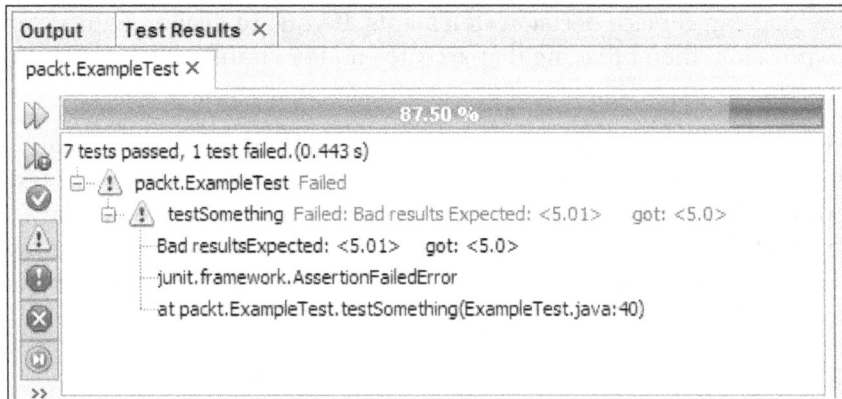

Success would appear as shown here:

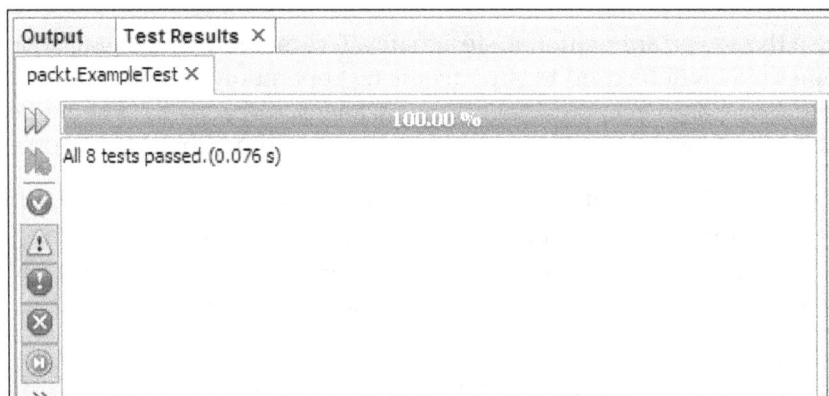

Copying the lambda expression

Copying the lambda expression to a test method is a simple way of testing the expression. In the next example, we use a lambda expression to either double or square a number depending on whether it is even or odd:

```
IntStream stream = IntStream.of(3, 15, 16, 12, 3);
int result = stream
        .map(n -> {
            if (n % 2 == 0) {
                return n * 2;
            } else {
                return n * n;
```

```
        }
    })
    .sum();
```

The expression is extracted and used in two test methods:

```
Function<Integer, Integer> function = n -> {
    if (n % 2 == 0) {
        return n * 2;
    } else {
        return n * n;
    }
};

@Test
public void testEven() {
    int result = function.apply(22);
    assertThat("Not even", result, equalTo(44));
}

@Test
public void testOdd() {
    int result = function.apply(3);
    assertThat("Not odd", result, equalTo(9));
}
```

As mentioned earlier, this does not test the expression within its execution context. In addition, it does not provide the flexibility to test various combination of integer values.

Using a method reference

Another approach is to copy the lambda expression to a method and use a method reference instead. In the next example, the body of the lambda expression has been moved to a method:

```
public static int processNumber(int number) {
    if (number % 2 == 0) {
        return number * 2;
    } else {
        return number * number;
    }
}
```

A method reference is then used to perform the test:

```
@Test
public void testMethodReference() {
    IntStream stream = IntStream.of(3, 15, 16, 12, 3);
    int result = stream
            .map(ExampleTest::processNumber)
            .sum();
    assertThat("Bad", result, equalTo(299));
}
```

The advantage of this approach is that we split the test of the stream into two sections. One for the stream and the second for the lambda expression. In addition, we can create a more flexible set of tests, as shown in the next section.

Reorganizing the test class

Ideally, we would like to test various combination of integers. We can facilitate this by reorganizing the previous set of methods. First, the stream is moved to a method called `computeSum` where it is passed a stream to process:

```
public int computeSum(IntStream stream) {
    int result = stream
            .map(ExampleTest::processNumber)
            .sum();
    return result;
}
```

The actual test cases are created using a `testPositiveNumbers` method and a `testNegativeNumbers` method, as shown here:

```
@Test
public void testPositiveNumbers() {
    IntStream stream = IntStream.of(3, 15, 16, 12, 3);
    int result = computeSum(stream);
    assertThat("Positive number failure", result, equalTo(299));
}

@Test
public void testNegativeNumbers() {
    IntStream stream = IntStream.of(-4, -13, -16, -2, -3);
    int result = computeSum(stream);
    assertThat("Negative number failure", result, equalTo(134));
}
```

The advantage of this approach is that it allows a specialized test to be created and reuses many of the computations.

We can rework these examples to perform tests on a slightly different problem. Let's assume that we have a series of lambda expressions we need to test. We can test them against the same set of data, as shown in the following code sequence. The testLambdaExpression method is passed a lambda expression, which is executed against a stream of numbers. The two test methods invoke the method using different lambda expressions:

```java
@Test
public void testDouble() {
    int result = testLambdaExpression(n->2*n);
    assertThat("Bad double results", result, equalTo(98));
}


@Test
public void testSquare() {
    int result = testLambdaExpression(n->n*n);
    assertThat("Bad square results", result, equalTo(643));
}


public int testLambdaExpression(IntUnaryOperator function) {
    IntStream stream = IntStream.of(3, 15, 16, 12, 3);
    int result = stream
            .map(n->function.applyAsInt(n))
            .sum();
    return result;
}
```

Additional flexibility is achieved using a method that is passed both a Stream and IntUnaryOperator instance, as shown here:

```java
public int testAll(IntStream stream, IntUnaryOperator
function) {
    int result = stream
            .map(n -> function.applyAsInt(n))
            .sum();
    return result;
}
```

The following test method illustrates how to use this method:

```
@Test
public void testStreamAndLE() {
    IntStream stream = IntStream.of(3, 15, 16, 12, 3);
    int result = testAll(stream, n -> 2 * n);
    assertThat("Bad results", result, equalTo(98));
}
```

Passing streams and lambda expressions makes it easier to create more succinct and useful test methods.

Testing exceptions using a fluent style

Methods will frequently throw exceptions that need to be tested. This is sometimes performed using the catch-exception library found at https://github.com/ Codearte/catch-exception. However, as detailed at http://blog.codeleak. pl/2014/07/junit-testing-exception-with-java-8-and-lambda- expressions.html?spref=tw, this technique can be replaced using a fluent style of interface. We will not try to duplicate this post, but rather point out the essence of this approach.

The post creates a class called ThrowableAssertion where a series of methods are implemented such as isInstanceOf, hasMessage, and hasNoCause. Each of these methods uses the assertThat method to perform some action and returns an instance of ThrowableAssertion, so as to support the fluent style of programming.

This allows test cases to be written as shown here. A method is invoked with a parameter or set of parameters, which throws exceptions. The ThrowableAssertion class's method will use the assertThat method and a matcher to test the method:

```
@Test
public void performTest() {
    assertThrown(() -> new SomeClass().someMethod(parameter))
        .isInstanceOf(RuntimeException.class)
        .hasMessage("Runtime exception occurred")
        .hasCauseInstanceOf(IllegalStateException.class);
}
```

The reader is encouraged to read this post. It not only offers insight into how exception handling can be tested, but also demonstrates the advantages of using a fluent style of programming.

Summary

We demonstrated techniques for refactoring, debugging, and testing code using NetBeans and Eclipse. Tools and techniques such as these make our lives as developers much easier.

Several refactoring techniques were explored. Converting an anonymous inner class to a lambda expression is a common technique when converting older code to use Java 8. This operation is easy to achieve and the IDEs provide several options for controlling the ultimate appearance and form of the results. The conversion of multiple occurrences of anonymous inner classes was demonstrated. We also illustrated other refactoring techniques in support of Java 8.

There are numerous application debugging approaches available. We illustrated several of these using IDEs. When in debug mode, the IDEs display the program stack and variables as it executes. This can be particularly useful when debugging recursion methods and lambda expressions. We also demonstrated the use of the peek method to help debug streams.

Testing is an important aspect of program development. We explored the use of JUnit and how it can be used to test functional programs. We also saw how several of Java's functional techniques can assist in developing test cases. We also saw how fluent interfaces can be used to make testing more readable.

In the last chapter, we will develop a program that ties together many of the new and old Java 8 features in an integrated manner. This will provide further examples of why Java 8 is an important advance.

Bringing It All Together

9

Now that we have examined the functional aspects of Java 8, we can use them to create more elegant and succinct applications. In this chapter, we will demonstrate many of the concepts discussed in this book to build a game engine. This application is simple enough to develop quickly, at least our version of a game engine, and has enough features to permit the use of functional programming techniques.

The game engine developed in this chapter is a Zork-like, text-based game. It will not be full featured, but will provide enough framework to demonstrate functional programming techniques and can serve as a basis for a more complete game should you desire to expand it.

We will begin with a discussion of the features of this game, which we will call functional Zork. The discussion is followed by a detailed explanation of the various parts of the game.

Functional Zork

In this game, there is a single character that moves around in a world. In this world, the player is able to examine the current location, move between locations, pickup objects, and drop objects. The list of commands are as follows:

- `Walk`: This moves from one location to another
- `Look`: This views the current location
- `Pickup`: This picks up an object
- `Drop`: This drops an object
- `Inventory`: This sees what the player is holding
- `Directions`: This determines the possible directions from the current location

Most commands have synonyms to make it easy to enter commands. These will be detailed as they occur and are quite easy to add or remove. A variation of the command pattern as developed in *Chapter 7, Supporting Design Patterns Using Functional Programming* is incorporated. As we will see, a Map class and lambda expressions are used to eliminate the need for individual command classes.

The world is made up of a series of locations. Each location has a name, a description, can hold items, and **Non-Player Characters** (**NPC**). There is no limitation on things such as how many items a player can hold at a time. These enhancements can be added, but were not included to simplify the presentation of the functional features of the game.

The locations, items, and NPCs making up the world are read from a text file. The file uses a simple format and is easy to modify.

Playing the game

A simple demonstration of the game follows. This will give you a feeling of how the game is played and some of the command variations possible. The game and the data file the game uses can be downloaded from Packt's website. The world defined in the file consists of four locations, as shown here:

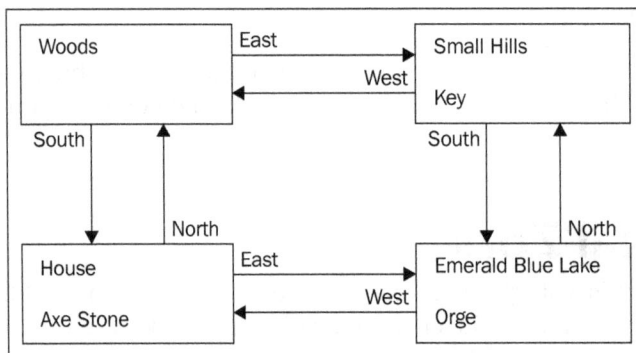

Woods	East → ← West	Small Hills
		Key
South ↓ ↑ North		South ↓ ↑ North
House	East → ← West	Emerald Blue Lake
Axe Stone		Orge

The game does not limit the locations to simply north, south, east, or west. As we will see in the *Initializing the commands* section, almost any text string can represent a command including directions such as up, down, backwards, or even quack if you choose.

When the game starts, the following will be displayed:

```
Welcome to Functional Zork!
```

```
You are standing outside a house sitting in the middle of a meadow. There
is a path leading north to the woods and a path leading east to a lake.

On the ground you see: Axe Stone

>>
```

You can use the command, `look`, to see where you are and what is around you. When you issue the command at the starting locations you get the following:

```
>> look
You are standing outside a house sitting in the middle of a meadow. There
is a path leading north to the woods and a path leading east to a lake.

On the ground you see: Axe Stone

>>
```

We can move about in the game using the `walk` command. There is one alias for `walk`: go. We use this command to move north, as shown here:

```
>> go North
You are standing in the middle of a dense woods. There is a path leading
south to a meadow and a path leading east to some small hills.

>>
```

The commands are case sensitive. If we use the following command instead, it will not work. Depending on the alias case may not be important. For items, directions, and NPCs, the case is significant:

```
>> Go north

Bad commmand

>>
```

We can get to the small hill by going east from the forest:

```
>> go East
You are standing on the top of a small hill. To the west you see a path
leading to a vast forest. To the south is a path leading to an emerald
blue lake.

On the ground you see: Key
```

One feature of the game is how it handles command arguments. Their use depends on the command. In the case of the `walk` command, using multiple directions can avoid issuing multiple `walk` commands to get to a location.

From the small hill, we can use the following command to get back to the house:

```
>> go West South
You are standing in the middle of a dense woods. There is a path leading
south to a meadow and a path leading east to some small hills.
You are standing outside a house sitting in the middle of a meadow. There
is a path leading north to the woods and a path leading east to a lake.
On the ground you see: Axe Stone
>>
```

The `pickup` command will pick up items and add them to the player's inventory. In the following command sequence, we pick up the `Axe` and eventually the `Stone`. The example illustrates how bad commands are handled, including the use of multiple arguments with the `pickup` command. As we will see later, certain words are ignored in commands. In this case, the word `and` was ignored:

```
>> pickup Axe
Picking up Axe
>> pickup Axe
Cannot pickup Axe
>> drop Axe
Dropping Axe
>> pickup Axe and Stone
Picking up Axe
Picking up Stone
>>
```

The `inventory` and `directions` commands are shown next. Both have aliases to make it easy to enter the command. The `directions` command is useful if you forget the paths leading out of a location:

```
>> inv
You are holding: Axe Stone
>> dir
If you go North you can get to Woods
If you go East you can get to Emerald Blue Lake
>>
```

The `quit` command terminates the game:

```
>> quit
Thank you for playing!
```

Now that we have a feel for how the game's commands work, we can explore how the game is constructed.

The game's architecture

The game uses several classes and interfaces. These are summarized here:

- `Character`: This represents the player
- `Command`: This represents a command and its arguments
- `Direction`: This holds a direction, such as north or south, and the corresponding location you will arrive at for the direction
- `FunctionalCommands`: This holds commands and executes them
- `FunctionalZork`: This is the main class containing much of the game mechanics
- `GameElements`: This holds collections of game elements and the current location
- `Item`: This represents an item
- `Location`: This represents a location in the game
- `NPC`: This represents an NPC

We will explore how each of these classes is implemented. For a few of the classes, we will not show the getter/setter methods. Otherwise, the critical elements of the classes will be explained.

Understanding the GameElements class

The `GameElements` class is composed of `HashMaps` for the game's locations, items, NPCs, and commands. In addition, the class holds a reference to the current location.

When a game element, such as items, is needed, it can be stored as a collection of `Item` objects or as a collection of strings holding the name of the item. When an item is referenced from a command, such as **pickup Axe**, the item is a string that needs to be associated with the actual `Item` instance.

We can either find the corresponding item in a collection of `Item` instances or maintain a list of string representing the item until the item is actually needed. For example, when picking up or dropping an item, it is not necessary to use the actual object. The name of the item is sufficient. We decided to maintain a list of `HashMap` of `Item` instances and look them up when needed. A location or the player maintains a collection of strings representing the items.

The GameElements class is shown next. The class has a few helper methods that are used when developing the game. They are not shown with the exception of the displayView method, which is used later:

```java
public class GameElements {
    public static Map<String, Location> locations =
        new HashMap<>();
    public static Map<String, Item> items = new HashMap<>();
    public static Map<String, NPC> npcs = new HashMap<>();
    public static final Map<String, Supplier<Boolean>>
        commands = new HashMap<>();
    public static Location currentLocation;


    public static void displayView(Location location) {
        System.out.println(location.getDescription());
        GameElements.currentLocation.displayItems();
        GameElements.currentLocation.displayNPCs();

    }
    ...
}
```

Introducing the Item, Direction, and NPC classes

There are several classes which represent game elements, including the Item, Direction, and NPC classes. These classes contain string variables for their fields. They also use a fluent style for many of their methods, as shown next:

```java
public class Item {
    private String name;
    private String description;

    public Item name(String name) {
        this.name = name;
        return this;
    }

    public Item description(String description) {
        this.description = description;
        return this;
    }
```

```java
    @Override
    public String toString() {
        return "Name: " + this.name + "  Description: "
            + this.description;
    }
    ...
}


public class Direction {
    private String direction;
    private String location;

    public Direction() {
        this.direction = "";
        this.location = "";
    }

    public Direction(String direction, String location) {
        this.direction = direction;
        this.location = location;
    }

    public Direction direction(String direction) {
        this.direction = direction;
        return this;
    }

    public Direction location(String location) {
        this.location = location;
        return this;
    }
    ...
}


public class NPC {
    private String name;
    private String description;

    public NPC name(String name) {
        this.name = name;
        return this;
    }
```

```
        public NPC description(String description) {
            this.description = description;
            return this;
        }

        @Override
        public String toString() {
            return "Name: " + name + "   Description: " + description
                    + "   Location: " + location;
        }
        ...
    }
```

With these element classes behind us, we can focus on the FunctionalZork class.

Implementing the FunctionalZork class

This is the heart of the application. The initialization of the game takes place here, and the player's commands are processed. The class is declared as follows:

```
public class FunctionalZork {

    private final Scanner scanner;
    private Character character = null;
    private final FunctionalCommands fc;
    private final Command command = new Command();
    ...
}
```

The instance variables are summarized here:

- scanner: This variable is used to access the keyboard
- character: This variable holds a reference to the class presenting the player
- fc: This will be used to control the execution of commands
- command: A single Command object is used for the game

The class uses several other instance variables that we will introduce when needed.

The main method is shown next. It initializes the game by creating an instance of FunctionalZork and then enters a loop that terminates when the user enters the quit command. The player's commands are returned in a Stream<String> instance and then passed to the parseCommandStream method, which sets up the command variable. The executeCommand method processes the command and then returns a string indicating which command was executed. The command string is used to control the while loop:

```
public static void main(String[] args) {
    String command = "";
    Stream<String> commandStream;
    FunctionalZork game = new FunctionalZork();
    while (!"Quit".equalsIgnoreCase(command)) {
        System.out.print(">> ");
        commandStream = game.getCommandStream();
        game.parseCommandStream(commandStream);
        command = game.executeCommand();
    }
}
```

Initializing the game

The game's initialization process starts with the creation of a `FunctionalZork` instance. Its constructor is shown next where the `scanner` variable is initialized along with the `fc` and `character` variables. The `initializeGame` method executes and initializes the `currentLocation` variable, which is used when the `Character` instance is created:

```
public FunctionalZork() {
    scanner = new Scanner(System.in);
    fc = new FunctionalCommands();
    initializeGame();
    character = new Character(GameElements.currentLocation);
}
```

The `currentLocation` method displays a welcome message, reads the `data.txt` file containing the specifics of the game's world, and then initializes the `currentLocation` variable.

Before we examine this method, let's examine the structure of the game's data file. The file is organized using a set of locations. Each location has a name, description, directions, and an optional list of items and NPCs located at that location. Each of these elements are found on separate lines. For example, the `House` location is organized as shown here:

```
Location

House

You are standing outside a house sitting in the middle of a meadow. There
is a path leading north to the woods and a path leading east to a lake.

Direction

North

Woods
```

```
Direction
East
Emerald Blue Lake
Item
Axe
A shape wooden handle axe
Item
Stone
A small round rock
```

The `initializeGame` method follows and expects the file to be in a specific order. Once the name of the location and its description are read in, one or more directions are processed. Following this is zero or more `Item` and `NPC` fields. The last section of the file should contain a `StartingLocation` field, which specifies where the game is to start. The last statement calls the `initializeCommands` method, which initializes the commands for the game. A fluent style of method invocation was used for several classes:

```java
public void initializeGame() {
    System.out.println("Welcome to Functional Zork!\n");
    File file = new File("data.txt");
    try (FileInputStream fis = new FileInputStream(file);
            BufferedReader br =
                new BufferedReader(
                    new InputStreamReader(fis))) {
        String line = br.readLine();
        while ("Location".equalsIgnoreCase(line)) {
            Location location = new Location()
                    .name(br.readLine())
                    .description(br.readLine());
            line = br.readLine();
            while ("Direction".equalsIgnoreCase(line)) {
                // Add direction
                location.addDirection(new Direction()
                        .direction(br.readLine())
                        .location(br.readLine())
                );
                line = br.readLine();
            }
            while ("Item".equalsIgnoreCase(line)) {
                // Add items
                Item item = new Item()
                        .name(br.readLine())
```

```
                    .description(br.readLine());
            location.addItem(item.getName());
            GameElements.items.put(item.getName(), item);
            line = br.readLine();
        }
        while ("NPC".equalsIgnoreCase(line)) {
            // Add NPC
            NPC npc = new NPC()
                    .name(br.readLine())
                    .description(br.readLine());
            location.addNPC(npc.getName());
            GameElements.npcs.put(npc.getName(), npc);
            line = br.readLine();
        }
        GameElements.locations.put(location.getName(),
        location);
    }
    if ("StartingLocation".equalsIgnoreCase(line)) {
        GameElements.currentLocation =
            GameElements.locations.get(br.readLine());
        GameElements.displayView
            (GameElements.currentLocation);
    } else {
        System.out.println("Missing Starting Location");
    }
    initializeCommands();
} catch (IOException ex) {
    ex.printStackTrace();
}
}
```

The Item, NPC, and Location classes support a fluent style interface. However, the previous code sequence using this style made it easier to read the code, but does not reduce the code size. For example, assume that we add the following setter methods to the NPC class:

```
public class NPC {
    private String name;
    private String description;
    ...
    public void setName(String name) {
        this.name = name;
    }
```

```
    public void setDescription(String description) {
        this.description = description;
    }
    . . .

}
```

Using this traditional approach, we can replace the previous fluent segment of code:

```
npc = new NPC()
        .name(br.readLine())
        .description(br.readLine());
```

With the following sequence:

```
NPC npc = new NPC();
npc.setName(br.readLine());
npc.setDescription(br.readLine());
```

The fluent style is easier to read, but uses the same number of lines of code. The best approach in this case is dependent on the preference of the programmer.

Initializing the commands

The `initializeCommands` method will initialize the commands used for the game. A series of `Supplier<Boolean>` instances hold specific commands. Each command is added to the `GameElements` command's `HashMap` instance. This declaration is duplicated here:

```
public static final Map<String, Supplier<Boolean>>
    commands = new HashMap<>();
```

The game uses a variation of the command pattern. A command is added to the `FunctionalCommands` class and then executed. This class is shown next and was detailed in *Chapter 7, Supporting Design Patterns Using Functional Programming*. The `clear` method has been added to remove older commands, since there is a single `Command` instance used for the application.

```
public class FunctionalCommands {
    private final List<Supplier<Boolean>> commands = new
    ArrayList<>();

    public void addCommand(Supplier<Boolean> command) {
        commands.add(command);
    }

    public void executeCommand() {
        commands.forEach(Supplier::get);
```

```
        commands.clear();
    }
}
```

> When we use the term, command, it can be found in several forms. There is the text form as entered by the user such as: **drop Axe**. There is the Command class that is created from the text command and consists of the command word and any arguments. Lastly, there is the command implementation in the form of a lambda expression.

Each command is implemented as a lambda expression. These commands are shown next and are declared as the FunctionalZork instance variables. Several of them use methods of the Character class and others use GameElements methods:

```
private Supplier<Boolean> dropCommand =
    () -> character.drop(command);

private Supplier<Boolean> pickupCommand =
    () -> character.pickup(command);

private Supplier<Boolean> walkCommand =
    () -> character.walk(command);

private Supplier<Boolean> inventoryCommand =
    () -> character.inventory(command);

private Supplier<Boolean> lookCommand = () -> {
    GameElements.displayView(GameElements.currentLocation);
    return true;
};

private Supplier<Boolean> directionsCommand = () -> {
    GameElements.currentLocation.displayPaths();
    return true;
};
private final Supplier<Boolean> quitCommand = () -> {
    System.out.println("Thank you for playing!");
    return true;
};
```

The `initializeCommands` method follows where they are added to the `GameElements` command's `map`. The key is a string, and the value is a `Supplier<Boolean>` instance. More than one command word is associated with a command. For example, the words `walk` and `go` are associated with the `walkCommand` command. This is an easy way of establishing aliases for commands:

```java
public void initializeCommands() {
    commands.put("drop", dropCommand);
    commands.put("Drop", dropCommand);
    commands.put("pickup", pickupCommand);
    commands.put("Pickup", pickupCommand);
    commands.put("walk", walkCommand);
    commands.put("go", walkCommand);
    commands.put("inventory", inventoryCommand);
    commands.put("inv", inventoryCommand);
    commands.put("look", lookCommand);
    commands.put("directions", directionsCommand);
    commands.put("dir", directionsCommand);
    commands.put("quit", quitCommand);
}
```

The Boolean value returned by these commands is not used in this version of the game. The return value has been retained for potential use in future versions of the game. With the commands initialized, we will see how the user input is processed.

Getting a command from the console

The input file structure used to initialize the game does not readily lend itself to parsing using a stream. However, for console input, we can use a stream. The `getCommandStream` method processes one command line at a time.

For each command, we will split it into tokens and then remove stop words. Using a stream makes this easier and permits other specialized operations to be performed if desired, such as converting each token to its lowercase equivalent.

Stop words are words that sound more natural to us, but are not necessarily important in a command. For example, the command, **pickup the Axe**, is more natural than **pickup Axe**. If we remove these stop words, it allows the player flexibility in how the command is expressed.

The regular expression, \\s+, is used with the compile method to tokenize the command line input. The `splitAsStream` method returns a `Steam<String>` instance. We can use this instance to remove stop words:

```java
public Stream<String> getCommandStream() {
    String commandLine = scanner.nextLine();

    // Stop words
    List<String> toRemove = Arrays.asList("a", "an", "the",
        "and");
    Stream<String> commandStream = Pattern
            .compile("\\s+")
            .splitAsStream(commandLine)
            //.map(s -> s.toLowerCase())
            .filter(s -> !toRemove.contains(s));

    return commandStream;
}
```

We did not convert the words to lowercase. If we had, then we could not match a command to pick up an item if the word for the item is stored using uppercase. Case-insensitive matching is possible, but will require modifications to how the data is stored.

The return value of this method is then passed to the `parseCommandStream` method.

We could have provided a similar imperative solution, as shown next:

```java
public List<String> processCommand(String commandLine) {
    List<String> toRemove = Arrays.asList("a", "an", "the",
        "and");

    List<String> tokens = new ArrayList<>();
    for(String token : commandLine.split("\\s+")) {
        if(!toRemove.contains(token)) {
            tokens.add(token);
            //tokens.add(token.toLowerCase());
        }
    }
    return tokens;
}
```

It is about the same size and returns a `List` instance instead of a stream. Returning a `List` instance does not provide as much flexibility as a stream does. The `List` interface does support a `stream` method if we wanted to use a stream instead. The most significant advantage the functional solution has over the imperative solution is its ability to add additional functionality more conveniently.

For example, if we wanted to perform additional processing if the token is `"drop"`. We can use the following method to encapsulate this processing:

```
public String additionalProcessing(String token) {
    if (token.equalsIgnoreCase("drop")) {
        // Additional processing
    }
    return token;
}
```

To incorporate this processing in the imperative solution, we can use a number of approaches. Two possible approaches are shown next. The first approach uses a temporary variable, while the second technique uses the output of the lowercase method as input to the `additionalProcessing` method:

```
// First appraoch
String tmp = token.toLowerCase();
tmp = additionalProcessing(tmp);
tokens.add(tmp);

// Second approach
tokens.add(additionalProcessing(token.toLowerCase()));
```

While the second approach is shorter, if we needed to perform more work, using the second approach results in a lengthy and harder to read solution.

To add the same processing to the functional solution requires adding a `map` method, as shown here:

```
.map(s->additionalProcessing(s))
```

If more work needs to be performed, then another `map` method can be used again. This results in a more readable and flexible approach, as opposed to the imperative solution.

Parsing the command

The purpose of parsing a command is to set up a Command object to hold the command and its arguments. The parseCommandStream command does this as shown next. A single Command instance variable is used and is cleared to erase any previous commands. If a command is found, it is assigned to the Command object. Otherwise, it assumes the remaining tokens are arguments to the command:

```java
public void parseCommandStream(Stream<String> tokens) {
    command.clear();
    tokens
        .map(token -> {
            if (commands.containsKey(token)) {
                command.setCommand(token);
            } else {
                command.addArgument(token);
            }
            return token;
        })
        .allMatch(token ->
        !"quit".equalsIgnoreCase(token));
}
```

The player can enter more than one command such as **pickup Axe and go North**. However, go is recognized as a command and will replace the initial assignment of pickup to the Command object. This results is an invalid command.

However, if a new Command instance is created each time a command is encountered, then the player will be able to enter multiple commands per line of input. This enhancement is left as a potential game enhancement.

Executing the command

The executeCommand method determines which lambda expression implementing the command is to be executed. It does this using the GameElements command's map to look up the expression using the name of the command. If the expression is found, then it is added to the FunctionalCommand instance, fc, and executed. The name of the command is then returned:

```java
public String executeCommand() {
    Supplier<Boolean> nextCommand =
        commands.get(command.getCommand());
    if (nextCommand != null) {
        fc.addCommand(nextCommand);
        fc.executeCommand();
```

```
            return command.getCommand();
        } else {
            System.out.println("Bad commmand");
            return "";
        }
    }
```

When the `quit` command is entered, the `main` method's loop will terminate.

By storing the command implementation as lambda expression, we eliminate the need for individual classes for each command. The use of the hash map, as implemented using the `commands` variable, eliminates the need for a series of if-then-else statements to select the command. The command's `get` method returns the corresponding command implementation without using if type statements. This makes the selection and execution of commands easier and succinct.

In contrast, if we had used an imperative approach instead, we would have needed to use a series of if-then-else statements similar to those shown here:

```
String cmd = command.getCommand();
if(cmd.equalsIgnoreCase("drop")) {
    // Setup drop command
} else if(cmd.equalsIgnoreCase("pickup")) {
    // Setup drop command
} else if(cmd.equalsIgnoreCase("go")) {
    // Setup drop command
} else {
    // Bad command
}
```

However, even this uses the lambda-based functions, as defined here:

```
private Supplier<Boolean> dropCommand =
    () -> character.drop(command);
private Supplier<Boolean> pickupCommand =
    () -> character.pickup(command);
...
```

These commands were added to the commands variable's hash table of `Supplier<Boolean>` entries. If we didn't use the `Supplier` interface, then we would need to rework the way we processed commands.

For example, the following method assumes a command line is passed to it. The command line is then tokenized and the first token is assumed to be the command. Only the code to process the `drop` command is provided. The `equalsIgnoreCase` method tests each command to determine which command was entered. The argument line arguments are then added to an `arguments` array. The command string and the `arguments` array are then passed to the `executeDropCommand` method for execution:

```java
public void executeCommandImperative(String commandLine) {
    String tokens[] = commandLine.split("\\s+");
    String arguments[] = new String[tokens.length-1];
    int index = 0;
    String cmd = tokens[0];
    if (cmd.equalsIgnoreCase("drop")) {
        // Setup drop command
        while (index+1 < tokens.length) {
            arguments[index] = tokens[index+1];
            index++;
        }
        executeDropCommand(cmd, arguments);
    } else if (cmd.equalsIgnoreCase("pickup")) {
        // Setup drop command
    } else if (cmd.equalsIgnoreCase("go")) {
        // Setup drop command
    } else {
        // Bad command
    }
}
```

The `executeDropCommand` method follows where we simply display the command. In an actual implementation, we will need to use a more involved solution:

```java
public void executeDropCommand(String command, String
        arguments[]) {
    // Execute command
    System.out.print("Command: " + command);
    for (String arg : arguments) {
        System.out.print(" " + arg);
    }
    System.out.println();
}
```

This approach requires more code and is more difficult to follow and maintain. In addition, we have not attempted to handle any errors that could occur, such as an invalid argument list.

The functional approach using a lambda expression for the commands and a hash table provides a more elegant and maintainable solution.

Implementing the Character class

Several of the commands are implemented by the Character class. We will examine each of these methods. The Character class maintains a list of items and its current location. As shown next, its constructor establishes this location and as we will see shortly, the walk method will change the location:

```java
public class Character {
    private final List<String> items = new ArrayList<>();
    private Location location;

    public Character(Location currentLocation) {
        this.location = currentLocation;
    }
    ...
}
```

Each of these methods is passed a Command instance. Not all of the commands will use arguments, but when needed they use the following statement to access them:

```java
List<String> arguments = command.getArguments();
```

If not needed, the statement is not used.

Implementing the pickup method

The pickup method converts the list to a stream by using the stream method. The filter method is used to determine if the item is available. If the item is available, then the method returns true passing the string to the forEach method. Otherwise, the method displays an error message and returns false, meaning that the string is not passed to the forEach method.

The lambda expression in the forEach method adds the item to the player's current inventory and removes it from the current location. A message is then displayed indicating success. The method easily handles multiple items, as shown next:

```java
public boolean pickup(Command command) {
    List<String> arguments = command.getArguments();
    arguments.stream()
```

```
            .filter(itemName -> {
                if (this.location.getItems()
                        .contains(itemName)) {
                    return true;
                } else {
                    System.out.println("Cannot pickup " +
                        itemName);
                    return false;
                }
            })
            .forEach(itemName -> {
                items.add(itemName);
                this.location.getItems().remove(itemName);
                System.out.println("Picking up " + itemName);
            });
        return true;
    }
```

Implementing the drop method

The drop method also works for multiple items. If the argument list is empty, an error message is displayed. For each item listed that can be dropped, the item is removed from the player's inventory and added to the current location. If an invalid item is encountered, an error message is displayed. The method is as follows:

```
public boolean drop(Command command) {
    List<String> arguments = command.getArguments();
    if (arguments.isEmpty()) {
        System.out.println("Drop what?");
        return false;
    } else {
        boolean droppedItem = false;
        for (String itemName : arguments) {
            droppedItem = items.remove(itemName);
            if (droppedItem) {
                this.location.addItem(itemName);
                System.out.println("Dropping " + itemName);
                droppedItem = true;
            } else {
                System.out.println("Cannot drop " + itemName);
            }
        }
        return droppedItem;
    }
}
```

For the `else` clause, we can use the following functional solution instead:

```
arguments.stream()
        .map(itemName -> {
            if (items.remove(itemName)) {
                this.location.addItem(itemName);
                return "Dropping " + itemName;
            } else {
                return "Cannot drop " + itemName;
            }
        })
        .forEach(System.out::println);
```

This is similar to the imperative solution, but it has the shortcoming of not modifying the `droppedItem` variable indicating whether any items were dropped or not. It is not able to use the variable without declaring *effectively final*, which defeats its intended use. In this case, the imperative solution is better.

Implementing the walk method

The `walk` method will move the player between locations in the game. It accepts multiple arguments allowing the player to move more than one location per command. If there are no arguments, an error is displayed. For each invalid direction, an error message is presented. For each valid direction, the current location is updated and the description of the new location is displayed.

The `Location` class's `getLocation` method returns an instance of `Optional<String>`, as shown next. This object is assigned to the `locationName` variable. This is a functional feature, which assists in handling null references. Each direction is passed to this method. The `map` and `orElse` methods are applied to `locationName`, which returns a string. In the `map` method, the `Location` object is obtained and assigned as the current location. The description for the new location is displayed. In the `orElse` method, an error message is displayed indicating that you can't go that way:

```
public boolean walk(Command command) {
    List<String> directions = command.getArguments();
    if (directions.isEmpty()) {
        System.out.println("Go where?");
        return false;
    } else {
        directions.forEach((direction) -> {
            Optional<String> locationName =
            GameElements.currentLocation.getLocation(direction);
            System.out.print(locationName
```

```
            .map(name -> {
                Location newLocation =
                    GameElements.locations.get(name);
                this.location = newLocation;
                GameElements.currentLocation =
                    newLocation;
                GameElements.displayView(
                    GameElements.currentLocation);
                return "";
            })
            .orElse("However, you can't go "
                + direction + "\n"));
    });
    return true;
  }
}
```

The use of the `Optional` class requires us to think explicitly about null references and their consequences.

Implementing the inventory method

The `inventory` method simply displays the items the player is holding. It uses a `forEach` method instead of a for-each loop:

```
public boolean inventory(Command command) {
    List<String> arguments = command.getArguments();
    if (items.isEmpty()) {
        System.out.println("You are holding nothing");
    } else {
        System.out.print("You are holding:");
        this.items.forEach((item) -> {
            System.out.print(" " + item);
        });
        System.out.println();
    }
    return true;
}
```

The last class to examine is the `Location` class, which has a number of interesting features.

Implementing the Location class

The Location class is responsible for maintaining information regarding each location in the game. As seen in the following declaration, in addition to a name and description, the class maintains a list of items, NPCs, and directions for that location. The directions list the paths from this location and normally does not change. However, the items and NPCs lists found at a location can change:

```
public class Location {
    private String name;
    private String description;
    private final List<String> items = new ArrayList<>();
    private final List<String> npcs = new ArrayList<>();
    private final Map<String, Direction> directions = new
        HashMap<>();

    public Location name(String name) {
        this.name = name;
        return this;
    }
    ...
}
```

The getLocation method used earlier returns an Optional instance:

```
public Optional<String> getLocation(String direction) {
    if (this.directions.containsKey(direction)) {
        return Optional.of(this
            .directions.get(direction)
            .getLocation());
    } else {
        return Optional.empty();
    }
}
```

The description method is written in a fluent style:

```
public Location description(String description) {
    this.description = description;
    return this;
}
```

Handling items

There are three methods dealing with items. The `displayItems` method uses a stream to list the items at a location:

```java
public List<String> getItems() {
    return this.items;
}

public void addItem(String item) {
    this.items.add(item);
}

public void displayItems() {
    if (items.isEmpty()) {

    } else {
        System.out.print("On the ground you see:");
        items.stream()
                .forEach(item -> {
                    System.out.print(" " + item);
                });
        System.out.println();
    }
}
```

Handling NPCs

There are three methods that assist with NPCs. With the `displayNPCs` method, the `forEach` method uses a method reference to display the NPCs at the location:

```java
public void addNPC(String npc) {
    this.npcs.add(npc);
}

public List<String> getNPCs() {
    return npcs;
}

public void displayNPCs() {
    if (npcs.isEmpty()) {

    } else {
        npcs.forEach(System.out::println);
    }
}
```

Handling directions

There is one method to add a direction and another one to display paths from the location. The `forEach` method in the `displayPaths` method requires two arguments, since it is used against a `Map` instance:

```
public void addDirection(Direction direction) {
    directions.put(direction.getDirection(), direction);
}

public void addDirection(String direction, String location) {
    Direction newDirection = new Direction(direction,
        location);
    directions.put(direction, newDirection);
}

public void displayPaths() {
    directions.forEach((way, direction) -> {
        System.out.print("If you go " + way);
        System.out.println(" you can get to "
            + direction.getLocation());
    });
}
```

This concludes the discussion of the game. There are many features that can be added to make the game more complete and playable. These are left as potential enhancements.

Summary

In this chapter, we demonstrated several of the Java 8 functional features to create a Zork-like game. Using console input, a player can navigate through a world picking up and dropping items along the way. New worlds can be configured using a file containing the description of the world.

We showed how to use the command pattern to handle commands. The commands were implemented using a combination of lambda expressions and other methods. Adding command aliases involved adding a different keyword to a hash map of commands.

Streams were used in a number of places to simplify processing and make the code more readable. Also used in conjunction with lists and maps was the `forEach` method, which replaced the need for imperative loops.

At several places in the chapter, we provided either an equivalent imperative solution or an equivalent functional solution for certain problems. In general, the functional approach was the better solution, as it was often cleaner and more maintainable. However, there are times where the best approach was imperative. By contrasting alternative approaches, you should be better able to select the best approach for future problems.

The application developed is a good start to a full-fledged Zork-like game. The use of the functional programming features will allow the application to be enhanced with less effort than a more imperative implementation.

Epilogue

Using a functional programming style often results in simpler and more elegant solutions to problems. We covered a number of different functional programming features available in Java 8. Lambda expressions provide the foundation for better ways of expressing application logic. Streams and the fluent style of method invocation make a program more readable and maintainable. Many of the other Java 8 additions complement and support functional programming in Java. It is hoped that you will apply this style to your future programming efforts.

Index

A

associativity, monads 171

B

Binary Search Tree (BST) 129
bounded recursion 120

C

catch-exception library
  URL 236
Character class, Functional Zork game
  drop method, implementing 259, 260
  implementing 258
  inventory method, implementing 261
  pickup method, implementing 258
  walk method, implementing 260, 261
classes, Functional Zork game
  Character 258
  Direction 244
  FunctionalZork 246
  GameElements 243
  Item 244
  Location 262
  NPC 244
closure 5, 38, 39
Collection interface 20
command pattern
  about 176, 185
  functional solution 188
  implementing 185
  object-oriented solution 186, 187
commands, Functional Zork game
  directions 239
  drop 239

inventory 239
look 239
pickup 239
walk 239
composite functions
  creating 56-58
  creating, in Java 8 58
  functional interface, using for function
    composition 59
concurrent processing 109
considerations, stream parallel
  non-inference 109, 110
  ordering, of elements 109, 113
  side effects 109, 112
  stateless operations 109-112
constructor references 18, 19
count-distinct problem
  reference link 86
currying process 5, 40-42

D

default method
  about 16, 80, 81
  in Java 8 81-83
  static default methods 81
  URL 81
  using 16, 17
design patterns
  about 175, 176
  command 176, 185
  execute-around 176, 177
  factory 176, 182
  strategy 176, 189
  template 176, 202
  visitor 176, 196

Direction class, Functional Zork game 244
direct recursion
  about 120
  using 120, 121
dynamic programming
  reference link 131

E

eager evaluation 106
Eclipse
  URL 220
  used, for debugging lambda
      expressions 225, 226
Eclipse support, for refactoring
  about 215
  anonymous inner classes,
      converting to 215, 216
  multiple code instances,
      refactoring 217-219
  other refactoring operations 219, 220
execute-around-method pattern
  about 176, 177
  functional solution 178-180
  implementing 177
  object-oriented solution 177, 178
  using, with stream 181

F

factory pattern
  about 176, 182
  functional solution 185
  implementing 182
  object-oriented solution 183, 184
filter method, Optional class
  using 155, 156
filter methods, Stream class
  about 96
  filter method, using 97
  skip method, using 98
first-class functions 31, 32
first-come-first-serve algorithm 191
fixed length streams 90
flatMap method 231
fluent interfaces 7, 8, 56, 64

function
  about 3-5, 80, 81
  composition 6, 7
  pure function 4
  returning 29, 30
functional code
  Eclipse support, for refactoring 215
  NetBeans support, for refactoring 211
  refactoring 210
functional interface
  about 17, 18, 47
  and method cascading, contrasting 67
  cascading 65, 66
  consumer-type functional interfaces 48-50
  creating 47, 68-72
  extending 76-80
  function-type functional interfaces 47, 48
  in Java 8 64
  instances, passing 61-63
  method chaining 65-67
  operator-type functional interfaces 48-52
  predicate-type functional interfaces 47-49
  supplier-type functional interfaces 48, 51
  used, for function composition 59, 60
  used, for hiding older
      interfaces/classes 72-74
  used, for supplementing methods 60, 61
  using 68-72
  using, with Properties class 74, 75
functional Java
  URL 56
functional method 47
functional programming
  about 1
  aspects 2, 3
  fluent interfaces 7, 8
  function 1-5
  function composition 6, 7
  monads 13, 14
  Optional class 13
  parallelism 11, 12
  persistent data structures 9
  recursion 10
  strict, versus non-strict evaluation 8
functional programming concepts, Java 8
  about 26
  closure 38

currying 40
first-class functions 31, 32
function, returning 29, 30
high-order functions 26-28
pure function 33
referential transparency 37
functional programs
exceptions, testing with fluent style 236
lambda expressions, copying 233
lambda expressions, testing 230-232
testing 230
functional solution, to
  command pattern 188
functional solution, to execute-around-
  method pattern 178-180
functional solution, to factory pattern 185
functional solution, to
  strategy pattern 194, 195
functional solution, to template
  pattern 205-207
functional solution, to visitor
  pattern 200-202
FunctionalZork class
command, executing 255-258
command, obtaining from
  console 252-254
command, parsing 255
commands, initializing 250-252
implementing 246
initialization process 247-250
Functional Zork game
about 239, 240
classes 243
commands 239
interfaces 243
playing 240-243
function composition 55, 56
Function interface
using 195, 196

G

GameElements class, Functional
  Zork game 243
generate method
used, for creating infinite stream 94, 95

H

head and tail recursion
using 128
head recursion
about 120-122
using 126
high-order functions 26-28

I

IDEs 210
infinite streams
about 90
creating, generate method used 94, 95
creating, iterate method used 91-94
inorder 124
intermediate methods 88
Item class, Functional Zork game 244
iterate method
used, for creating infinite stream 91-94
iterative factorial solution 119
iterative loop
converting, to recursive solution 131
iterative solution
about 119
reference link 119

J

Java
closure 38
Java 8
collections 20
composite functions, creating 58, 59
constructor references 18, 19
default method 16, 17, 81-83
functional interface 17, 18, 64
functional programming concepts 26
lambda expressions 15, 16
method 18, 19
multiple inheritance 83, 84
JUnit
URL 231

L

lambda expressions
  about 4, 15, 16, 43, 44
  copying 232
  debugging 220
  debugging, with Eclipse 225, 226
  debugging, with NetBeans 222-224
  exception handling 46
  Java 8 type inference 44-46
  method reference, using 233, 234
  recursive lambda expressions,
      debugging 227-229
  test class, reorganizing 234-236
  testing 230-232
  using 24, 25
lazy evaluation
  about 106
  demonstrating 106-108
lazy loading 106
left identity, monads 171, 172
lists
  merging 132
  reference link 132
Location class, Functional Zork game
  directions, handling 264
  implementing 262
  items, handling 263
  NPCs, handling 263
longest-task-first algorithm 191

M

map method, Optional class
  using 156
mapping methods, Stream class
  about 100
  flatmap method, using 103-106
  mapping operation 100
  map-reduce paradigm,
      implementing 101-103
map-reduce paradigm
  implementing 101-103
maybe monad 163
maybe type 147
memoization 33

Memoizer
  about 35
  URL 35
monads
  about 13, 14, 160-162, 168-171
  associativity 171
  bind operation 163
  left identity 171, 172
  reference link 163, 168
  right identity 172, 173
  unit operation 163
monads, in Java 8
  about 163
  flatMap method, using 164
  map method, using 165
  of method, using as unit function 164
  Optional class, using with string 166
  using, with Part class 167
multi-recursion 120
mutual recursion 120

N

NetBeans
  used, for debugging lambda
      expressions 222-224
NetBeans support, for refactoring
  about 211
  anonymous inner classes, converting to
      lambda expressions 211, 212
  multiple code instances,
      refactoring 212-214
  other refactoring operations,
      support 214, 215
Node class
  using 124, 125
Non-Player Characters (NPC) 240
NPC class, Functional Zork game 244
N-Queens problem 119

O

**object-oriented solution, to command
      pattern 186, 187**
**object-oriented solution, to execute-around-
      method pattern 177, 178**

object-oriented solution, to factory
 pattern 183, 184
object-oriented solution, to strategy
 pattern 190-193
object-oriented solution, to template
 pattern 203, 204
object-oriented solution, to visitor
 pattern 197-199
Optional class
 about 13, 147
 disadvantages 159, 160
 filter method, using 155, 156
 map method, using 156
 missing values, handling 153
 orElseGet method, used for obtaining
  substitute value 154
 orElse method, used for obtaining
  substitute value 153
 orElseThrow method, used for throwing
  exception 154
 reference link 159
 solution, to Customer problem 157, 158
 used, for supporting return
  values 149-152
 using 147, 148
 values, filtering 155
 values, transforming 155
Optional instances
 creating 148
option type 147

P

parallelism 11, 12
parallel streams
 debugging 229
peek method
 used, for assisting debugging 222
persistent data structures 9
pipelines 160
postorder 124
preorder 124
println method
 used, for assisting debugging 221, 222
program stack 133-136

Properties class
 fluent interfaces, using with 74, 75
 URL 74
pure function
 about 4, 33
 advantages 4, 33
 dependencies, eliminating between
  functions 36, 37
 lazy evaluation, supporting 37
 support repeated execution 33-36

R

recursion
 about 10, 117, 123
 criticisms 143
 Node class, using 124, 125
recursion humor
 about 144
 references 144
recursion implementation techniques
 about 139
 converting, to tail call 142
 short circuiting, using 140, 141
 tail call optimization 141, 142
 wrapper method, using 140
recursion types
 about 120
 direct recursion 120, 121
 head recursion 120-122, 126, 127
 multi-recursion 120
 mutual recursion 120
 tail recursion 120-122, 127
recursive acronyms
 about 145
 reference link 145
recursive data structure
 about 118
 examples 119
recursive descent parsers
 reference link 120
recursive lambda expressions 137
recursive solution
 about 118, 119
 base case 121
 creating, based on formula 129, 131

iterative loop, converting to 131
recursive case 121
reference link 119
recursive solutions, issues
  about 137
  absence, of base case 138
  instance variables, using 138, 139
  post-increment operators, using 139
  pre-increment operators, using 139
  static variables, using 138, 139
refactoring 209
referential transparency 4, 37, 38
return values
  supporting, Optional class used 149-152
right identity, monads 172, 173

S

short circuiting
  using 140, 141
short-circuiting methods 108
shortest-task-first algorithm 191
state full 109
strategy pattern
  about 176, 189
  functional solution 194, 195
  implementing 189
  object-oriented solution 190-193
Stream class
  about 86
  benefits 86, 87
  filter methods 96
  intermediate methods 88
  mapping methods 100
  terminal methods 88
stream processing 109
streams
  about 85
  creating 89
  execute-around-method pattern,
    using with 181
  fixed length streams 90
  infinite streams 90
  sorting 99
strict evaluation
  versus non-strict evaluation 8, 9

T

tail call 141, 142
tail call optimization 141
tail recursion
  about 120-122
  using 127
template pattern
  about 176, 202
  functional solution 205-207
  implementing 202
  object-oriented solution 203, 204
terminal methods 88
terminating method 67
testing 210
type inference 18

U

unbounded recursion 120

V

variable capture 38
visitor pattern
  about 176, 196
  functional solution 200-202
  implementing 196
  object-oriented solution 197-199

W

wrapper method
  using 140

Thank you for buying
Learning Java Functional Programming

About Packt Publishing

Packt, pronounced 'packed', published its first book, *Mastering phpMyAdmin for Effective MySQL Management*, in April 2004, and subsequently continued to specialize in publishing highly focused books on specific technologies and solutions.

Our books and publications share the experiences of your fellow IT professionals in adapting and customizing today's systems, applications, and frameworks. Our solution-based books give you the knowledge and power to customize the software and technologies you're using to get the job done. Packt books are more specific and less general than the IT books you have seen in the past. Our unique business model allows us to bring you more focused information, giving you more of what you need to know, and less of what you don't.

Packt is a modern yet unique publishing company that focuses on producing quality, cutting-edge books for communities of developers, administrators, and newbies alike. For more information, please visit our website at www.packtpub.com.

About Packt Open Source

In 2010, Packt launched two new brands, Packt Open Source and Packt Enterprise, in order to continue its focus on specialization. This book is part of the Packt Open Source brand, home to books published on software built around open source licenses, and offering information to anybody from advanced developers to budding web designers. The Open Source brand also runs Packt's Open Source Royalty Scheme, by which Packt gives a royalty to each open source project about whose software a book is sold.

Writing for Packt

We welcome all inquiries from people who are interested in authoring. Book proposals should be sent to author@packtpub.com. If your book idea is still at an early stage and you would like to discuss it first before writing a formal book proposal, then please contact us; one of our commissioning editors will get in touch with you.

We're not just looking for published authors; if you have strong technical skills but no writing experience, our experienced editors can help you develop a writing career, or simply get some additional reward for your expertise.

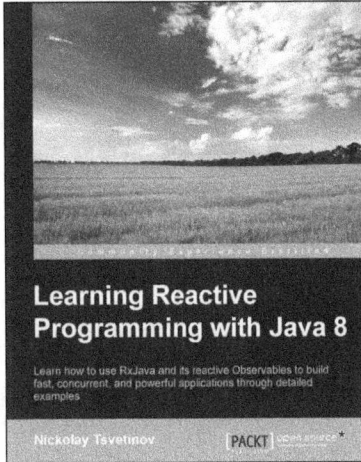

Learning Reactive Programming with Java 8

ISBN: 978-1-78528-872-2   Paperback: 182 pages

Learn how to use RxJava and its reactive Observables to build fast, concurrent, and powerful applications through detailed examples

1. Learn about Java 8's lambdas and what reactive programming is all about, and how these aspects are utilized by RxJava.

2. Build fast and concurrent applications with ease, without the complexity of Java's concurrent API and shared states.

3. Explore a wide variety of code examples to easily get used to all the features and tools provided by RxJava.

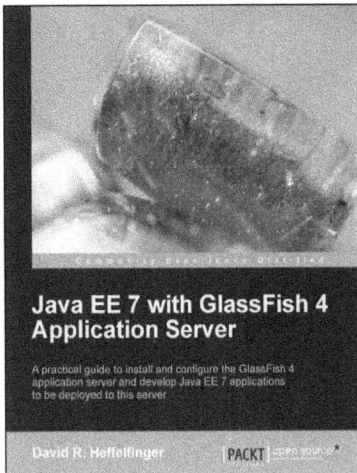

Java EE 7 with GlassFish 4 Application Server

ISBN: 978-1-78217-688-6   Paperback: 348 pages

A practical guide to install and configure the GlassFish 4 application server and develop Java EE 7 applications to be deployed to this server

1. Install and configure GlassFish 4.

2. Covers all major Java EE 7 APIs and includes new additions such as JSON Processing.

3. Packed with clear, step-by-step instructions, practical examples, and straightforward explanations.

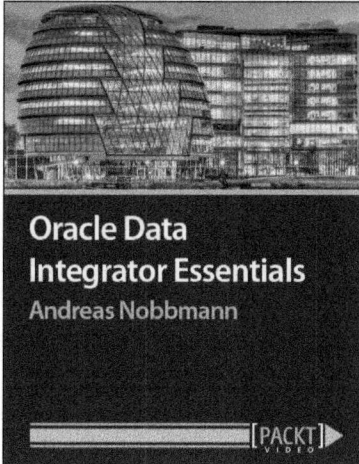

Oracle Data Integrator Essentials [Video]

ISBN: 978-1-78217-048-8   Duration: 02:08 hours

Develop, deploy, and maintain your own data integration projects with a clear view of Oracle Data Integrator essentials and best practices

1. Develop the necessary skills for effectively carrying out data integration and transformations in ODI interfaces.

2. Understand the use of ODI development objects with methods and concepts illustrated from real projects.

3. Master the key concepts of ODI's physical and logical architecture and the use of Knowledge Modules and data models.

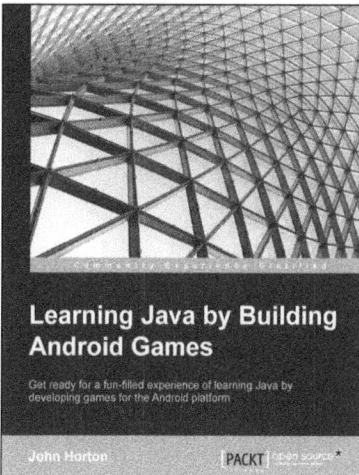

Learning Java by Building Android Games

ISBN: 978-1-78439-885-9   Paperback: 392 pages

Get ready for a fun-filled experience of learning Java by developing games for the Android platform

1. Acquaint yourself with Java and object-oriented programming, from zero previous experience.

2. Build four cool games for your phone and tablet, from retro arcade-style games to memory and education games, and gain the knowledge to design and create your own games too.

3. Walk through the fundamentals of building games and use that experience as a springboard to study advanced game development or just have fun.

Please check **www.PacktPub.com** for information on our titles